PAINTING, POETRY, POLITICS

Some other books by the author:

PROSE

Cells: Prose Pieces (*Grosseteste* Press, 1967)
Beats, Bohemians and Intellectuals (Trent Books, 2000)
Radicals, Beats and Beboppers (Penniless Press, 2011)
Brits, Beats and Outsiders (Penniless Press, 2012)
Bohemians, Beats and Blues People (Penniless Press, 2013)
Artists, Beats & Cool Cats (Penniless Press, 2014)
Rebels, Beats and Poets (Penniless Press, 2015)
Anarchists, Beats and Dadaists (Penniless Press, 2016)
Paris, Painters, Poets (Penniless Press, 2017)

POETRY

Some More Poems (R Books, 1966)
The Store of Things (Phoenix, 1969)
A Single Flower (Andium Press, 1972)
Leben in Preston (Palmenpresse, 1973)
Playing it Cool (Galloping Dog Press, 1976)
The Goldfish Speaks from Beyond the Grave (Salamander Imprint, 1976)
Fred Engels bei Woolworth (Rotbuch Verlag, 1977, reprinted 1990)
Aristotle's Grill (Platform Poets, 1977)
Catullus in Preston (Cameo Club Alley Press, 1979)
Internal Memorandum (Rivelin Press, 1982)
Notizen von Einem Schmerigen Loffell (Palmenpresse, 1982)
Out of the Past: Selected Poems 1961-1986 (Rivelin Grapheme, 1987)
The Gift (Redbeck Press, 1989)
Confessions of an Old Believer (Redbeck Press, 1996)
As Good a Reason as Any (Redbeck Press, 1999)
Take it Easy (Redbeck Press, 2003)
Short Statements (Redbeck Press, 2006)
Laying Something Down: Poems 1962-2007 (Shoestring Press, 2007)
Streetsinger (Shoestring Press, 2010)

PAINTING, POETRY, POLITICS

JIM BURNS

PENNILESS PRESS PUBLICATIONS

www.pennilesspress.co.uk

Published by

Penniless Press Publications 2018

ISBN 978-0-244-64982-1

Cover: Some books reviewed

CONTENTS

ACKNOWLEDGEMENTS

Many of these pieces were written for the on-line *Northern Review of Books*. The appropriatc details are listed below:

Degas, Impressionism and the Paris Millinery Trade. April, 2017
The Pen and the Brush: Art and French Novels. March, 2017
L'Affichomania: The Passion for French Posters. August, 2017
Alphonse Mucha. July, 2017
Australia's Impressionists. March, 2017
Italian Futurism and the First World War. March, 2017
Nordic Painting. December, 2016
John Minton. July, 2017
Inventing Downtown: Artist-run Galleries. May, 2017
Bohemian Lives: Three Extraordinary Women. August, 2017
Free as Gods: Reinventing Modernism. July, 2017
Becoming Americans in Paris. April, 2011
Trotskyism in the USA. January, 2017
No Pasarán! The Spanish Civil War. February, 2017
Revolutionary Yiddishland. December, 2016
First Thought: Conversations with Ginsberg. August, 2017
The Hippies. June, 2017
The Red and the Black: 1950s Film Noir, April, 2017
Finks: The CIA and Writers. June, 2017
Hardboiled, Noir and Gold Medals. September, 2017
Weimar in Exile. March, 2017
Coal Mine Disasters in Britain. February, 2017
Angel Meadow: Britain's Savage Slum. March, 2016
1919: Britain's Year of Revolution. November, 2016
Running Commentary. October, 2010
Penguin Parade. September, 2017
Hank Williams. February, 2017

Depression Folk: Music in 30s America. January, 2017

Essayism. July, 2017

Browse: The World in Bookshops. December, 2016

Douglas Hayes. July, 2017

Clancy Sigal. July, 2017

Roy Fisher (obituary). June, 2017

Other acknowledgements are listed below:

Published in Paris. *Tribune,* London, 12th December, 1975 and 10th September, 1976

Paris Magazine. *Beat Scene* 85, Coventry, Winter, 2017

Jack Kerouac. *Tribune*, London, 20th April, 1973; 16th November, 1973; 30th November, 1973; 13th September, 1974

Lew Welch; The Letters. *Stony Hill* 10, New Sharon, Maine, 1981

Burroughs and Bax. *Tribune*, London, 5th June, 1970; 30th June, 1972; 19th April, 1974; 3rd September, 1976

W.H. Manville. *Beat Scene* 86, Coventry, Summer, 2017

Poets in Translation. *Ambit* 102, London, 1985; 191, 2008

A Few Good Poets. *Ambit* 177, London, Summer, 2004; 186, Autumn, 2006; 187, Winter, 2007; 191, Winter, 2008; 192, Spring, 2008; 207, Winter, 2012

Crime Time. *New Statesman,* London, 3rd March, 1972

Roy Fisher (review). *Tribune*, London 3rd September, 1971

Thoughts on Music and Literature. *Jazz & Blues*, London, September, 1972

Thanks to the editors concerned and to Ken Clay and Joan Mottram

INTRODUCTION

As in the previous collection, Paris has a place in this one, with reviews/essays about various artists, writers, expatriates, editors, and others who were in the city at one time or another. I have to admit that I'm generally looking back in these pieces to the Paris of the 1890s or the 1920s, "golden periods", as they're called, though in a review of poets in translation I do briefly comment on a collection of more-contemporary French left-wing poets. I doubt that they will be familiar to most British poetry readers, and that seems to me a good reason for reviewing them in the first place, and reprinting the review in this book.

In case I'm accused of overlooking interesting British poets, there are reviews of several of them. These are from a list of several hundred books of poetry that I reviewed during a fifty years stint as a reviewer for the magazine, *Ambit*, edited by Martin Bax. One of the pleasures of writing for *Ambit* was that I wasn't asked to only deal with books from established poets. Many of the volumes I was sent came from small presses and featured little-known and new writers, together with some who had, perhaps, been around for a long time, but who were forgotten or unfashionable. It was always more fun to write about these people than knock out another piece about a poet who was sure to be noticed by the weeklies and the literary pages in *The Guardian* or *The Times*.

Staying in Britain, I've included several reviews looking at certain aspects of its history. I make no claim to complete objectivity in these pieces, and my social and political sympathies will be obvious. I refer to some loose personal connections to the subjects concerned. History fascinates me, and I don't mean the sagas of kings and queens.

The Beats make an appearance, of course, with material about Kerouac, Ginsberg, and Burroughs. And I include a short essay about George Whitman and *Paris Magazine*. It has relevance in connection with the Beats, though I'd mostly see Whitman in an older, bohemian tradition, just as the obituary for W.H. Manville does. He was one of those fringe figures who, for a short time, got associated with the Beats and bohemia. There might be links, also, to the long review of artist-run galleries in New York. And to the Hippies, though I've always had my doubts about the relationship between them and the literary side of the Beat activity.

Art is covered in reviews of books about painting in Italy, France, the Scandinavian countries, Australia, and the work of the British painter, John Minton. He was always a fascinating figure for me, and seeing the exhibition of his work that I reviewed was a great pleasure.

Politics, inevitably. I don't suppose the subject of Trotskyism in America will seem exciting, but it strikes me that, apart from its appeal to the few who will like to read about the subject, it raises some interesting questions about the nature and likely effect (if any) of minor political factions. But, as I've remarked elsewhere, it's Trotskyists rather than Trotskyism that interest me, and I draw some parallels with religious groups and their tendency towards sectarianism.

The political also crops up in reviews of books about film noir, folk music in 30s America, and the tangled web surrounding CIA involvement with publications such as *Partisan Review, Encounter*, and *The Paris Review* (not to be confused with *Paris Magazine*).

I think it should be obvious that much of my life revolves around books, and the review of a couple of books about bookshops touches on my love of browsing in them. It also brings in the Paris connection again, when it discusses the history of the famous bookshop, Shakespeare and Company.

Finally, a few words of explanation about one or two of the items may be of value. There's a review of several crime novels published in 1972, and it might reasonably be asked why bother to try to revive interest in books that weren't all that important at the time and have now been forgotten. My reason for using the review is that it highlights how British crime fiction, and probably crime fiction generally, has changed in the past forty or so years. It's unlikely that the books reviewed would be published now, or reviewed widely if they were. Readers require much more dynamic stories, with what some might see as a tendency towards sex, graphic violence, and sensation of one kind or another.

With regard to the reviews of Jack Kerouac and William Burroughs, they were written for *Tribune,* and the nature of that publication meant that space was limited. In each case I've linked together a number of short pieces to provide a wider picture of what these writers were doing. I've also added a review from *Tribune* to my Roy Fisher obituary.

DEGAS AND MILLINERY

An early biographer of Pierre-August Renoir commented that he was fascinated by women's hats, and would buy them regularly from various milliners: "He never came home empty-handed; he was a maniac, a sort of erotomaniac of women's hats: toques, bonnets, felts, straws, various kinds of lace, flowers. He also delighted in multicoloured fabrics". Someone else, talking about Edouard Manet, remarked: "The next day, it was the hats of a famous milliner, Madame Virot, that enthralled him……On his return to the rue d'Amsterdam, he could not stop talking about the splendour of the things he had seen at Madame Virot's".

As for Edgar Degas, he was clearly interested in millinery and the people who practised it, though coming from a thoroughly bourgeois background, with emotional reticence built in, he doesn't seem to have displayed the kind of outward enthusiasm that others noted in relation to Renoir and Manet. It was hard to imagine Degas standing in front of a shop window, talking excitedly about what was on display. But he knew about hats and, as this splendid book makes clear, he pictured them in more than a few of the paintings and pastels he produced.

People have always worn hats, of one kind or another, and a quick tour of 18th century paintings by artists such as Gainsborough, Romney, Fragonard, and Elisabeth Louise Vigée-LeBrun, will turn up numerous portraits of fashionable ladies wearing flamboyant headgear. But the 19th century appears to have spread the word beyond a selection of aristocrats and their followers. The rise of the bourgeoisie with money to spend, new methods of communication (magazines, newspapers, catalogues) which could disseminate information about the latest fashions, and advertising. They all combined to promote new markets for milliners: in Paris alone, "Around one thousand milliners created a rich and diverse array of hats, often covered with extravagant trimmings, such as silk flowers and ribbons, ostrich plumes, and even whole birds".

The 19th century also saw the rise of department stores (see Zola's novel, *The Ladies Paradise),* though most milliners operated from small shops. It's interesting to note that artists like Degas, Renoir, and Manet do not seem to have taken much interest in department stores where mass-produced hats were sold at relatively low prices. They preferred to visit the smaller shops, where hats were individually designed and made for clients who could afford them. And there was an awareness among the painters that the people who made the hats were, in their own way, creative artists. Questions of colour relationships could be just as important for a hat as for a painting.

It's relevant to note that very often the artists were living and working in close proximity to the milliners' shops: "Over his lifetime Degas's eight studios were all located in the Montmartre area: he regularly visited milliners' shops on the rue de la Paix (although frustratingly their names are unknown to us today)". It's true that, on the whole, Degas and other artists, such as Renoir, Manet, Mary Cassatt, Toulouse-Lautrec, and Federico Zandomeneghi, mostly focused on what might be termed the "front of shop" aspect of millinery. There were few insights into the workrooms where hats were made and working conditions not necessarily ideal. One or two photographs do show how cramped they could be, with women crowded together at benches and piles of material scattered around the room. Milliners were considered among the elite workers in the garment trade, so it's easy to imagine what life was like for those lower down the scale.

But can we really blame the artists for failing to focus on the lives of the workers, and largely concentrating instead on the people who wore the hats?: "This environment – at once familiar and artistic – during the years 1875-1890 – attracted many painters, who portrayed these young and elegant Parisian *modistes* as an expression of the reality of modern life that so fascinated them". It was more than probable that a painting of an attractive and fashionably dressed woman would be likely to find a buyer than one of a badly-dressed and hungry worker.

It's true that the *modiste,* perhaps seen delivering one of her creations to a client, might well have had a sideline in occasional prostitution. Her work was not well-paid, especially when compared to what the hats sold for, and selling her body might have been a necessity in hard times. There are a couple of reproductions of early prints which give a rather romanticised picture of *modistes* at their employment, and I suspect the reality was much darker. Of one of these prints, Pierre de La Mésangère's *Atelier de modistes,* it is said that it codes the women as "both elegant ladies and erotic objects, both creative artisans and disorderly tarts".

Later artists could sometimes hint at the weariness that would overcome women working long hours in less than-perfect environments. One of Degas's canvases, *The Milliners*, has a woman whose "apparent exhaustion" is obvious from her fixed stare and "greyish pallor". Compare it to Louise Catherine Breslau's pastel on paper. *The Milliners,* which has two tidily dressed women working on hats. They appear less tired than the woman in Degas's painting, though the level of concentration they're displaying, and their body postures, might well point to an eventual exhaustion.

The main intent of most painters was to show how women wore their hats at the theatre, on the street, and elsewhere in public: hats were very much a status symbol, hence the permanent demand for new creations. Besides the paintings there are numerous illustrations of hats from the period concerned, and they give an idea of the styles available and the imaginative designs involved. They range from the relatively simple - limited decoration on a hat could sometimes be as effective as more ornate trimmings – to hats that probably had little obvious use beyond being worn for show at a recital, the opening of an exhibition, or a similar social gathering. It's hard to see them being employed for more-mundane purposes. They just wouldn't have been practical.

It might seem that women's hats fascinated the artists most of all, and it's obvious that the designs and the colours provided them with inspiration. Renoir's paintings are awash with colourful representations of attractive young girls and women wearing gaily-decorated hats. And it's not difficult to know why men's hats got less attention. They just didn't have the range (of design or colours) that women's hats presented. Gone were the days when men wore hats with plumes. There's a painting by Manet, *Masked Ball at the Opera*, and it's amusing to see the row of black top hats which spreads from left to right across the canvas. Was Manet being satirical about bourgeois conformity?

The top hat was replaced to a degree by the bowler, invented in London in 1849 "as a sturdy riding hat for gamekeepers", though it soon went into general use in both England and France. Degas's painting, *Standing Man in a Bowler Hat* illustrates how it became a part of men's general street wear, as does Toulouse-Lautrec's portrait of

Gaston Bonnefoy. Both paintings show how "By the 1890s top hats had been relegated to formal wear". Men did also wear straw hats on occasion, and there's a painting by Berthe Morisot entitled, *Eugène Manet on the Isle of Wight*, with him sporting a straw hat. Men in straw hats can also be seen in Renoir's *Le Moulin de la Galette*. The settings, however, indicated leisure activities, so straw hats were appropriate.

It's the women's hats that inevitably capture the attention. Top hats and bowlers simply can't compare with them. And it's hard to accept that any sort of creative impulse lay behind designs for men's hats. As mentioned earlier, the bowler came about because of a practical need for useful head coverings for gamekeepers. There may have been some hats that men wore that broke away from the top hat or the bowler. There's a self-portrait by Degas which shows him in a soft hat of some sort which was perhaps meant to indicate a bohemian inclination. It was done when Degas was young and the bohemian angle was relevant. It's also said that Degas's *Portrait of Zacharian* shows him wearing a "a bowler hat with upturned brim a hat that by the 1890s not only carried working-class associations but also conveyed bohemian status for artists and intellectuals". Presumably it represented a way of separating oneself from the bourgeoisie and their top hats?

Not everyone thought the hundreds of milliners' shops, and the department stores, were forces for the good. Shopping may, in some eyes, have been a way for women to assert their independence, but other people saw it as distracting them from their domestic responsibilities. They were "frivolous" and carried away with "uncontrollable desires" and "placed personal shopping satisfaction before family commitments". A now-obscure novel, *Histoire d'un agent de change,* told the story of a woman who destroys her family because she is addicted to shopping.

It occurs to me to speculate on the taste for hats among working-class women in Paris. Obviously, when they could afford to buy them it would be from a department store or from milliners' shops in the poorer districts of the city. Prices would be lower and the goods of a lesser quality. And the designs, though perhaps essentially copied from the hats on sale in high-class shops, would not be as inventive. Still, a nice-looking hat would probably be cherished by a working-class woman who was able to purchase one, though moralists would no doubt have condemned her for spending money on such an item. Some paintings do show other women besides the society ones favoured by many artists. The woman in the famous painting by Degas, *L'Absinthe*, looks drab and defeated, but is noticeably wearing a hat, though it's difficult to tell what condition it's in.

Although Degas is a key figure in this book it's sometimes another artist who perhaps captures the mood of the moment, even if the painting is less well-regarded than those by Degas. There is a work by Jean Béraud, *Fashionable Woman on the Champs Élysées,* that might be seen as a typical, if sentimentalised, version of Parisian street life during the Belle Époque. The woman is carrying a couple of hatboxes, which suggests she's either a customer who has been shopping, or alternatively a *modiste* who is delivering hats. She's hitching up her skirt at one side and revealing her white petticoat. And there's a smile on her face that could indicate that she's recognised someone, or alternatively that she's aware that a top-hatted man behind her is looking at her questioningly. Dare he approach her, or not? Some observers might think that it's a painting now best-suited to a calendar, or a picture-book about life in Paris, but it tells a story that might have a basis in reality. Or did it just help to create a myth about fashionability and elegance? And sex?

Another Béraud painting, *Paris, rue du Havre,* also presents a view of street life, and again a woman in the foreground is carrying hat boxes and lifting her skirt at one side. It did strike me that there i*s* a practical reason for this, and it's that she's ensuring that the skirt isn't likely to trail on the wet ground. Both paintings give the impression that there has recently been rain.

There's an anecdote about Béraud and Degas, who "once likened his contemporary's paintings to the art of accompanying his fashionable friend, the *salonnière* Geneviève Straus on a shopping trip: `Like a Béraud, I attended the fitting of a most impressive dress' ". What precisely did Degas mean? Was he being complimentary about the accuracy of Béraud's canvases, or possibly a little more cryptic and suggesting that they were as dull as a dress-fitting might be for an onlooker?

Degas, Impressionism, and the Paris Millinery Trade is such a stimulating book that I could happily carry on looking at individual paintings and drawing conclusions from them. One of its intentions is to focus attention on Degas's millinery works which, the editors contend, are often overlooked in favour of his studies of ballet dancers and racehorses, but are as important: "Millinery represents a central element of Degas's broader artistic project of the exploration of Parisian modern life".

It will appeal to enthusiasts for his work generally for that reason. It will also appeal to those who find the subject of the Belle Époque and the artists associated with it of interest. And it will, no doubt, fascinate anyone curious about changing fashions in hats. It is intelligently written, beautifully illustrated, and extensively documented. It should be noted that it was published for the exhibition, *Degas, Paris, and the Paris Millinery Trade,* at the Saint Louis Art Museum (February 12th to May 7th, 2017) and the Legion of Honour, San Francisco (June 24th to September 24th, 2017).

DEGAS, IMPRESSIONISM, AND THE PARIS MILLINERY TRADE
by Simon Kelly and Esther Bell
Prestel Publishing. 296 pages. £50. ISBN 978-3-7913-5621-1

THE PEN AND THE BRUSH

Why were nineteenth-century French novelists often "obsessed with painters and painting"? That question is asked at the very start of Anka Muhlstein's book, and she goes on to say that numerous writers "explored not only how a painter sees things but also how he looks at them, and this produced a new way of writing".

According to Muhlstein, the "visual nature of novels at the time", was "essentially a French phenomenon", and "has no real equivalent in England, Germany, or Russia". I did, at first, wonder whether or not something similar had happened in England, but on reflection I found it difficult to think of an English novelist who dealt with a painter's preoccupations in terms of how he sees things. Yes, there are plenty of novels in which a painter is one of the characters, sometimes with even a central role to play. But it's the painter as a person who seems to intrigue English writers.

There is a book by Bo Jeffares, *The Artist in 19th Century English Fiction* (Humanities Press, 1979), which discusses a wide range of writers, some of them forgotten or obscure, and it's noticeable that it's the social side of the artists' experiences that predominates. The titles of some of the chapters perhaps indicate the book's tendencies: "The Artist Versus Society", "The Artist's Appearance as Romantic Hero", "The Artist's Tragic Temperament". I can't claim to have read most of the books Jeffares refers to, but from her comments I get the impression that few, if any, of them say much about the painting process as opposed to the personalities of the artists. But I may be wrong.

I'm not suggesting that French novelists weren't involved with a question like the "Artist's tragic temperament". Zola's *His Masterpiece* surely deals with the "tragic temperament" of an artist in a highly-detailed manner. But Zola had worked as an influential art critic and was a leading advocate for the work of the Impressionists. Muhlstein says that, "some passages in his novels read like descriptions of Impressionist paintings", and she cites the following as an example: "Everything blazed, the new foliage on the trees, the fountains in the pools springing up and wafting away like gold dust. They watched Paris go by as if through a divine light, the carriages with their wheels shimmering like stars, the great yellow omnibuses more golden than triumphant chariots........"

Zola knew many artists, and Cezanne had been a friend since boyhood. It's often said that the artist in *His Masterpiece* was based on Cezanne, and that his portrayal was the cause of a breakdown in their relationship. Muhlstein suggests that this was not necessarily the case, and claims that some passages in the book can be read to suggest aspects of paintings by Monet, Manet, and even the Symbolist painter, Gustave Moreau, as providing a basis for the work of Zola's fictional painter, Claude Lantier.

Muhlstein essentially focuses on five writers – Balzac, Zola, Huysmans, Maupassant, and Proust - though she stresses that others (Stendhal, Flaubert, the Goncourts) could also be drawn into the survey. It was Edmund de Goncourt, incidentally, who said of Zola: "It is a perilous undertaking for a man who is a complete stranger to art, to write an entire book about it". I've never read the Goncourt's novel about 19th century artistic circles, *Manette Salomon,* though Jerrold Siegel, in his *Bohemian Paris: Culture, Politics, and the Boundaries of Bourgeois Life, 1830-1930* (Viking Penguin, 1986) says that it "provides a portrait of nineteenth-century artistic life and an image of Bohemia unequalled in its combined hostility and insight". But Zola's novel has lasted, whereas I would guess that *Manette Salomon* may now only be read or referred to by scholars, and readers with a specialist interest in nineteenth-century French bohemia.

Muhlstein says that Balzac "was the first novelist to grasp how much of a painter there is in any writer". He had a lifelong interest in art, and "Paintings often sowed the seeds for the novelist's narratives". There is an anecdote about Balzac looking at a painting of a "melancholy winter scene steeped in fog, dotted with shacks and scrawny peasants". He studied the painting, and said it was beautiful, and then added, "but what do they do in that shack? What do they think about, what are their problems? Did they have a good harvest? They probably have debts to pay".

Did the painting suggest all that, or was it just Balzac's imagination that projected the questions onto it? The painter may only have had the scene in mind and what it represented in terms of shapes, colours, etc. He may have had no thoughts at all about the implications of the setting – winter, scrawny peasants, shabby huts – though it's perhaps underestimating an artist's capacity for social concerns, and a way to represent them, to suggest this.

Balzac's most significant study of art and artists was probably *The Unknown Masterpiece*, a novella described by Muhlstein as his "major work about art, artists, and the creative act". It involves three artists, one of them, Frenhofer, a fictional character, and the other two, Poussin and Pourbus, real-life painters. The story gives Balzac an opportunity, through the character of Frenhofer, to discourse at some length about creativity. It isn't sufficient to just have a first-class technique. A genuine artist has to invest his work with something that goes beyond it and gets to the essence of the subject, no matter what it is. Balzac tells a story, of course, and doesn't merely theorise, and there is irony in it, in that Frenhofer, despite all he says about art, in the end fails to succeed when attempting to transfer his ideas to the canvas.

It would seem that Balzac, unlike Zola and other writers, was not the friend of any artists, nor did he ever attempt to become a painter, as did Gautier, Vigny, Musset, and Sue. He did visit art galleries, particularly The Louvre which was open to everyone, much to the chagrin of the respectable who objected to crowds of scruffily-dressed workers wandering around the rooms. The National Gallery in England opened some time later and probably drew the same negative comments from the polite and prosperous, assuming that working people in England annoyed them by venturing into galleries.

I can accept that both Balzac and Zola displayed influences from art and artists in their work, but Maupassant may be a more difficult example to deal with. His novel, *Strong as Death*, is about an artist, a quite successful one compared to the struggling and ill-fated painters who occur in many other books. Maupassant knew artists, and had reviewed exhibitions for the Parisian papers, but his story isn't concerned with the artistic process. It's a social novel, in the sense that it's the characters' actions in relation to each other that matters, and not the painter's feelings about what he's putting on his canvases. He's a society painter. Art may be a job for him, not a conviction.

It's interesting, and of relevance, to look at a Maupassant short-story, "The Model", which opens:

"The little crescent-shaped town of Étretat, with its white cliffs, white shingle and blue sea, was dozing peacefully in the brilliant July sunshine. At the tips of the crescent two arches of rock jutted out into the calm water, the smaller to the north like a dwarf foot, the larger to the south like a giant leg; and beyond it the needle, tapering upward from a broad base almost to the height of the cliff. towering skyward".

Now let me quote a passage from *Portalone,* a long out-of-print novel, published in 1904, by a minor British writer, C. Ranger-Gull:

"They turned out of the station and walked a few yards till they came to the inn. It stood on the banks of a wide, shallow estuary, an arm of the sea which had come far inland. Except for one narrow strip of horizon, where something white fell and tumbled, suggesting the sea outside the bar, the scene was grey and sad. The inn was a square house of granite without ornamentation, or, indeed, anything which might seem to suggest much hospitality or cheer".

That seems to me as visual as the Maupassant, and I'm not drawing argumentative comparisons between French and British writers, simply pointing to the fact that writers "painting scenes" were not unusual. I will accept that 1904 was a few years after Maupassant was active (he died in 1893), and his work was known to many British writers. In fact, the style and mood of the story, which concerns an artist more or less pushed reluctantly into marriage when his model attempts to commit suicide, reminds me of the work of the ill-fated British writer, Hubert Crackanthorpe. But then, he was a great admirer of Maupassant's novels and stories.

It's perhaps worth noting that *Portalone* is a novel based on the artists' colony of St Ives in Cornwall. I'm not about to claim that it bears comparison with Balzac, Zola, or Maupassant. Ranger-Gull was a popular novelist of his day, facile, sentimental, and easy to read. But scattered throughout his book are descriptive passages which point to his being alert to the land and the sea around him and, possibly, to the work of the artists he was associating with.

J.K.Huysmans was descended from a line of Dutch artists and had worked as an arts columnist. His novel, *Against the Grain,* revolved around an aesthete, Des Esseintes, whose preferences in painting run to Gustave Moreau and Goya. Huysmans himself seems to have liked the work of Degas and Whistler among nineteenth-century artists. Muhlstein refers to "the most beautiful passage in *Against the Grain*", which is a description of Moreau's *Salomé.* According to Muhlstein, when Maupassant reviewed Huysmans', novel he praised it but also thought it "uproariously funny," not perhaps a judgement that the author would have welcomed. But from my own reading of

Against the Grain many years ago, I can understand why Maupassant saw it that way. It did often strike me that Des Esseintes' aestheticism was so extreme that it couldn't help but lead to laughter.

Proust had a taste for classical art, but liked the Impressionists and painters such as Whistler and Steer. He seems not to have cared for Cezanne, Matisse, Bonnard, and Picasso. Muhlstein says that it is clearly Monet who inspired Proust when his narrator at one point admires "the places where the sea is so calm that the reflections feel almost more solid and real than the hulls of boats vaporised by the effects of the sun".

There is a strong argument in *The Pen and the Brush* for the singularity of French nineteenth-century novels in terms of their use of art and artists, not only as subject-matter but also as influences relating to how things are described. It's certainly true of Zola. It did occur to me, however, to keep thinking about whether or not British novelists didn't also emphasise the visual (people as well as landscapes) in some ways, though without necessarily insisting on being influenced by paintings.

There are many descriptive (of faces and places) passages in Dickens, for example. I recently came across a reference in George Eliot's *Daniel Deronda*, where someone is likened to a Titian portrait. The same novel also has a passage where the play of light on water is emphasised and adds to the mood of the situation described. I have a feeling that, had I the time and energy to track down and read all the novels mentioned in Bo Jeffares' *The Artist in Nineteenth-Century English Fiction*, I might well be able to come up with some more examples of English writers doing "literary painting".

This is not a criticism of Anka Muhlstein's book, and I have to emphasise that the points raised in my review were brought about by the clear and provocative (in the best sense) nature of her writing. Her ideas are interesting, and her selections from the work of the novelists she writes about are always apt. I enjoyed *The Pen and the Brush*. It pushed me into questioning some of my assumptions about writers and writing, and opened my eyes to themes worth taking into consideration. And in an age of overlong books it is refreshingly short and concise.

THE PEN AND THE BRUSH: HOW PASSION FOR ART SHAPED NINETEENTH-CENTURY FRENCH NOVELS

By Anka Muhlstein (translated by Adriana Hunter)

Other Press. 228 pages. $18.95. ISBN 978-15905-1805-2

L'AFFICHOMANIA

I recently saw an exhibition of Alphonse Mucha's work at the Walker Art Gallery in Liverpool, England, and admired his skill at combining commercial requirements with artistic accomplishments. In their way, Mucha's posters are possibly the most representative in terms of being identified with Paris of a certain period in the minds of many people. Henri de Toulouse-Lautrec probably demands attention when it comes to Montmartre and the bohemian world of the Moulin Rouge and its performers, but Mucha commanded the fashionable scene with his famous posters for Sarah Bernhardt, and those concerned to advertise cigarettes, drinks, and other commodities.

There were other producers of posters, and several of them are alongside Mucha and Lautrec in this handsome book that accompanies an exhibition at the Richard H. Driehaus Museum in Chicago (February 11, 2017 to January 7, 2018). Driehaus, a businessman and philanthropist, is an avid collector of posters and has built up a fine collection which provides the basis for the exhibition.

Jeannine Falino, its curator, says that the "Golden Age" of French poster art was during the period from the 1880s through to the late-1890s. There were some practical reasons for this. In 1881 a law was passed which opened up the freedom of the Press, including the unlimited production of posters, prints, etc. Around the same time, Jules Chéret had made advances in the use of colour lithography. The result was that "colour-printed posters were exhibited in that most public of galleries – the street – where they began to blur the boundaries between fine and popular art". Someone described them as "frescoes, if not of the poor, at least of the crowd".

It's interesting to note that, almost from their first appearances, the posters were collected. There had been posters before, of course, but they were mostly in basic colours and simply stated the appropriate information they were designed to disseminate. With Chéret's posters, and those of his contemporaries like Mucha, Eugène Grasset, Theodore Steinlen, and Lautrec, the artistic value of them was immediately recognised. There are stories of them being stripped from the walls and hoardings almost as soon as they were posted there. Special kiosks were built to display them. Dealers began to sell posters, catalogues were printed, and there were exhibitions of poster art.

There are a couple of illustrations which point to the profusion of posters in the Paris of the period in question. A painting by Jean Béraud simply entitled *The Kiosk* shows a smartly-dressed woman looking at posters on a kiosk while a well turned-out man is likewise peering at them. The other painting, *Posters on a Wall and a Man Mending Metal Pots* by Louis-Robert Carrier-Belleuse, has a bourgeois couple inspecting posters on a wall, some of which are peeling away. There may be some implied social commentary in this painting. Not everyone welcomed the idea of posters being displayed everywhere and they probably did become tattered and torn and unsightly. It may also be correct to assert that showing the working-class man busy at his job, while the couple have time to indulge in checking on what the posters are advertising, indicates that they were essentially there to sell things that the low-paid couldn't afford. But perhaps I'm reading too much into the painting?

Chéret has been described as the "king of the poster," and the writer J.K. Huysmans is said to have "preferred his originality and energy to the stifling and unimaginative academic painting of the state-sponsored Salon of the Society of French Artists". He had been trained as a lithographer and was skilled at the use of colour techniques. As for influences, he referred back to painters such as Watteau and Fragonard, with their "idealised qualities of pleasure, leisure, and reverie". The attractive and always-happy young women portrayed on Chéret's posters became popularly known as *chérettes.* And he "strove to integrate subject and text", which according to Jeannine Falino, "was an improvement on traditional poster design where text was not visually connected to the image".

Eugène Grasset, from the examples of his posters, was nowhere near as flamboyant as Chéret, and appears to have been influenced by the English arts and craft movement. His women are appealing, but seem more-mature than Chéret's, and there are no displays of bare shoulders and plunging necklines. One poster, advertising bicycles, offers only a hint of the actual machine and it's the woman holding the handlebar who essentially attracts attention. This might be seen as using sex to sell a product, but it doesn't really come across in that way. She is too demure. The accompanying note refers to her as "smartly dressed and self possessed", and I was put in mind of the contrast afforded by a poster, also advertising bicycles, in the aforementioned Liverpool exhibition, where the curves of the handlebar might have some relationship to the curve of the cleavage seen because of the low-cut dress the woman is wearing.

I have to admit to a personal prejudice in favour of Théophile-Alexandre Steinlen, perhaps because he loved cats, but also because of his links to bohemian Montmartre and its radical inclinations. The Montmartre Museum in Paris has examples of his work, and some years ago, visiting an exhibition in Giverny, I made a short detour to Vernon to look at several paintings by American Impressionists, and to my delight found that the gallery there was also showing a Steinlen exhibition. He was clearly more politically aware than the others, and had a "more compassionate realistic style". There is a Steinlen poster, *La Rue,* done to advertise the work of a printer, which shows a cross-section of Parisian society, ranging from workers to obviously-affluent bourgeoisie. It isn't overtly political, but the placing of the different characters might indicate some sort of confrontational situation, albeit not a violent one.

A more-direct social comment was made in Steinlen's advertisement for the novel, *La Traite Des Blanche (The White Slave Trade),* which shows a self-satisfied pimp with three prostitutes, one of whom has collapsed crying, another who appears to be howling in misery, and a third who might have accepted her fate. This third figure had bare breasts in Steinlen's original design, but the censor intervened and the published version shows her covered up.

One of Steinlen's most-famous posters advertised *Le Chat Noir*, the "bohemian outpost for the avant-garde". It's suggested that he used this illustration to also poke fun at Mucha's "penchant for placing haloes around the heads of his female subjects", the large black cat in Steinlen's image having what appears to be one around its head. Like Mucha and Grasset, he also helped publicise bicycles, and for his poster introduced some humour, with the lady riding her machine into a gaggle of startled geese.

The swirling long locks of hair so characteristic of many of Mucha's women, as seen on his posters, are what may persuade people to almost-immediately identify his work, and relate it to their ideas about Paris around 1900. Described as "One of Mucha's best-known images, the *Job* poster is a beloved symbol of art nouveau". *Job* was a brand of cigarette paper, and the inference was that smoking was a "sensual experience". It's interesting that the one woman in the book who actually designed posters as opposed to being shown on them, was Jane Arché, whose *Hors Concours* also used a sophisticated woman to highlight the pleasures of smoking and the quality of *Job* cigarette papers.

In 1894, *La Plume,* a Parisian literary magazine, started *The Salon des Cent*, an annual exhibition that continued until 1900 and was meant to show the work of one hundred poster artists. Mucha did the poster for the 1897 exhibition, with a somewhat pensive-looking lady holding what she is working on and peering at the viewer. The reference to the number of artists producing posters gives an indication of how widespread their use was. Not all of the artists were necessarily active all of the time in poster production. In a book I recently found in a second-hand bookshop, *Paris 1900: The Art of the Poster* by Herman Schardt (Bracken Books, London, 1987), there were examples of posters by Pierre Bonnard, Maurice Denis, and the Spanish painter, Ramon Casas, but none of these artists went beyond creating a handful of examples of the genre. Another bookshop-find was Alain Weill's large *The Art Nouveau Poster* (Francis Lincoln Ltd., London, 2015), which gives Paris a central place in its survey, but goes outside it to take in Austria, Great Britain, the United States, and other countries.

One of Henri Toulouse-Lautrec's classic images is his striking poster of Aristide Bruant, a singer of "realist songs," who "gave eloquent voice to the downtrodden who were living on the margins of city life". He hurled insults at the well-to-do people who slummed it in Montmartre, and they, no doubt, lapped it up, knowing full well that their lives and property would be protected by the police, and the army, if necessary. It wasn't all that many years since the Commune had been savagely repressed and thousands of working-class men and women shot.

But Lautrec specialised in posters which portrayed entertainers like May Milton (an English performer with a limited range who quickly disappeared from sight), La Goulue, and Jane Avril, a particular favourite of his. There was an excellent exhibition, *Toulouse-Lautrec and Jane Avril: Beyond the Moulin Rouge*, at the Courtauld Gallery, London in 2011.There is an amusing difference to be noted between Lautrec's version of Yvette Guilbert and the way she is shown on a poster by Chéret. In the latter she is slender, graceful, and quite pretty, but Lautrec didn't see her that way. There is a story that she once said to him, "For the love of heaven, don't make me so appallingly ugly! Just a little less so!".

Jane Avril was herself interested in posters for their own sake, and not just because they advertised her performances. One of Lautrec's illustrations shows her at the printer's shop, examining a poster, while the man works at his machine in the background. Lautrec could, of course, come up with a darker picture of life in Montmartre, when he showed what life was like in the brothels he frequented, but those illustrations were never likely to appear on public posters around Paris.

Posters didn't suddenly disappear after 1900 or so, but they began to decline in importance as new technologies and popular interests (the cinema was starting to attract attention) came into play, and the relevance and importance of posters began to diminish. Artists moved on to different things. Mucha, always a Czech patriot, was increasingly involved with producing work "aimed at elevating awareness and admiration for Slavic culture". Grasset devoted his time to teaching. Chéret concentrated on murals. And Lautrec had died.

L'Affichomania is a beautifully-produced and fascinating book that works in its own right to provide a picture of aspects of Paris during the Belle Époque. It isn't the whole picture, of course, and some might argue that the posters largely appealed to the affluent or the bohemians, and that the working-class population of Paris, certain individuals apart, probably took little notice of them from an artistic point of view, and could only dream about most of what they publicised or promoted. I'm not sure about this, and it would be useful to have some information about where the posters were placed. Advertising of any kind is usually aimed at people who can afford to purchase the products on offer.

These are questions for a social historian, and shouldn't be allowed to distract from an appreciation of the skills of the artists concerned, and the sheer attractiveness of what they produced.

L'AFFICHOMANIA : THE PASSION FOR FRENCH POSTERS
by Jeannine Falino
Richard H. Driehaus Museum (distributed by The University of Chicago Press). 127 pages. $32.50. ISBN 978-0-578-16802-9

ALPHONSE MUCHA

I have a suspicion that a lot of people may not be prepared to accept that Alphonse Mucha's work, or at least that part of it he produced for "commercial", as opposed to "fine art" purposes, deserves to be given serious consideration as "art". His posters and other designs were usually commissioned and were created to promote plays, magazines, bicycles, brands of beer or other alcoholic beverages, biscuits, and train journeys.

It's true that various of his contemporaries, Toulouse-Lautrec perhaps most famously, also did commercial work, though in his case it was often to advertise the kind of establishment, and its performers, where bohemians were said to congregate. So, there isn't a problem if his posters are displayed in exhibitions of his work alongside his paintings. They're seen as part of a whole that includes brothel studies, portraits, and more.

With Mucha it might be a little different. He did paint some pictures and murals which weren't meant for advertising purposes, and a few of them are included in the exhibition. But I have to admit that I found them of less interest than the commercial posters.

Mucha was born in Ivancice, then a part of the Austro-Hungarian Empire, in 1860. He didn't have a very distinguished school record, and though he showed some talent for drawing, his application to enter the Prague Academy of Fine Arts was rejected. In 1879 he moved to Vienna to work as an apprentice scene painter. He attended evening art classes and visited art galleries, but lost his job in Vienna and then made a living painting portraits of local notables in South Moravia.

He was sponsored by several titled people, spent time as a student in Munich, and in 1887 moved to Paris to study at the Académie Julian. In 1889 he started to work as an illustrator for publishers in Prague and Paris. He mixed with the painters associated with the Nabis, and also met and became friends with Gauguin. His breakthrough came in late-1894 when he designed a poster advertising the famed actress Sarah Bernhardt's appearance in the play, *Gismonda*. It was displayed across Paris and attracted a great deal of attention. As a result, Mucha was asked to create sets, costumes and posters for Bernhardt's theatre productions on a regular basis.

By 1897 Mucha was holding solo exhibitions and expanding his circle of friends to include many well-known writers, artists, and musicians. And his career went from strength to strength. He visited the USA several times, taught at art schools in New York, Chicago, and Philadelphia, and was commissioned to decorate a theatre. He had similar successes in Europe, and was asked to work on murals for the Municipal House in Prague. He did make another visit to New York in 1913 and attended the famous Armoury Show which introduced a range of European modern art to America. He also went to Poland and Russia to research for the project, *The Slav Epic*, "a series of twenty murals painted on enormous canvases and depicting "the history of all the Slavic peoples".

Mucha was always a Czech patriot, and when Czechoslovakia came into existence as an independent country in 1918 he stayed there, and designed postage stamps and bank notes for the new state. He died in Prague in 1939, shortly after the Nazis had moved into Czechoslovakia and he had been arrested and questioned by the Gestapo because of his involvements as a Freemason.

As I remarked earlier, I don't find his historical paintings, relevant though they may be from a documentary point of view, as interesting as the posters and designs for books, etc., he produced during his Paris years. That could be because I have a particular liking for the art emanating from the French capital in the late-nineteenth and early-twentieth centuries. But it would be useful to know how many other people visiting the gallery inclined towards my point of view.

It's said that Mucha's poster designs (120 between 1895 and 1904) are now regarded as "icons of Art Nouveau", and that he "left an enduring legacy through his style.......which is characterised by the image of a beautiful woman in an elegant pose arranged in a harmonious composition with flowers and other decorative motifs taken from nature". He had perhaps been influenced by what he knew about the Pre-Raphaelites, particularly Edwards Burne-Jones, and he was aware of the work and ideas of William Morris. He had a firm idea that the "aim of art is to glorify beauty", and it is obvious that he found beauty particularly expressed through the faces and forms of many women.

In commercial terms this, of course, came down to "using" women to advertise almost everything, which raises the question of whether or not Mucha exploited the sexual angle to emphasise the qualities of what was being sold. In a way, he did, though the sensuality on show is mild by modern standards. Usually the most that can be seen are bare arms and shoulders, though occasionally there is a glimpse of a bare breast. It's always possible to read phallic symbols into paintings, of course, though they may only exist in the eye of the beholder. Likewise with other references. An advertisement for a bicycle appears to draw a relationship between the curves of the handlebars and the curve of a cleavage made evident by the low-cut dress of the girl in the illustration. One wonders what today's Advertising Standards Authority might make of Mucha's proclivity for using attractive women to advertise goods and services? Would they find him guilty of perpetuating gender stereotypes?

Alphonse Mucha: In Quest of Beauty is a colourful exhibition, with an excellent accompanying catalogue which has some stimulating essays about Mucha and the general background to his work. It may be of interest to mention a couple of relevant recent publications. Alain Weill's large *The Art Nouveau Poster* (Frances Lincoln Ltd., 2015) sets Mucha in context, alongside the brilliant Jules Chéret, Eugène Grasset, Théophile Alexandre Steinlen, and many others. Jeannine Falino's *L'Affichomania: The Passion for French Posters* (The Richard H. Driehaus Museum, Chicago, 2017) looks at the Richard H. Driehaus collection. Driehaus is a contemporary collector, but people have valued the posters almost from the start, and it wasn't unusual for them to be stripped from walls and hoardings within a short time of their being displayed. And gallery exhibitions of poster art were held around the time of their employment for the purpose of advertising. It's obvious that they were recognised as having artistic qualities that raised them above mere commercial use.

ALPHONSE MUCHA: IN QUEST OF BEAUTY
An exhibition at the Walker Art Gallery, Liverpool, 16th June, 2017 to 29th October, 2017

ALPHONSE MUCHA: IN QUEST OF BEAUTY
Edited by Tomoko Sato.
Mucha Foundation Publishing. 168 pages. £15.99. ISBN 978-0-9536322-99

AUSTRALIA'S IMPRESSIONISTS

I doubt that much is known about the four artists covered in this exhibition. Charles Conder may be someone recognised by those who are curious about the fin-de-siècle circles associated with writers and artists like Oscar Wilde and Aubrey Beardsley. Condor was born in England, grew up in India, moved to Australia as a teenager, went to Paris, where he knew Toulouse-Lautrec, in 1890, and then to England, where he died in 1909 at the early age of forty-one. He painted in places like Swanage and Newquay in England.

If Conder may only be recognised by a limited number of people, what about Tom Roberts, Arthur Streeton, and John Russell? Roberts was born in England in 1856, moved to Australia as a teenager, was in London between 1881 and 1885 to study art, and became friendly with and was influenced by Whistler. He also spent a short time in Paris. Roberts returned to London in 1903 and stayed there until 1923. He then went back to Australia and died in 1941.

Arthur Streeton was born in Australia. He was the first Australian-born artist to have a painting exhibited at the Royal Academy in London (it was also shown at the Paris Salon), but when he moved to England in 1897 he found it difficult to achieve any sort of recognition for his work. Nonetheless, he stayed in England for thirty or so years before returning to Australia, where he died in 1943.

John Russell, seems to be the artist most favoured by the curators of the National Gallery exhibition. Born in Australia in 1858 he became financially independent when his father died, and he then moved to London to study art in 1881 before going to Paris. Russell stayed in Europe for around forty years, and became associated with many of the leading modern artists in France. His painting reflected that fact. He did eventually return to Australia, dying in Sydney in 1930.

I've sketched in some basic biographical details because they seem to me to be relevant in terms of the sort of work produced by each of the painters. Russell, for example, was highly thought of by artists such as Matisse and Monet, and by the sculptor, Rodin. Unlike the others, he never painted scenes of Australian life and locations, and that, perhaps, caused him to be neglected in his native country, while the fact of his not being French probably meant that he would be overlooked when histories of Impressionism and other Parisian art movements were written. Russell was wealthy enough to be able to build a house on an island off the Brittany coast and live there with his family for many years. He had no need to sell his work, so didn't market it widely. It's said that when his wife died he was so grief-stricken that he destroyed much of it.

I have to admit that, looking around the National Gallery exhibition, I found Russell's paintings less interesting than those by Roberts and Streeton. They quite clearly demonstrate that he was aware of what was happening in France, and that may have been, for me, something of a problem. I could see Monet in one painting, Cezanne in another. What I couldn't see was any kind of real individuality. It may be true that what Russell was doing now appeals to art historians and critics, and they can talk about his brushwork and colour sense, and the fact of his being "the most impressionist of Australia's impressionists", which may be true enough, but doesn't make his canvases any more interesting.

Tom Roberts and Arthur Streeton were much more to my taste, and their work, while showing some influences from Europe, seemed firmly located in the landscapes and urban scenes of a developing and energetic Australia. Unlike Russell, and Conder (though he did seem to share some of Roberts and Streeton's concerns before leaving the country), they wanted to record what was around them. They also wanted to use the natural colour and light to heighten the effect of their paintings. It wasn't that they were unaware of impressionist techniques, but they didn't feel the need to follow them slavishly. In some ways, it may be that lumping all four artists under the "Impressionist" label doesn't do them justice. It has become a catch-all term that appears to be applied to almost everyone painting in a non-academic way in the late-19th century. The catalogue quotes an American art historian, Norma Broude, on the subject of "international impressionism" which she defines as "the impulse to paint contemporary life and experience directly from nature, to study the effects of light, and to use a lighter palette and looser brushwork". It occurs to me that it's a quite broad definition which could be linked to any number of late-19th century artists.

Fine paintings such as Roberts's *A Break Away!* (a wonderfully movement-packed picture of horsemen trying to stop thirsty sheep stampeding towards a water hole) and *Allegro Con Brio: Bourke Street West* (a street scene in which you can almost feel the heat and the dust rising) attract the attention, as does his quieter *The Camp, Sirius Cove.* Streeton's *Fire's On* is a large canvas in which workers near the entrance to a mine seem dwarfed by the rocks towering above them. His *The Railway Station – Redfern* reminds me of Norman Garstin's Cornish painting, *The Rain It Raineth Every Day* in the way a wet day is shown, while *'the purple's noon's transparent might'* beautifully captures the vastness of the landscape we see.

There are paintings by Conder from his days in Australia. *Departure of the Orient – Circular Quay* is darker than many of the pictures by Roberts and Streeton, where they worked on "the glare" (the impact of the bright sun) to heighten their canvases, but it is striking in the way it captures the crowds on the quayside clustered in the rain. His *A Holiday at Mentone* is much brighter and perhaps anticipates some of the paintings he produced in Newquay and Brighton. Conder was the tragic one of the four, and often criticised for his bohemian lifestyle. It's said that other "Australian artists in London and Paris kept their distance from him", and his death was ascribed to "general paralysis of the insane", in other words the long-term effects of syphilis.

Australia's Impressionists is a relatively small exhibition, but is full of interesting paintings. As I said earlier, it did occur to me, looking around the exhibition, reading the catalogue, and watching a useful short film about the artists, that there is a desire among curators, critics, and art historians, to revive interest in John Russell. I had the feeling that because he moved to France, knew Monet and many others, and picked up on new ideas, he's now being seen as somehow more adventurous than Roberts or Streeton. He didn't impress me that way. While I was looking at his paintings, the friend I was with pointed to one of them, (*Madame Sisley on the Banks of the Loing at Moret*) and remarked, "Wynford Dewhurst".

Dewhurst, known as the "Manchester Monet", lived in France and, like Russell, knew Monet and other impressionists. He was a talented painter, but not very original, and there have been some moves towards reviving interest in him, including a current exhibition at Manchester City Art Gallery. I'm all for revivals of interest in forgotten or obscure painters, poets, novelists, and musicians, but there is a danger that, to satisfy the interests and needs of curators, critics, and academics, anxious to find some fresh ground to explore, they may sometimes be over-rated.

AUSTRALIA'S IMPRESSIONISTS
An exhibition at the National Gallery, London, 7th December, 2016 to 26th March, 2017

AUSTRALIA'S IMPRESSIONISTS, edited by Christopher Riopelle
National Gallery Publications. 128 pages. £16.95. ISBN 978-1857-096-125

ITALIAN FUTURISM AND THE FIRST WORLD WAR

It isn't true to say that Filipo Tommaso Marinetti single-handedly created the Futurist movement in the early 1900s, but it's difficult to get away from the idea that, without him, it may never had the impact that it did. He co-ordinated activities, put people in touch with each other, drew up manifestos, helped start magazines and newspapers, wrote novels and critical essays, publicised Futurist events, and generally shaped the direction that it would take. Other artists and writers were present, but it was Marinetti who represented Futurism in the minds of the general public.

It was certainly Marinetti who first drew international attention to Futurism when, in 1909, he published a manifesto on the front page of the Parisian daily newspaper, *Le Figaro*. It was a manifesto designed to shock the bourgeoisie with its many outrageous statements:

"We want to glorify war – the only cure for the world – militarism, patriotism, the destructive gesture of the anarchists, the beautiful ideas which kill, and contempt for women. We want to demolish museums, libraries and academies of all kinds, fight morality, feminism and all opportunist and utilitarian cowardice".

There was much more, including an advocacy of "a new beauty: the beauty of speed", and "great-breasted locomotives, puffing on the rails like enormous steel horses", and "the gliding flight of aeroplanes". It was the modern world that Marinetti was celebrating, in order to deliver Italy from "that spineless worshipping of old canvases, old statues and old bric-à-brac", and to stand "against everything which is filthy and worm-ridden and corroded by time".

It might be worth noting what Gino Severini, one of the signatories of the manifesto, recalled of its publication when writing his autobiography, *The Life of a Painter* (Princeton University Press, 1995). Severini, who was living in Paris, claimed that he only signed because his friend, Umberto Boccioni, asked him to lend support to the fledgling Futurist movement. He talked to the Italian artist, Amadeo Modigliani, who advised against participating. When the manifesto appeared in print: "The art world had a good laugh about the whole thing, and I was not spared their jibes. Modigliani was fierce; as for Picasso, with whom I later discussed it, his opinion is easily imagined".

The demonstrations, performances, and other activities staged by the Futurists in Italy were designed to antagonise. And they succeeded, though sometimes the reactions ranged from mockery to anger. They were, in many ways, precursors of the Dadaists and Surrealists. But the liveliness and inventiveness of Futurist artists shouldn't be underestimated. Painters such as Gino Severini, Umberto Boccioni, Giacomo Balla, and Cario Carrà were producing fascinating work, with an influence from Cubism, before the First World War. Severini, in particular, had spent time in Paris, knew various painters, and so was familiar with all the latest innovations in art.

When the war broke out in August, 1914, Italy was not initially involved. However, there was a significant surge of anti-German, and particularly anti-Austrian feeling which lent itself to demands for Italy to throw in its lot with France, Britain, and Russia. Marinetti and some other Futurists were active in calling for the country to go to war, as might be expected if one took their manifesto at face value. When Italy did declare war on Germany and Austria in May, 1915, they quickly volunteered. Not all of the Futurists were as keen to be involved in fighting as Marinetti was, and Carrà and Severini distanced themselves from Marinetti. In a way, this early rift in the group perhaps hinted at later differences about the role of the Futurists. Were they artists or political activists, and could the two commitments be productively combined?

It's interesting that, during the pro-intervention period prior to May, 1915, the figure of Benito Mussolini appeared on the scene, and it is suggested that Marinetti, knowing that Mussolini "was one of the most well-known agitators for intervention on a national scale attempted to attach himself to Mussolini's name and persona in order to attract maximum attention at the demonstration". I have to say that, from what I've read about Marinetti, he was always an opportunist, even if it seemed to be to further the cause of Futurism rather than himself. Mussolini was also an opportunist, so they had much in common, both personally and politically.

Selena Daly's well-researched and documented account of the Futurist involvement in the First World War doesn't spend a lot of time looking into what Futurism was in terms of its artistic aims. Her intention is to focus on how Marinetti and the others responded to the call to arms, and how Futurism fared in a war setting. Marinetti, Boccioni and several others were quick to enlist and joined the Lombard Battalion of the Volunteer Cyclists and Motorists, a unit which attracted writers, artists and, intellectuals, and was not looked on kindly by officers of the regular Italian Army. The volunteers tended to be less amenable to discipline than other soldiers. Artists, writers, and intellectuals frequently have an individual approach to rules and regulations that obviously clashes with military ideas of good order.

After a time, the Volunteer Cyclists and Motorists unit was broken up and its members transferred to various regiments of the Italian Army. Marinetti eventually became an officer and served with an Alpine Battalion. It's interesting to note how he saw the war in the mountains:

"Marinetti transformed the Alpine landscape so that the experience of mountain combat would conform to Futurist visions of technologically advanced and industrialised modernity. The man-made environment transformed by war, surpassed the traditional religious and nostalgic associations of nature and landscape".

Marinetti also used his military service as an opportunity to promote the Futurist cause, giving talks and encouraging soldiers to read Futurist texts. It's not easy to know what kind of responses he received when he spoke of the wonders of war, and warned against the duplicity of women who might get up to all sorts of mischief while their men were in the trenches. Daly more than once says that: "Futurist testimonies are often unreliable sources of evidence", so we have to be careful when reading their accounts of success in persuading people to be interested in the Futurist programme. Marinetti may have convinced a few officers, who perhaps already knew about Futurism from its pre-war antics, but there appears to be little or no records of how the rank-and-file reacted. I'd guess that most ordinary soldiers, especially conscripts, might have come up with a fairly robust reaction when told about the glory to be gained from losing a leg or being killed.

To be fair to Marinetti, he wasn't just a behind-the-lines propagandist, encouraging others to do what he would never do himself, and he served with distinction at the front. His military involvements worked in his favour after the war, as did those of some other Futurists. People were more-inclined to look favourably on Futurist art and performances, though it helped that there had been a general toning down of the anti-bourgeois rhetoric that had characterised Futurist activities before 1914. There was a turn towards what was termed, "moderate Futurism".

For obvious reasons, Futurist painting had taken something of a back-seat during the war, but there were several publications which, in one way or another, continued to further the interests of the Futurists. The immediate post-war period found Marinetti forming a Futurist Political Party. And in 1919 he stood for election as a Fascist candidate. There was a strong Futurist presence when Mussolini formed his Fasci di Combattimento. The Futurist Political Party was never popular in the sense of attracting a wide membership, or achieving substantial votes at elections, though it did have some support among the Arditi, the elite troops (and proto-Fascists) that Marinetti favoured. But he soon dissolved the Party, and began to announce that he had no interest in politics.

He returned to the artistic side of Futurism and saw potential for advancing its interests through theatrical performances and the new-medium of film. And he continued to write.

Futurism didn't fizzle out after its brief moment of fame during and just after the war. It's not within Daly's remit to tell us what happened to the Futurists, but it's worth making a few observations on the later activities of one or two of the leading lights of the movement. As noted earlier, Carrà and Severini had drifted away from Marinetti, and Daly points to Carrà's "conversion to metaphysical painting". Boccioni had died during the war, as had Sant'Elia. Balla moved towards designing furniture and clothing which took the Futurist idea in a decorative direction. Fortunato Depero did a variety of things, including interior decoration, furniture design, and tapestries. Gino Severini, who had moved to France at the start of Italy's venture into war, came back to Italy and turned to religious paintings later in life. Although the Futurists were still producing manifestos (Marinetti, Balla, Depero, and some younger artists, were behind one in 1929), I very much have the feeling that people were operating more as individuals, rather than as members of a functioning and influential movement.

It needs to be acknowledged that the Futurists' links to Italian Fascism can be disturbing. Marinetti's pronouncements on the virtues, as he saw them, of violence, war, emphatic modernisation, and similar topics, may appear foolish now, but at the time they certainly seemed to correspond to some of the aims of the Fascists. They wanted to turn Italy into a more modern country, though their methods might not have appealed to everyone. Economically, they thought that a corporate state, with labour and business combining to boost production and eliminate class differences, could lead to modernisation. So, in some ways, the interests of the Futurists in wanting to use all the elements of modernism – mechanisation, speed, etc. – did, on the surface, seem to have a relationship of sorts to Fascism. And, of course, the Fascists' militarism would have appealed to Marinetti, at least, as would the Fascist desire to create a new Italian Empire. I'm simply trying to suggest why some impressionable young men might have been inclined to see certain virtues in Fascist theories.

Selena Daly's account is, as stated in the title of her book, essentially about Futurist fortunes around the time of the First World War. And, from that point of view, it is highly successful. With a multitude of notes, and a large bibliography (the two total over one hundred pages) it will surely become a standard work on the subject.

Before leaving the Futurists, it occurs to me to point out that, however one feels about Marinetti's views on war, the art work produced by several of the Futurist painters is still worth looking at. In fact, I'd go as far to say that the best of it can stand comparison with most of the work by Cubists, Surrealists, and others from the same period. We perhaps don't get too many opportunities to see Futurist work in Britain, though I recall an excellent Fortunato Depero exhibition at the Lowry in Salford in 2001. And a visit to the small, but fascinating Estorick Collection in North London is always a pleasure. It specialises in 20th century Italian art and has some good examples of Futurist paintings. Later this year, there will be an exhibition of work entitled *Giacomo Balla*: *Designing the Future.* Marinetti's shrill and often silly demands for blood and thunder are now just a matter of historical record, and can be treated as such, but the paintings of the Futurists continue to intrigue.

ITALIAN FUTURISM AND THE FIRST WORLD WAR
By Selena Daly

University of Toronto Press. 265 pages. £44.99. ISBN 978-1-4426-4906-4

NORDIC PAINTING

How well-known is Nordic art in Britain? By Nordic art we're essentially talking about paintings from Denmark, Sweden, Norway, Finland, Greenland, and Iceland. And I suspect that most people, leaving aside art critics and academics, might be hard pushed to put forward more than a handful of names for consideration. Edvard Munch (Norway) would most likely be the obvious one, though I wonder which of his paintings, other than "The Scream," might come to mind at the mention of his name? Anders Zorn (Sweden), could be included in a list of Nordic artists who some people, at least, would know. And perhaps Vilhelm Hammershøi (Denmark) would receive a nod of recognition. August Strindberg (Sweden)? Yes, but would it be for his work as a painter rather than as a playwright?

I think it is true to say that there haven't been a great many exhibitions devoted to Nordic art in recent years. I recall the excellent, *Dreams of a Summer Night: Scandinavian Paintings at the Turn of the Century* at the Hayward Gallery, but that was in 1986. Munch and Strindberg have both been exhibited at Tate Modern since the beginning of this century. There was *Hammershøi: Poetry of Silence* at the Royal Academy in 2008. I'm not claiming that what I've mentioned covers everything that has been available to British audiences, but compared to galleries on the Continent and in the USA (see the bibliography in *Nordic Painting*), we do seem to have been poorly served with what has generally been on offer over the years.

The same could well be true of books relating to the art of the countries concerned. Leaving aside the publication under review, I can think of *Nordic Art: The Modern Breakthrough, 1860-1920* (Hirmer, 2012), edited by David Jackson, though that related to an exhibition of the same name shown in Groninger and Munich in 2012. We could buy the book, but not easily visit the exhibition. There is also Patricia G. Berman's splendid *In Another Light: Danish Painting in the Nineteenth Century* (Thames & Hudson, 2007 and 2013). I can think of a few other books that help throw light on Nordic artists in the context of 19th and early-20th century painting generally. Michael Jacobs' *The Good and Simple Life: Artist Colonies in Europe and America* (Phaidon, 1985) and Brian Dudley Barrett's *Artists on the Edge: The Rise of Coastal Artists' Colonies, 1880-1920* (Amsterdam University Press, 2011) might be useful for what they say about Nordic painters.

Again, I make no claim to completeness in what I've said about literature relating to Nordic art. There are, no doubt, other books on the subject, though some of them may be relatively little-known, and I've been focusing on publications that are, or have been, fairly easy to access.

My purpose in spending a little time talking about the availability of material, or lack of it, is to welcome *Nordic Painting* as something that will surely help to broaden our knowledge of artists from Denmark, Sweden, and the other countries concerned. Obviously, it can't cover the whole range of artistic activity over a wide period, and the emphasis is largely on the late-nineteenth and early-twentieth centuries. In other words its very title, *Nordic Painting*, indicates a degree of selectivity in what is involved. The thrust of the argument is to pick out certain paintings either from a specific artist's career, or from a period, and often analyse them in some detail. What do they say, and how do they say it? And how do they represent certain tendencies in the development of art in the region?

Despite what I said about a possible lack of awareness of art from the Nordic countries, it may be true that, where some familiarity with the paintings does exist, it's probable that it might rest on an assumption that among the chief characteristics of Nordic art are a propensity for works that involve open spaces, often in a coastal location, and plenty of natural light. "Northern Light", in fact, is almost a kind of semi-substitute word for describing Scandinavian paintings. Or there are closely perceived interiors with what we think of typical Scandinavian furnishings. It may be worth quoting in full some comments that occur near the beginning of *Nordic Painting*, and which perhaps point to the direction much of the critical commentary in the book will take:

"This attribute follows a common interpretative schema of Nordic painting that has dominated (at least) international art history until the present day: climatic and geographic characteristics of the Nordic countries – such as light spectacle of the midnight sun – are combined with stereotyped ideas of naturalness, authenticity, and purity and are mythically or even magically charged. Idealising topoi of longing serve a kind of branding specific to the region ("region branding"). They are functionalised as self-images or public images to create a region-spanning identity of the North."

It's pointed out that, in contrast to the "region-spanning identity" certain people (critics, curators of exhibitions, etc.) are accused of fostering, the "cultural diversity of the North is reflected in the art production which participated in various ways in the avant-garde currents of modernism." Nordic artists travelled to widen their awareness of modern trends. The Swedish artist, Sigfrid Hjerton, went to Paris, where she studied at the Matisse Academy. Her 1914 painting, *Flag Parade,* reproduced in the book, shows her to have been influenced by the Fauves. The Dane, Jais Nielsen's *Departure*, dating from 1918, has obvious influences from Futurist and Cubist painting.

It can, of course, be argued that by spending time in Paris, and picking up on the new ideas then being circulated in the city, artists were possibly losing their individual identities. And some would say their national identities, too. The counter-argument could be that, in actual fact, it was only when the artists liberated himself or herself from the bonds of nationality that they could truly express themselves as individuals. It might all depend on what one wanted from art, and there may have been a divergence of expectations between the artist and the audience. Some people might desire an art that has evident links to national ideas of what it can express. And they might view modern art, especially of the abstract kind, as losing that sense of identity and becoming almost bland in its willingness to give up representation and take on international characteristics.

There is an interesting discussion of the work of the Finnish painter, Tyko Sallinen, who had visited France and the United States. Claims were made to the effect that Sallinen had taken little from anything he encountered on his travels. But Sallinen got into trouble when his paintings, particularly one called *The Tradesman's Daughters*, seemed to suggest that there were allusions to "a racial classification of the Finns as Mongolians". This did not fit in with a need among the general populace for "membership in the `Indo-German race', so as to achieve a higher place in the racial hierarchy. Sallinen's painting appeared to present a "threat to the young nation's narrative of identity formation," as the Finns freed themselves from Russian influences and also fought a bloody civil war to defeat a communist attempt at a coup. As the authors of *Nordic Painting* point out: "The reception of Sallinen's paintings shows how strongly ideological and political convictions could come to the fore."

Something significant that comes across when reading *Nordic Painting* is the number of women involved in the production of works of art. The point is made more than once that women ran into difficulties in terms of the reaction of bourgeois society in Stockholm, Copenhagen, and other cities where there was a concentration of respectable middle-class families. Women were expected to stay at home, carry out their domestic duties, and look after the children. When they instead turned to painting and went off to Paris and elsewhere they defied the conventions of the time. Cora Sandel (real name, Sara Fabricus) wrote three novels, largely autobiographical, which told the story of a young Norwegian woman from a provincial town in Norway who dares to first of all head for Oslo and art school, and then goes to Paris. These books *(Alberta and Jacob, Alberta and Freedom, Alberta Alone)* may at least give an idea of what it must have been like for a woman to take the decision to strike out on her own. Other women were luckier and encouraged to become artists with grants to study abroad.

A painting by Elin Danielson-Gambogi, *The Finished Breakfast,* is interesting from the point of view of what it says in terms of portraying a woman (the sister of the painter) and her attitude, as expressed in the painting, towards conventional notions of domesticity. She's leaning on the table, cigarette in one hand, and clearly not in any rush to start clearing the pots away. There has presumably been someone else at the table, and what appears to be a still-lit cigarette looks like it could easily burn the tablecloth. There is a wine glass on the table (did it have wine? At breakfast?) and some paintings tacked on the wall. All in all, it would suggest bohemianism to any soberminded citizen. It's an interesting painting, too, in that it doesn't fit into the accepted notions of Nordic paintings by not focusing on a landscape with light, or a tidily organised interior scene.

Other paintings likewise play up the idea of the artist as someone who, if not antagonistic towards convention, is certainly mocking it. Gustav Wentzel's *The Day After* has a figure lying in bed with a nearby table full of empty bottles and glasses. A small statue, a drawing pinned to an otherwise bare wall, and one or two other items, leave the viewer in no doubt that it's an artist's room. Hanna Hirsch Pauli's *The Artist Venny Soldan-Brofeldt* has the subject of the painting sitting on the paint-stained floor of a studio, and the accompanying commentary asserts that: "The painting presents the studio as a space in which middle-class conventions are suspended, which goes hand in hand with the topos of the studio in general." Hirsch-Pauli and Soldan-Brofeldt shared a studio in Paris. It's relevant to note that the painting was shown at the Paris Salon, and favourably commented on, but when put on display in the Nordic countries, "reception of the work was not uniformly positive".

A chapter on the painters who came together in Skagen is particularly valuable, though in saying that I have to admit to an interest in the subject of artists' colonies. They appear to have been a feature of late-19th century artistic life – there's a reference to them being a "Europe-wide phenomenon" – and soon spread widely to Newlyn and St Ives in Britain, Pont-Aven and Concarneau in France, Worpswede in Germany, and numerous other places, including Skagen in Denmark. The attractions of such locations tended to be similar. There was the light, of course, and the relatively low cost of food and housing. But most of all, there was the opportunity to paint people and their way of life which hadn't yet been touched (tainted?) by modern ideas and appliances. Painters thought that they could, perhaps, capture something before it was lost forever.

However, as is pointed out in *Nordic Painting,* "Ethnological precision is not central to these depictions of rural life. The stylistic execution also contributes to the impression of a domesticated reality, which was intended to satisfy the aesthetic demands of a well-off middle-class". It was highly doubtful that someone living comfortably in Copenhagen would want a picture which really portrayed the poverty and hard lives of many fishermen, and others, hanging on their wall. But a painting which might have been acceptable, is Michael Ancher's *Will he Round the Point?* With its hint of a possible problem (not seen), albeit all the people shown look healthy and well-fed, it's a canvas that could probably find a buyer. I'm not criticising the Skagen artists when I refer to their wanting to sell their work. The same applied to similar paintings I've seen in Penzance and elsewhere. The rough edges have mostly been removed to make palatable what's portrayed. Most artists are not innovators or experimentalists and have to take note of the market in order to make a living.

Not all artists went to the coastal art colonies, and some stayed in the cities where they felt "an attunement to the urban night, which was established at the time through the emergence of electrical street lighting". Eugene Jansson's *Dawn over Riddafjarden,* with its skyline tinged with red, the buildings below it having a string of lights along the seafront, and the overall scene framed with blue, might be a classic example of what some artists were seeing in towns and cities. Others, however, were less inclined to be "colourful," and in Vilhelm Hammershøi's *Christianbourg Palace, Late Autumn*, the effect is primarily what the book describes as "monochromatic." And the painting is further said to have, "gray shrouded colouration and almost dystopian, uninhabited atmosphere."

Hammershøi is a particularly interesting artist, and it's possibly significant that he's one of the few from the Nordic countries to have had a major British exhibition in recent times (the Royal Academy show in 2008 referred to earlier). He had visited London during his lifetime and painted cityscapes there. I have a postcard of one of his London paintings, *Street in London,* which I think may be in Bloomsbury, near the British Museum. Perhaps it's just my imagination, and I'm projecting too much onto the painting, but whenever I look at it I think of George Gissing's novel, *New Grub Street*, and its cast of often slightly shabby and depressed characters scurrying to their places in "the valley of the shadow of books." The scene doesn't have any such people in it, but it's as if they're about to appear at any moment.

I recall that some people found the Hammershøi exhibition at the Royal Academy dull, even boring, but it didn't strike me as lacking substance. His interior scenes suggested a great deal, even when they were devoid of human figures. And when they did have someone in them it was often noticeable that the women, which they mostly were, always seemed to be viewed from behind. One painting was even called, *Interior with Young Woman Seen from Behind.* And the painting on the back cover of *Nordic Painting, Interior with Woman at Piano,* again shows the woman from behind. I wasn't the only visitor to the exhibition to notice how often the women were, in a sense, "faceless."

I'm conscious of having moved quickly around the contents of *Nordic Painting*, and it may be that in doing so I've neglected certain aspects of what is covered. The book does look at those artists who pushed the boundaries of art in the Nordic countries to take in influences from Cubism, Surrealism, and other modern movements, though surprisingly there is little about what I would think of as social/political art, which must have existed in the region. There is one painting, Christian Krohg's *Tired*, which the commentary says refers to "the growing poverty in the increasingly industrialised cities". Krohg is an interesting person and wrote a novel, *Albertine*, about an impoverished seamstress sliding into prostitution, which fell foul of the censors. In the book, *Nordic Art: The Modern Breakthrough, 1860-1920,* mentioned earlier, there is a painting by Krohg entitled *Albertine*, which shows a woman being arrested by a policeman while some other better-dressed women appear to be looking at her disapprovingly. And there is also H.A. Brendekilde's *Worn Out*, a bleak comment on the hard lives of the rural poor. It could be useful to look at this book in conjunction with *Nordic Painting*.

I don't want to be seen as criticising *Nordic Painting* for not including something that I'm personally curious about. The book does offer a wide view of the range of forms of painting that took place in the countries concerned. There is a great deal of insight and information to be gleaned from the various short chapters which look at numerous painters and their work. Extensive notes and a decent bibliography provide for the usefulness of the book. Added to which there is the pleasure of being introduced to paintings that aren't known in Britain. They certainly ought to be.

NORDIC PAINTING
By Katharina Alsen and Anika Landmann
Prestel Publishing. 303 pages. £50. ISBN 978-3-7913-8131-2

JOHN MINTON AND JEAN COOKE

Artists are sometimes remembered by the majority of people more for their links to other painters and places than for their own work. John Minton's name crops up in all the books about Soho in the 1940s and 1950s, drinking alongside Francis Bacon and Lucian Freud In the Colony Room, being photographed by John Deakin, and tragically committing suicide at the age of 39. Jean Cooke was, for many years, overshadowed by her husband, John Bratby, who abused her in more ways than one, and was jealous of any sort of success she had with her paintings. But it would be a pity if Minton and Cooke were only known for their personal involvements with other artists. Both had something of value to offer in their own right.

John Minton was born in 1917 into a middle-class family and in later life was a trust beneficiary, so "was never dependent purely on his art, and he could be remarkably generous to his friends". He had a good education, and in 1936 was awarded s scholarship at the St John's Wood Art School. He exhibited at the Westheim Gallery in London in 1938, and thanks to his private income he was able to spend several months in France with Michael Ayrton. In 1939 he collaborated with Ayrton on designs for a production of *Dido and Aeneas* that was never realised.

The outbreak of war in 1939 found Minton at first attempting to register as a conscientious objector, but then enrolling for service in the army. He continued to exhibit and worked with Ayrton on designing sets and costumes for John Gielgud's *Macbeth* at the Piccadilly Theatre. He was discharged from the army on health grounds in 1943, and for the next three years shared a studio with the Scottish artists, Robert Colquhoun and Robert MacBryde.

I don't think it's necessary to outline all of Minton's activities in the post-war period. He exhibited regularly here and there, and contributed cover illustrations to publications like *Penguin New Writing* and for numerous novels. The exhibition in Chichester includes examples of his work in this line. He also travelled to France and Spain. And taught at various institutions, including the Royal College of Art. What also impresses is the range of people, especially artists, that Minton knew and mixed with. They included Lucian Freud, Keith Vaughan, Francis Bacon, the two Roberts, Rodrigo Moynihan, Richard Chopping, Denis Wirth-Miller, and many others. The Soho bohemia of the late-1940s and 1950s was, in many ways, his natural habitat when he wasn't teaching or painting.

Minton's seeming gregariousness and love of drinking and dancing may well have been signs of a basically insecure disposition that led to his suicide in 1957. Minton was openly homosexual at a time when it was a criminal offence and the police were actively attempting to entrap men into committing acts that would lead to their arrest. There is a dark painting in the exhibition that shows a figure loitering in the shadows as if in anticipation of some sort of assignation, or encounter, no matter how dangerous.

The material on show in Chichester encompasses a broad sample of Minton's work, from colourful paintings, to some splendid pen and ink drawings, to illustrations for magazines and books, and film posters. And it's especially encouraging to see that his skills as an illustrator are given their fair share of attention. There may be a tendency, in certain circles, at least, to relegate book and magazine covers, and other forms of what some will consider tantamount to advertising matter, to a lower category than canvases, but it strikes me as unfair if that is the case.

There is much to be gained from looking at an apt jacket design for a novel, and Minton had a flair for such things. It may be that his best-known book covers are those he did for some Elizabeth David cook books, and that those for what are, in many cases, fairly obscure and forgotten novels, are consequently destined to be overlooked. But there are sufficient of them in the exhibition to persuade a fair-minded observer that Minton excelled at illustrating a variety of subjects.

With regard to his paintings, they often have an immediate impact because of their bright colours, particularly when Minton travelled to Corsica or Jamaica. But there are also some London scenes from 1946/47 in which, the catalogue suggests, "the strong colours suggest neither daytime nor night". They certainly don't adhere to a popular notion of post-war Britain as a grey and dismal place, though it has been suggested that they do point to a decline in the country's fortunes, with its industrial base shattered. The picturesque is ultimately going to take over from the commercially busy. And the skies appear to indicate impending storms.

By 1957 or so tastes in art were beginning to change. Abstraction was coming to the fore and in 1956 the Tate staged a show of American Abstract Expressionism. Minton was strongly opposed to abstraction, and it could have been that an awareness that his style of painting was being overtaken and likely to go out of fashion, combined with his alcoholism and his chaotic personal life, pushed him into suicide. For a deeper consideration of Minton's mental state at the time of his death I'd recommend Frances Spalding's *Dance till the Stars Come Down: A Biography of John Minton* (Hodder & Stoughton, 1991). It could also be useful to read the chapter on Minton in Malcolm Yorke's *The Spirit of Place: Nine Neo-Romantic Artists and their Times* (Constable, 1988).

Back in 1987, when I saw the exhibition, *A Paradise Lost: The Neo-Romantic Imagination in Britain 1935-55* at the Barbican, John Minton had a prominent place in it. For obvious reasons he's not included among the Neo-Romantic artists like MacBryde, Colquhoun, John Craxton, John Piper, Paul Nash, and several more, on show in Chichester. It's instructive, though, to have a look at their work in order to see the kind of context Minton was operating in. In 1987 it was suggested that Neo-Romanticism had been "repressed and edited out of the history of British art and culture", and it was true that abstraction and Pop Art and other post-1960 movements had more or less consigned Neo-Romanticism to, if not the dustbin, then the storage room of history.

It's good that recent years have seen the paintings being brought out and put on display again. I've seen an exhibition of Colquhoun and MacBryde in Edinburgh, another of Robin Ironside in Chester, and earlier this year there was an exhibition, *The Romantic Impulse: British Neo-Romantic Artists at Home & Abroad 1935-1959* at the Osborne Samuel Gallery in London. An informative catalogue was published in connection with the exhibition.

If Neo-Romanticism is "a difficult term to define" and its "boundaries and content" have more to do with "a spirit of place" and an "impulse to convey a sense of Britishness", then this might be a useful time for looking again at the work of Minton, Craxton, Leslie Hurry, Prunella Clough, and their contemporaries, not just to set the historical record right, but also to highlight the work of several imaginative artists. They can be looked on as members of a loosely-defined group, but perhaps more as individuals with characteristic, and sometimes similar, content ("the lyrical....the mystical, the romantic, and the preoccupation with linear rhythms....") in their paintings.

Jean Cooke can't be grouped with the Neo-Romantics, but she's a neglected figure and deserves to be recognised for her own work and not just because she was at one time married to the roaring boy of the British art world, John Bratby. Life with him wasn't easy and he wasn't averse to painting over her canvases, and even damaging something of hers that he didn't approve of. Bratby was, of course, the leading light of the so-called "kitchen-sink" school of artists, and even when he allowed her to paint he tried to get her to adhere to that style.

There is a 1958 painting by Jean Cooke in the Hastings exhibition, and it is very much akin to what John Bratby was doing. It shows him looking through an open window into the kitchen from outside. It has all the acknowledged signs of a "kitchen-sink" canvas, the bottles and packets, the glimpse of a sink. A later portrait of Bratby has him white-bearded and looking rather glum. Perhaps it was payback time for when he forced her to act as his model and, to suit the kitchen-sink image, usually made her appear downtrodden and miserable, which she most likely was, anyway.

When she finally broke away from Bratby she left the kitchen sink behind, and had a reasonably successful career under her own name. The exhibition has some attractive nature scenes set in gardens and woods, and one or two conventional but likeable portraits. Jean Cooke wasn't a major painter, but she could be an interesting one. The critic Andrew Lambirth said: "A characteristic Cooke painting takes the real world and views it from a slightly odd angle – as if musingly with head on one side". It's an accurate description of her approach to painting.

JOHN MINTON: A CENTENARY
An exhibition at the Pallant House Gallery, Chichester, 1st July to 1st October, 2017

JOHN MINTON: A CENTENARY
by Simon Martin and Frances Spalding
Pallant House Gallery. 128 pages. £24.95. ISBN 978-1-8698-2786-1

A DIFFERENT LIGHT: BRITISH NEO-ROMANTICISM
An exhibition at the Pallant House Gallery, Chichester, 10th June to 24th September, 2017

JEAN COOKE: DELIGHT IN THINGS SEEN
An exhibition at the Jerwood Gallery, Hastings, 24th May to 10th September, 2017

INVENTING DOWNTOWN

"Tenth Street, the whole block on Tenth Street became the hangout. One hung out at the galleries and Friday nights were big social occasions, and it got to be very much the Downtown scene ......That world was very small then – a few hundred people".

Al Held

In the 1950s in New York it was Abstract Expressionism that held sway in the art world. Newer, younger artists, and even some older ones, who perhaps leaned more towards figurative painting, had difficulty in getting their work shown in the established commercial galleries in uptown Manhattan. Without critical approval, and that could only come when they exhibited, they weren't likely to be asked to provide paintings for consideration by dealers and others in positions of power and influence.

It needs to be also acknowledged that, despite some attention being paid to painters like Jackson Pollock and Willem de Kooning, there wasn't widespread interest in contemporary art on the part of the general public and the media. If people wanted to buy paintings they mostly looked to the past, and often to European artists. A concern for the new would come later, but in the early and mid-Fifties, even in New York, working artists inhabited, as Al Held recalled, a small world.

Faced with indifference from the public, likely patrons, and critics, young painters and sculptors considered their position and, in some cases, decided that opening their own galleries might not be a bad idea. Their work would then be seen, if only by a small audience of fellow-artists, and, hopefully, by a critic or two curious enough to venture into what could be somewhat shabby and run-down areas of downtown New York.

Harold Rosenberg, one of the leading writers on art, and a critic who was partly responsible for promoting the so-called Action Painters (another name for the Abstract Expressionists) wrote an article for the *Art News Annual* in 1954 in which he talked about "Tenth Street: A Geography of Modern Art" (reprinted in his *Discovering the Present: Three Decades in Art, Culture, & Politics*, University of Chicago Press, 1976). In it he described an area of pawnshops, liquor stores, cheap restaurants, a poolroom, an employment agency for restaurant workers. And, for the artists, cheap studios in old factories, warehouses, shops, and other empty buildings.

There had been some attempts at drawing attention to new work by young artists when certain coffee-house owners in Greenwich Village hung paintings on their walls. But the numbers and sizes of the selected canvases were inevitably limited by the space available. Having their own galleries would obviously provide better facilities for the artists. The aim was that the galleries would be run on a co-operative basis, with members donating a fixed amount each month to pay for rent, lighting, and other necessities. Initially, artists would take turns looking after the gallery concerned during opening hours. After a time, a regular assistant might be hired, assuming that funds were available to pay a modest wage.

Irving Sandler provides a vivid picture of the time he spent in such a role at the Tanager Gallery in his *A Sweeper-Up After Artists: A Memoir* (Thames & Hudson, London, 2004), and also writes about the need to accept that functioning in the Downtown milieu meant acknowledging that poverty was a way of life, at least for a time. It wasn't that anyone wanted to be poor, and in fact, opening a co-operative gallery was usually a means to an end. Most artists saw "Downtown galleries as transitional. Nearly all the artists strove for commercial representation uptown". This shouldn't be held against them, and they weren't all ready to compromise on their ideas and ideals about art in order to succeed. But artists, most of them, anyway, produce works that they want to be seen and sold, and there was a better chance of that happening in the commercial galleries.

The Tanager Gallery, which ran in one location or another (mostly 90 East Tenth Street), from 1952 until 1962, was "the most influential of all the co-op galleries". Other leading co-op galleries were the Hansa (1952-1959) and the Brata (1957-1962), and all three helped to "redefine the parameters of artmaking and challenged the definition of art by critics and museum curators". It would take up too much space to list all the painters and sculptors involved with these galleries, but among them were William King, Angel Ippolito, Lois Dodd, Wolf Kahn, Jan Muller, Nicholas Krushenick, and Al Held. It was, on the whole, a male-dominated scene. Rosalyn Drexler, asked about her experiences at the Reuben Gallery (1959-1961), talked about being "aware that there were things that happened to women", meaning that their work was often looked on as less relevant or interesting than that produced by men.

Each gallery had a distinctive approach to what was exhibited. The Tanager's "juxtaposition of disparate styles often defied logic", with "representational art alongside abstraction". The City Gallery (1958-1959), with Red Grooms and Jay Milder involved, focused on "life in New York as a core subject". The March Group (1960-1962) was located at 95 East Tenth Street in "the basement, a squat, cramped space with exposed pipes, tin ceiling, and whitewashed brick walls". With artist Boris Lurie, photographer Sam Goodman, and poet-artist Stanley Fisher participating, the exhibitions there were heavily politicised. There are some of Lurie's provocative collages in the collection of poems and paintings, *Beat Coast East: An Anthology of Rebellion* (Excelsior Press, New York, 1960) that Fisher edited.

Another significant outlet for experimental art was the Judson Gallery (1959-1962), linked to "the progressive Judson Memorial Church on Washington Square South". The gallery was in "an approximately 1,000 square feet room in the basement of Judson House, an interracial student dormitory at 239 Thompson Street, around the corner from the church". Claes Oldenberg took over "programming for the Judson", "and arranged for a joint show with Jim Dine in November 1959 that featured new figurative work inspired by the streets, Brutalism, and children's drawings". The Judson Gallery also became a centre for what became known as "Happenings", forms of performance art in which Oldenberg, Dine and Allan Kaprow were heavily involved.

It was an especially lively time for the church as a little magazine, *Exodus* (1959-1960), edited by Bernard Scott and Daniel Wolf, was published from the gallery. Some of Oldenberg's pictorial work appeared in *Exodus*, as did that by Red Grooms and Richard O.Tyler. There was also prose from Ivan Karp, who worked at the Hansa Gallery for a time and recalls its struggle to survive in an interview in *Inventing Downtown*. There are photographs by Fred McDarrah from an event at the Judson Gallery for a new issue of *Exodus* in *The Beat Scene,* edited by Elias Wilentz (Corinth Books, New York, 1960). It's also worth looking at McDarrah's *The Artist's World in Pictures* (Dutton, New York, 1961), which has material on the Tenth Street galleries.

It's noted that another venture which took place at the Judson Gallery was artist Phyllis Yampolski's "Hall of Issues"(1961-1963), described as a strategy for "merging art and politics". It invited anyone "who has any statement to make about any social, political or aesthetic concern" to participate by displaying art work or poetry or other forms of expression. It tapped into a growing need to say something as the restrictive effects of the McCarthy Era wore off, and what Melissa Rachleff, quoting Daniel Bell, refers to as the "end of ideology", struck a chord with many artists and writers. But as she further notes: "Such openness promoted diversity, but lack of a clearly defined political goal kept the project as an art initiative diffuse, fractured, and ultimately uneven".

The Hansa Gallery had stayed afloat largely due to the efforts of Richard Bellamy, and when it finally closed he "drifted and looked for a job". Eventually, Ivan Karp introduced him to Robert Scull, a wealthy businessman who was prepared to put up the money needed to open an uptown gallery. The Green Gallery (1960-65) was the result, and led to some of the Downtown artists moving uptown, something that wasn't always looked on kindly by those left behind. But Claes Oldenberg was of the opinion that "The Green Gallery was a way to feel at home on Fifty-Seventh Street for the first time. It was a very unpretentious place. The installations were very straight ahead. There was nothing fancy about it; it was like the downtown moving uptown".

The full story of the Green Gallery and its backer, Robert Scull, would provide material for a book in itself, with shady financial dealings and much more to complicate the day-to-day operations of an art gallery. Scull's wife had a significant role in what happened: "Ethel clearly had no patience for Bellamy's personal conduct or managerial style. And unlike her husband she did not find him fascinatingly bohemian. It was only a matter of time before her discontentment coupled with Bellamy's disinterest in business and her husband's limited finances would come together and bring the gallery to an end".

Before it closed, Green Gallery had played a part in promoting the work of James Rosenquist, Tom Wesselmann, and George Segal, all three of them soon to become leading figures in the Pop Art movement. The rise of Pop Art, its popularity with dealers and collectors (if not initially with the critics), and with the public, led to the boom in the art market that essentially started in the 1960s and continues. Leaving aside the question of money, and as Rachleff notes, there is a "subservience to wealth at the heart of most art enterprises", there is no doubt that Pop Art gained a wide audience. As the artist Lucas Samaras said, "the images were easily assimilable by the whole country". And the media liked to run stories on the wealthy collectors who bought Pop Art and displayed it in their homes. Samaras credits Robert Scull with helping to further Pop Art by having it in his own house, and inviting other wealthy people to view it "and see how nice it looked and think how nice it would look in their house".

It's relevant to mention that the Downtown activity throughout the 1950s and early-1960s had often inter-related with the other arts, such as poetry. Some galleries had poetry readings to help draw attention to their exhibitions. It's mentioned that: "Poetry was integral to the creative life of the Lower East Side, where the main venues for readings in the early 1960s were Le Metro, on Second Avenue between Ninth and Tenth Streets, and Le Deux Megots, on East Seventh Street. The informality of the café setting transformed Downtown poetry from a solitary endeavour to a performative art". There's a photograph of Jack Micheline, a socially-conscious poet sometimes associated with the Beats but really out of an older bohemian tradition, reading at one of Phyllis Yampolski's "Hall of Issues" events. The black poet, Amiri Baraka (formerly known as Leroi Jones) is acknowledged as a leading light of the Spiral Group (1963-1965), a group of black poets and painters discussed in *Inventing Downtown.*

The accounts of the various galleries are fascinating to read, and there were others besides those I've mentioned. The Reuben Gallery (1959-1961) featured "anti-ceremonious, anti-formal, untidy, highly-physical (but not highly permanent)" exhibitions which were later credited with leading towards "Pop". Some "iconic projects" by Jim Dine, Claes Oldenberg, Allan Kaprow, and others took place at the Reuben, and were designed to "shift away from traditional artistic categories" and explore "space, performance, and process to the hilt". The Center (1962-1965) had Aldo Tambellini "working in his building's backyard", and using found objects (pipes, joints, discarded washbasins, beer cans) for his sculptures. He treated his studio as "a community space", and involved local people in what he was doing.

That the period concerned was a vital one is made clear in *Inventing*

Downtown, but it wasn't all smooth sailing. There is some evidence that, by around 1960, the notion of co-operative-operated galleries was declining. Financial limitations inevitably affected what could be done. And there were clashes of temperament and egos. John Gruen, writing about his time at the Hansa Gallery in *The Party's Over Now: Reminiscences of the Fifties – New York's Artists, Writers, Musicians, and their Friends* (Viking, New York, 1972) had this to say: "The Hansa group may have been compatible as far as art was concerned, but not as regards its members' personalities. As the gallery began to function any number of violent personal clashes took place, with hysterical outbursts by the more high-strung artists. Countless decisions had to be voted on, and there was always someone totally against one policy or another. Tempers invariably ran high".

I imagine that what happened at Hansa was probably similar to what took place in other co-op galleries, especially the bigger ones, where there were likely to be a variety of ideas and opinions about personalities and policies. *Inventing Downtown* mentions some disagreements, and there were resignations from groups and bickering about who was to be included in exhibitions.

Generally, however, there does seem to have been a great deal of co-operation, and the interviews in *Inventing Downtown* do elicit some almost-wistful memories of a time when, poor and un-recognised as they were, the artists appeared to be relatively content. Wolf Kahn claimed that "There was no frantic careerism in those days. It was amazing how idealistic we were, and unself-interested". Jim Dine remembered, "There was a kind of bohemia". Jean-Jacques Lebel thought that "Those years in New York felt like paradise. Art was life, daily life was intense art". And Irving Sandler reckoned that "Most artists were living on air, and elegantly. I don't know how they did it.....Poverty had an upside. There wasn't then the division between the successful artists and the unsuccessful artists. It was an open situation".

Inventing Downtown is an engrossing and informative book, wonderfully illustrated and massively documented. It should be essential reading for anyone interested in the New York art scene of the 1950s and early-1960s. For those lucky enough to be in the city, it accompanies an exhibition at the Grey Art Gallery, New York University, which opened in January and runs until 10th December, 2017. It then moves to the Kunstmuseum Luzern,Lucerne, Switzerland from 28th September, 2018 to 25th November, 2018.

INVENTING DOWNTOWN: ARTIST-RUN GALLERIES IN NEW YORK CITY 1952-1965
By Melissa Rachleff
Prestel Publishing. 296 pages. £50. ISBN 978-3-7913-5558-0

BOHEMIAN LIVES

Bohemianism was once, according to Amy Licence, "a philosophy of opposition", and not just the almost-meaningless concept that has now been hi-jacked by the fashion industry, pop cultural commentators, and other current arbiters of taste. Going hungry in a garret while creating is no longer the necessary or desirable thing to do in a world where instant success is sought after. And it would probably be difficult these days to find a garret at a price a struggling poet or painter could afford.

Amy Licence's *Bohemian Lives* looks at the trials and tribulations of three women who, by accident or design, found themselves in a bohemian environment in the years before the First World War. What does become obvious is that, for them, as opposed to the men they were involved with, the experience was not often a satisfactory one. At best, they perhaps got to know some engaging personalities and, for a time, may have been able to share in the excitement of a fervent and fertile artistic period. At worst, they watched their own potential decline as the demands of looking after male artists took precedence over anything they had planned to do.

Ida Nettleship was a talented student at the Slade when she met the swaggering and highly-regarded Augustus John. Born in 1877 into a respectable middle-class family, she was encouraged by her parents to develop the skills she had for drawing and painting. Her father was an artist and Amy Licence says that: "For generations, Ida's family had been advocates for personal freedom. They were among the first Victorian bohemians". Ida grew up in a house where "artists and poets including Walter Sickert, William Rothenstein, Max Beerbohm, the Yeats brothers, and Robert Browning" were among the visitors. It needs to be noted, though, that the bohemianism in evidence was of a restrained and polite kind, and wasn't that of cheap cafes, near-destitution, shabby rooms, and dubious relationships.

When Augustus John came into her life she no doubt knew of his reputation, both as an artist and as a womaniser, but she was starry-eyed enough to think that marrying him would lead to a situation where her own work would thrive alongside his, and she would be able to curb his excesses outside the studio. She should, perhaps, have looked for examples of women artists marrying male painters, and studied what became of them. It was difficult enough for a woman to make her way in the male-dominated art world, and even more so if her male partner insisted that his work take precedence over whatever she had in mind to do.

Once they were married, Ida began to realise just what sort of trap she'd fallen into. John was never going to be a homebody of any kind. He continued as before, drinking with friends, pursuing various women, and expecting Ida to look after the domestic side of things. Pregnancy added to her dilemma, and she was unable to find time to apply herself to painting or producing anything artistically creative. And money problems soon embroiled her in the kind of bohemia – of debts and life in dreary lodgings – she wasn't used to.

More pregnancies and John's insistence that another woman, Dorelia, come to live with them in a ménage-à-trois arrangement, caused Ida a great deal of pain, both mental and sometimes physical. The "family", Ida, Dorelia, John, various children (their maid had left because John had also got her pregnant), shuttled around England and France, until Ida, pregnant again, fell ill, and died from peritonitis in 1907. I've given a very sketchy account of Ida's life, and Amy Licence provides a much more detailed version, but whichever way it's looked at, Ida's brief encounter with bohemia was a sad one, and an example of how someone from a sheltered background could so easily be drawn into circumstances that she just wasn't prepared for. Ida was worn out with child-bearing, and the vicissitudes of certain aspects of bohemianism, when she died at the age of thirty.

A tougher-minded woman, one who had not known a happy and comfortable upbringing, might have been more equipped to assert her individuality and leave Augustus John before it was too late, or at least learn how to survive in bohemia. Fernande Olivier, who was to live with Pablo Picasso for some years, had never had it easy in life before she met him. An illegitimate child, brought up by mostly unsympathetic relatives, married young to an insensitive and sometimes violent husband, she lived until she was eighty-five, despite having to struggle to make a living most of the time.

When Fernande left her husband and moved into bohemia she initially had a series of affairs while earning money modelling for various artists in Montmartre: "she derived pleasure from her friendships, associations with art students, and developing her own painting". As someone said: "Once past Rue Lepic, normal behaviour was thrown overboard. Everyone did just as they pleased, not giving a damn". She met a young sculptor, Laurent Debienne, and lived with him, though the relationship ended when she discovered that, while she worked, he did little to bring in any money, and spent most of the time in bed, which is where she found him one day with a young girl.

According to Licence, Debienne's response to her objections to his behaviour was to tell her that his life-style was essential to his creativity, and that "I could have created a masterpiece, but you stifle me completely". It was a typically male bohemian's excuse for acting badly. Augustus John no doubt used it when he neglected his wife and pursued other women, though he did at least also produce numerous admired paintings.

They had been living at the Bateau-Lavoir, a "rambling, ramshackle complex," housing a number of artists and writers. And it's where. after leaving Debienne, she met Picasso, though in between she had short relationships with other men. She may have been promiscuous, but Licence says that she "longed for stability". Not everyone took advantage of her. Fernand Cormon, an artist she modelled for, told her: "marry a young man who's rich. Think of your future. Don't get sucked into this Bohemia".

Fernande did manage to establish a degree of stability with Picasso, though possibly like Ida Nettleship, she may have had some idealistic notions about bohemia and life with an artist : "Here, life is preserved by hope, love and intellect……..I really have been won over by the madness of the people I'm going to be living with now". She would eventually learn that high hopes could easily be brought low by the day-to-day demands of even a basic domesticity, and that most male artists expected women, on the whole, to support them in various ways. There were very few women artists who were respected for their achievements. Licence mentions Suzanne Valadon, Berthe Morisot, and Marie Laurencin as among them.

Life with Picasso seemed to proceed smoothly at first, though being poor brought its problems. And there were different difficulties. Picasso had fears of her faithlessness and tried to keep her away from other men, though it's more than probable that he was still seeing other women. And, though she had ambitions to make a name for herself as an artist, she lacked the drive and determination to succeed. Was it the bohemian life that distracted her from the hard work of producing a painting? If so, she would not be the only one affected by "riotous nights and opium smoking", and time spent at the Lapin Agile, the club where "Derain, Matisse, Jacob, Apollinaire, Marie Laurencin, and Modigliani" were frequently seen unwinding from the hours in their studios.

It was inevitable that the relationship between Fernande and Picasso would eventually come to an end. It had often been tempestuous, and as Picasso's fame increased and he began to earn more money, and explore different areas of art, he started to lose interest in Fernande: "As would be the case with his life-long artistic development, a new style required fresh inspiration and Fernande's influence belonged to the flourish that had led him out of the rose period. She was a muse of the past; now he was looking in a different direction".

Fernande's life after the break with Picasso found her mostly doing mundane jobs and eventually eking "out a living as a teacher of drawing, French and elocution". In later life, she contacted Picasso to ask for help, and she began to write her memoirs of life with him. He tried to stop them being published and came to an agreement with her to provide financial assistance provided she accepted that the memoirs would not appear until they were both dead. She died in 1966.

Sophie Brzeska, though she had ambitions as a writer, would probably not be remembered today had it not been for her association with the ill-fated young sculptor, Henri Gaudier-Brzeska. They had what was, to put it mildly, an unconventional relationship, which largely involved her, as a woman twice his age, declaring her love for him while at the same time refusing to have any sort of sexual involvement with him. She often referred to herself as his "mother" or "sister", and encouraged him to frequent prostitutes to satisfy his needs in that direction. He seems to have been obsessed with her.

Bohemian Lives probably gives as full an account as we need of Brzeska's life. She was born in 1872 into a Polish aristocratic family that had fallen on hard times, and when young immersed herself in literature, so much so that her own "fiction later came to cloud her reality". She "had constantly fought against the expectations of her family and society, determined to live life on her own terms, making her a bohemian in aspiration and practice". She refused to follow her parent's wishes and engage in a marriage to someone with money. She had positions as a governess, but wasn't happy in them, and her "intense and sensitive responses often elicited the opposite reaction in those whom she most wished to provoke love".

She was in Paris in the late-1890s, went to New York as a governess, was in Philadelphia for a time, and back in Poland in 1908. She did have relations of a sort with several men, though none of them seemed to have involved complete sexual activity, and there are references to illnesses which resulted from emotional stress. She sometimes thought of suicide as a way out of her problems. It might be relevant to quote Katherine Mansfield's opinion of Brzeska, who she saw as "neurotic and disturbing". And Enid Bagnold thought her "treacherous, suspicious, easily affronted, violently hurt".

It was in Paris in 1910 that Sophie met Henri Gaudier, then a nineteen-year old thinking of himself as "in the midst of Bohemia, a queer mystic group but happy enough, there are days when you have nothing to eat, but life is so full of the unexpected that I love it as much as before I used to detest the stupid regular life of employment". Licence refers to the "unlikely friendship" that developed between them. It was a friendship perhaps destined from the beginning to move into a closer relationship with attached problems, neither party being of a practical enough frame of mind to ensure any kind of day-to-day ability to deal with basic matters like food and rent. This was to become obvious when he moved to London. She followed him, and they struggled to find places to stay and earn enough to buy meals. Both were ill because of lack of food and poor living conditions. They also had violent arguments because Henri was finding it difficult to do any creative work. A routine clerical job he had taken meant that he could only paint in the evenings and at weekends. And the lack of sexual contact between them further exacerbated their delicate situation.

Gaudier-Brzeska, as he became even though they never married, was very much a part of the London art scene before the First World War, and involved with the Omega Workshop and the Bloomsbury circle, and with Wyndham Lewis and the Vorticists. His work showed great promise, with people like Joseph Epstein speaking well of him as "a picturesque, slight figure with lively eyes and a slight beard" who had "any amount of talent and great energy". But he also said that he was "confrontational" and got into fights. He was less impressed with Sophie and thought that her "outbursts of frenzied jealousy and hatred of anyone who approached Gaudier" were indications of mental instability. She was suspicious of Nina Hamnett, for example, when she appeared to become too friendly with Henri.

When the First World War broke out in 1914, Henri, after some hesitation, went back to France and enlisted. He was killed in action in 1915. Sophie's behaviour after his death became increasingly erratic as she sought to obtain some recognition for her writing. but often rejected offers of help from well-meaning friends. She also fought with Henri's family regarding ownership of his work. A few people, such as Nina Hamnett, tried to keep in touch with her, but even she eventually thought it impossible "to stay with a lunatic". Sophie's condition deteriorated and she was taken to a mental hospital in 1922 and died there in 1925.

There are, perhaps, many differences to be drawn between the experiences of the three women dealt with in *Bohemian Lives* though all three clearly suffered from male dominance in relation to their artistic aims. Ida and Fernande might have been able to achieve more had they been prepared to stand up to Augustus John and Pablo Picasso and assert their right to some independence. When it comes to Sophie Brzeska, however, I have my doubts, and suspect that her personality was such that she would have found it difficult to be more than she was and do more than she did, even given different circumstances. The examples of her literary work provided in the book don't convince me that she was of any great consequence as a writer.

Amy Licence has written an intriguing and informative book. She writes well about Paris and London in the years leading up to 1914, and provides a convincing backcloth to the stories of her three subjects.

BOHEMIAN LIVES: THREE EXTRAORDINARY WOMEN, IDA NETTLESHIP, SOPHIE BRZESKA AND FERNANDE OLIVIER
by Amy Licence
Amberley Publishing. 255 pages. £18.99. ISBN 978-1-4456-7064-5

PUBLISHED IN PARIS

Paris between the wars was a place of dynamic artistic endeavour, and not only among French writers, artists, and musicians. It also attracted many American and British expatriates, and it is these or, to be precise, the literary figures among them, who are the substance of Hugh Ford's lively and often informative study.

It attempts a closely detailed survey of their activities, and is marred only by Ford's failure to explain fully why the people he describes went to Paris, and why they wrote, printed or published what they did. He's very good at stringing together facts and anecdotes, but not too good at using them to help establish an overall picture of his subjects' needs, aims, and achievements.

It's unfair to criticise too much, however, because he has performed a valuable service by providing a series of accounts which can form the basis for further research. He thankfully gives the much-maligned Robert McAlmon a fair amount of space, and is also interesting on the question of Caresse and Harry Crosby and their Black Sun Press. My only complaint about Ford's approach is that much of the material he mentions is tantalisingly impossible to obtain, unless you're an avid and well-heeled collector. It may be true to say that some of it is also difficult to locate in libraries in Britain if my own minor experiences of finding a full set of the magazine *This Quarter* is anything to go by.

Not all the Parisian writers wrote, nor did all the Parisian publishers bring out, now-forgotten books, though the bibliography sometimes reads like a catalogue of failure or neglect. Such people as James Joyce, Ernest Hemingway, Gertrude Stein, and Henry Miller, first found fame, or notoriety, depending on your point of view, with their small-press publications from Contact Editions, Obelisk Press, and others.

It's interesting that money played such a significant part in the publishing activities. And I don't only mean the favourable exchange rates which allowed foreigners to live cheaply in Europe, for a time, at least. The Crosbys were very much rich dilettantes, Nancy Cunard had obvious wealthy connections, Edward Titus was married to Helena Rubenstein, and Barbara Harrison could afford to indulge her whims by backing limited editions. Even the sardonic McAlmon, though often personally impoverished from ploughing his resources into his press, had money because of a curious, if ill-fated marriage to a member of the rich Ellerman family.

But why Paris? One can take account of the money, the Twenties mood, the explosion of new ideas in the arts, and possibly even just a desire to be fashionable, and still not arrive at a single, satisfactory answer. There perhaps isn't one. After all, the Thirties brought a different kettle of economic fish, but some small presses still carried on. *Published in Paris* won't be the last word on this topic, but it does fill in some gaps overlooked by previous publications.

Little magazines tell the stories of literary eras. To look back at them is to discover worlds in which the famous first made their appearances in print, and the later-forgotten had their brief moments in the sun.

There are specific periods of little magazine activity, and generally speaking, they can be related to the social and economic circumstances surrounding them. But *transition* challenges glib assumptions about these matters. Although born in the Twenties (one of the heydays of non-political littles) it managed to survive throughout most of the Thirties, a time when many energies were diverted into social and political channels.

transition was political in a way, however, and the Nazis publicly burned a copy during one of their campaigns against "decadent" literature. They hated its independence and its preference for the personal, the unusual, and the irrational. After all, how can a totalitarian state control writers and artists operating outside the easily identifiable? A surrealist poem, or an abstract painting, can be just as subversive as a social-realist statement, but they're not as easy to pin down.

During its lifetime, *transition* spotlighted such writers as James Joyce, Hart Crane, Gertrude Stein, and Samuel Beckett. Most English and American editors ignored or dismissed these people, and Eugene Jolas, the driving force behind the magazine, carried on a one-man struggle to bring their works to the attention of the reading public. That he was more alert than many of his contemporaries is shown by the importance now attached to the writers mentioned and others like them.

transition also attempted to link material by British and American moderns to European forays into Dadaism, Surrealism, and related experimental forms. And its idea of the arts was healthily wide-ranging, taking in cinema and photography as well as writing, painting, and music.

Douglas McMillan's useful coverage of *transition* concentrates heavily on a handful of the important writers it published, and I personally would have welcomed a broader account of the magazine's history. But that's a minor complaint, and the book should prove valuable to those who find little magazines a constant source of interest and pleasure.

PUBLISHED IN PARIS: AMERICAN AND BRITISH WRITERS, PRINTERS, AND PUBLISHERS IN PARIS, 1920-1939 by Hugh Ford. Macmillan.

TRANSITION 1927-38: THE HISTORY OF A LITERARY ERA by Dougald McMillan. Calder & Boyars

FREE AS GODS

Paris in the 1920s. Le Dome, Le Select, La Coupole. Ernest Hemingway boxing with Morley Callaghan, and Scott Fitzgerald as an incompetent timekeeper between rounds. Gertrude Stein telling everyone that they are a "Lost Generation". Hart Crane getting drunk and falling foul of the French police. Sylvia Beach's bookshop and her heroic support for James Joyce's *Ulysses*. Robert McAlmon publishing Hemingway's first book. The little magazines, *transition, This Quarter, The Transatlantic Review*. It's a period and a place that lends itself to the recounting of anecdotes.

It's a fascinating story and numerous books with titles like *The Crazy Years* have documented the personalities and events in a lively way. There's nothing wrong with such accounts, which often emphasise the experiences of the American expatriates who flocked to the French capital, but it is essential to know that much more was going on than the merely anecdotal evidence suggests. A lot of important and inventive work was being done in the fields of literature, art, and music.

Charles A. Riley's *Free As Gods* is a wide-ranging account that goes a long way towards redressing the balance in terms of the manner in which it deals with the various disciplines, demonstrates how they often inter-acted with each other, and points to some lesser-known (to most people, I would guess) figures around Paris in the 1920s. It is his contention that: "To read a poem or examine a painting in isolation from the cultural history is especially inadvisable because this was an era of collaboration more than of individual genius toiling in seclusion". And he further states: "This study argues that the form-shattering tendencies of modernist art, music, and literature were accompanied by a concomitant will to create form". The 1920s witnessed "a march towards abstraction through expressionism but also a resurgence of figural and still-life painting, realism in fiction, and classical ballet on stage".

To emphasise his point about how the various branches of the arts frequently interconnected, Riley says that, in the 1920s, minds and tastes were changing at "an accelerated pace" and the boundaries among media were "blurring": "Some of the greatest writers, such as Hemingway and Stein, were also contemporary art insiders, just as

Gershwin, Porter, cummings and Dos Passos were serious painters. Pound was writing an opera in the twenties. Le Corbusier was painting as well as designing buildings and laying out a revolutionary new magazine. Léger was making movies, and Picasso was designing sets for the theatre". Add to all this the fact that, according to Riley, jazz musicians had encouraged people to "take improvisation as the gold standard of originality" and everyone felt free "to be gay, straight, black, Jewish, bohemian, or aristocratic," and so "slipped into fluid roles that defied specialisation".

If Riley is to be believed, "a working knowledge" of jazz is essential to an understanding of the "cultural history of the period". He seems to be knowledgeable about music generally, though perhaps a bit hazy about jazz history, and I'm not sure how Dizzy Gillespie's "bent trumpet" altered the "physical culture of music". There are various explanations about why Gillespie came to use his distinctive "bent" instrument in the 1950s (the popular, though unlikely one is that someone trod on it and bent it out of shape and Gillespie found that he achieved a better sound with the bell pointing upwards), and it does seem to be accepted, in jazz circles, that Gillespie got the idea from a British musician at the Ritz Ballroom in Manchester, England, in 1937 (see Alyn Shipton's *Groovin' High: The Life of Dizzy Gillespie,* Oxford U.P., 1999). And it's said that a trumpeter/comedian named Merwyn Brogue who played with Kay Kyser's novelty band in America in the 1930s under the name of Ishkabibble, used a similar instrument. But perhaps I'm being unnecessarily pedantic? On the other hand, it bothers me that what appears to be a statement of significance about the influence of jazz seems to lose its impact when its factual basis is questioned. Gillespie was hardly introducing anything new when he appeared with his "bent" trumpet. In any case, his inclusion in a discussion about the 1920s seems a bit odd. He only appeared on the jazz scene in the late-1930s.

On the question of jazz generally, Riley again arouses my suspicions when he talks about "Understanding the thrill in 1924 of what it meant to import jazz from club to concert hall...". Some might argue that in doing so the essence of jazz as an improvised music, with audience reaction almost a part of the performance, was likely to be lost. What Riley seems to be talking about is a watered down version of jazz, tailored to make it respectable. I enjoy Gershwin but his music isn't jazz. And as for Paul Whiteman, Riley quotes the French jazz critic, Robert Goffin, who referred to Whiteman's music as "weak dilution devoid of all real musical character". And did Gershwin really write "history's greatest serious jazz?" What is "serious jazz"? I have an uneasy feeling that Riley thinks jazz is "serious" when it takes on some of the orchestral characteristics of classical music.

Riley brings in some well-known names, such as F. Scott Fitzgerald, Hemingway, Malcom Cowley, Harry Crosby, and Gerald and Sara Murphy, all of them regularly mentioned in other accounts of Paris in the Twenties. I have to admit that I've never been able to get too excited by the Murphys. They were rich and could afford to invite a select band of musicians, artists, and writers to stay at their villa on the Riviera. Gerald Murphy had some talent as an artist, working in the Cubist style, but he was hardly all that original or inventive (Murphy "was not all that important to Picasso"). But as Scott Fitzgerald knew, people tend to be fascinated by the rich. They are different, even if it's only because they have more money. Riley does have a point when he says that "private patronage is often the most auspicious guarantee of avant-garde freedom".

Of more interest is the chapter about Archibald MacLeish. "It is a pity that nobody reads or teaches the poetry of Archibald MacLeish anymore," Riley plaintively says, and with that kind of statement it's only fair to wonder why? Poets come and go, and fade from sight as fashions change, but there may also be a case for suggesting that it's perhaps because their poems are not very interesting. Riley doesn't offer any complete poems, or even substantial extracts from them, for us to consider. I turned to some anthologies and couldn't get excited by most of what I read, which is, of course, a purely personal response and my judgement may be at fault. I have to say that Riley makes a persuasive case for at least looking at MacLeish's work again.

Nancy Cunard, Ernest Ansermet, Eugene Jolas, Picasso, Hart Crane, even Oswald Spengler, all receive attention from Riley, and one way or another, he does manage to build up the idea of a period in ferment. I did notice a few errors along the way. On page 55 there's a reference to the "1929 film version of *American in Paris*", with a dream sequence "staged by Vincent Minelli and Gene Kelly". Riley presumably means the 1951 film version, and at the risk of again being called pedantic, isn't it Vincente? On page 58 John Dos Passos' novel, *One Man's Initiation*, published in 1922, is said to be about the Spanish Civil War, which didn't break out until 1936. Dos Passos was writing about the First World War. A later novel, *Adventures of a Young Man*, published in 1939, did touch on the war in Spain. On page 166 Riley says that "Veterans unleashed the grim details of trench warfare in novels and memoirs", and lists several items, including Hemingway's *For Whom the Bell Tolls,* which, as it's set during the Spanish Civil War and was only published in 1941, doesn't belong with books about the First World War.

I've raised some queries about aspects of *Free As Gods*, but it still seems to me a stimulating book, partly because it takes a different approach to its subject, Paris in the 1920s, than many other books. And it looks at some of the lesser-known, or less talked about, writers and others who were around, but perhaps not noticeably so.

A couple of the writers who were in Paris for a time in the 1920s, and later wrote about their experiences, were the Canadians, Morley Callaghan and John Glassco. Neither rates a mention in Riley's book, but they are both dealt with in detail in *Translocated Modernisms.* As the sub-title of the book suggests, it isn't only the Paris experience that is dealt with, and even when the focus is on that city, as it is in the case of Mavis Gallant, for example, who went there in the late-1940s and stayed for most of her life, Paris as a place is not necessarily of key importance. Gallant's *Paris Stories* were written in the city, but were not always located there.

Neither Glassco nor Callaghan produced anything of major significance about their Paris experiences, though both wrote interesting and useful memoirs about them, Callaghan's *That Summer in Paris* is tidily written and probably reliable when it comes to telling how it was. He met Hemingway, Robert McAlmon, John Glassco, and many others from the Paris expatriate community. But, as far as I know, he wrote only one short story, "Now that April's Here," which had what might be called a Paris basis, and that was produced in response to a request by Edward Titus, Editor of *This Quarter,* for a piece inspired by an encounter that Titus, Callaghan, and Robert McAlmon had with John Glassco and his companion, Graeme Taylor. McAlmon was also asked to write something, but typically failed to come up with a suitable story. Callaghan's account was published in the December, 1929, issue of *This Quarter.*

It is suggested, in the essay about Callaghan in *Translocated*

Modernisms, that he revised many of his stories to make them fit in with writings by "more well-known American modernists who lived in Paris". I happen to have a copy of the issue of *This Quarter* in question, and out of curiosity checked the text of "Now that April's Here" with the version in *Morley Callaghan's Stories* (Macmillan, Toronto, 1959). There are only one or two minor amendments to the original version, and nothing that would suggest anything other than tidying up some punctuation and similar small points.

Callaghan's story certainly satirised Glassco and Taylor, and within the conventions of the time, clearly indicated that they were homosexuals. McAlmon was, too, but Callaghan played down that side of the character based on him. When Glassco's *Memoirs of Montparnasse* was published in 1970 he painted a somewhat condescending portrait of Callaghan, picturing him as provincial and not very imaginative. This was probably an act of revenge on Glassco's part because he had been annoyed by the way Callaghan had portrayed him in his story. The question of how truthful or accurate Glassco's memoirs are needs to be asked. It's suggested that "*Memoirs of Montparnasse* is grounded in a self-reflexive engagement with fabrication. He intentionally destabilises the factuality of his memoir in favour of the performative and the fictional". In other words, Glassco wasn't trying to present a true and accurate picture of what he had experienced, but instead wanted to get across how it felt to be in Paris in the 1920s.

I mentioned earlier that *Translocated Modernisms* isn't solely about Paris in the 1920s. Mavis Gallant moved to Paris in the early 1950s and died there in 2014. She wrote two novels, but was mainly known for her brilliant short stories, many of which were published in *The New Yorker*. When asked if she was a Canadian or international writer, she replied, "I'm a writer in the English language". And she said that she didn't enjoy the company of other writers and preferred to mix with painters.

Brion Gysin was associated with William Burroughs and the coterie at the so-called Beat Hotel in Paris in the 1950s, though he had a more varied career than that implies. He seemed determined to be at home wherever he was in a process of "unsettling identity at the individual level as a formalised global ideological critique". But he might well be best remembered for his time with the Beats, as recounted in his novel, *The Last Museum* (Faber, 1986), and in the interview and related material in *Here to Go: Planet R-101* (Re/Search Publications, 1982). He's a genuine avant-gardist, perhaps one of the few that Canada has produced.

Other essays focus on Wyndham Lewis, Katherine Mansfield, and Malcolm Lowry, with the emphasis being on how they "translated and dislocated cultural practices across oceans and continents".

Translocated Modernisms is a useful addition to the library of books engaging with the history of modernism. There were moments when it seemed to be in danger of sliding into the quicksands of academic theorising and jargon, but on the whole it's readable, though not designed for a non-specialist readership looking for entertaining anecdotes about expatriate escapades.

FREE AS GODS: HOW THE JAZZ AGE REINVENTED MODERNISM
by Charles A. Riley II
University Press of New England. 271 pages. $29.95. ISBN 978-1-61168-850-4

TRANSLOCATED MODERNISMS: PARIS AND OTHER LOST GENERATIONS
Edited by Emily Ballantyne, Marta Dvořák and Dean Irvine
University of Ottawa Press. 255 pages. $39.95 CA. ISBN 978-0-7766-2380-1

BECOMING AMERICANS

Paris in the 1920s. Well, of course, it's Hemingway and Gertrude Stein, Sylvia Beach's bookshop, expatriate drinkers, and little magazines that carried the message of modernism, and dozens of books have been written to tell the tales of literary experiments and entertaining escapades. It's all fascinating but in reality was just a small, if important, part of the total experience of the city in the period concerned. Paris, after all, is in France, so what were the French doing while the Americans lived it up? And were those artists and writers in Montparnasse the only Americans in town? Also, what was happening in the political arena? Most accounts have little or nothing to say about French politics but they did impact on the Americans in more ways than one.

The inter-war years saw the rise of confidence in what was said to be the "American way of life." As Brooke L.Blower puts it: "Before, Americans had looked to Europe for cultural models. Now, celebrating their own arts and traditions - cultivating self-consciously American styles and postures - they were becoming a more self-aware and integrated population while simultaneously building up their economic and political clout around the world." And she goes on to suggest that Paris became central to the way in which "modern American culture would be defined, and how Americans would be imagined as critical players in global affairs." To emphasise her thesis about Paris being more than just a location for a Hemingway novel she asserts: "All but forgotten are the thousands of businessmen, journalists, scholars and others who poured into Paris alongside the more famous expatriates. And beyond the artistic impact of musicians, painters, and writers, little attention has been paid to Americans' influence in the city or the ways in which Parisians protested their presence, sometimes violently." The number of permanent American residents rose from 8,000 in 1920 to 32,000 in 1923 and around 40,000 in the mid and late-Twenties These figures did not include tourists and special occasions such as when over 20,000 members of the American Legion held their convention in Paris in 1927.

To explode another myth, that of the Left Bank being where most Americans congregated, it's pointed out that the Right Bank was much more popular. The place de l'Opéra became "the prime reference point. This imposing square emerged during the 1920s as the main hub for the rapidly growing American colony - a nexus around which the grand hotels did a brisk transatlantic business, where tour buses lingered and scores of American companies set up shop." The financial benefits for the French capital are obvious and it's also significant that the Americans brought with them speciality goods and services previously unknown, or at least with little presence, in Paris. Not all Parisians welcomed the American influence which, they thought, led to the "French way of life" coming under threat. Blower reckons that reactions to foreigners, including Americans, "ranged widely from tolerance or more likely avoidance and indifference, to outright hostility." Some French writers went into print with lamentations for the decline of "the old Paris." André Warnod said: "Our guests, welcomed too eagerly, have spoken like masters and we have listened to them," meaning that things were becoming more and more Americanised.

There were allegations that the influx of foreigners (not only Americans, though they were probably the biggest and most obvious contingent) had driven up the cost of living: "There are too many of these parasites here, eating our food, drinking our wine, going untaxed, and paying ridiculously little for everything they consume, thanks to the exchange." The fall in the value of the franc meant that Americans benefited but Parisians suffered, and a spate of attacks on tourists took place along with demonstrations against manifestations of American culture. Magazines and newspapers ran articles which claimed that Paris was becoming "a copy of America" and the city was "a conquered land."

Critics attacked American films, seeing them as "potentially dangerous vehicles of cultural imperialism." And the American attitude towards eating and drinking horrified the French: "American customers threatened cherished routines - by demanding faster service, by promoting the abbreviated cocktail hour instead of the lingering aperitif, and, rather than adopting the protracted midday meal, by spreading the much-dreaded habit of the quick lunch."

The cultural clashes referred to, along with the currency problems, altered relations between many Americans and the French. American foreign policy also disturbed Parisians, especially when it meant helping to revive the German economy while pushing France into quicker repayment of its war debts. Large economic and political concerns combined with small matters relating to social habits to create a climate of anti-Americanism. It was this climate that allowed extremists from both right and left of the political spectrum to manipulate crowds into street action. All it required was a trigger and that was provided in 1927 by the execution of Sacco and Vanzetti, two Italian anarchists who were convicted of an armed robbery in the USA during which two people were killed. The case had dragged on for several years and had attracted world-wide attention, and when they were finally put to death left-wing mobs took to the streets in Paris and a night of rioting followed, with hundreds of rioters and police injured and many arrests made. Restaurants and bars frequented by Americans were attacked and individual Americans seen on the streets were often targeted by the rioters.

If the Sacco and Vanzetti affair gave the left an opportunity to indulge in a display of anti-Americanism, the right, too, seized on an opportunity to oppose "the liberalism linked with Americans and the districts that catered to them." The Paris police were noted for their brutality and were controlled by a reactionary Prefect, Jean Chiappe. He decided to launch what Blower describes as "a purging or cleansing" of certain areas of the city, and she hints that behind this operation lay a suspicion of the "Americans' presence and the kinds of values they were believed to embody." Chiappe was quoted as saying that "fear of the police is the beginning of wisdom," and his purge was said to be for the benefit of decent, well-behaved citizens. His men focused on anyone seeming to be outside a norm established in Chiappe's mind. The working class were seen as a threat, especially if they were politically active on the left. Blower, alluding to Chiappe's right-wing associations, refers to his cultivation of "reactionary cultural politics" which opposed communists and the like and also meant that "right-wing activists like Chiappe could hold together in their minds a cluster of enemies, including foreigners, homosexuals, Jews, Americans, and other purported undesirables, all imagined as agents of an economic and cultural liberalism that would undermine the health of the nation." The police may have kept a close watch on working-class areas of Paris, but they paid equal attention to parts of Montmartre and Montparnasse where Chiappe saw "cosmopolitanism in turmoil."

Blower's account of the visit by well over 20,000 members of the

American Legion in 1927 is particularly interesting. The Legion had been formed in Paris in 1919 when thousands of American servicemen were awaiting demobilisation. It established itself in America in the 1920s as an ultra-patriotic organisation that, its preamble said, aimed to "maintain law and order; to foster and perpetuate a one hundred percent Americanism," and much more. It had some positive aspects, in that it "piloted civic improvement schemes, contributing to child welfare services and disaster relief efforts." But the Legion also tried to exert control over what was taught in schools, insisted on loyalty oaths, chased radicals out of town, intimidated journalists, and helped break strikes. When they decided to stage their convention in Paris they met with opposition from French left-wingers but were welcomed by conservative elements in the Government and business community. A planned parade down the Champs-Élysées, and a national holiday declared by the French Government for the opening day of the convention, particularly aroused the anger of communists, socialists, and anarchists. Blower works hard to indicate that the Legion had some disturbing similarities to aspects of European fascist movements like those in Italy and Germany, something that French left-wingers and American liberals were aware of. As she says, it wasn't an outright fascist organisation but "exhibited key fascist elements."

Not all Americans who lived in Paris were in favour of the Legion's visit, feeling that it would exacerbate anti-American sentiments. But, despite threats from the left, the parade passed off peacefully and, in fact, seemed to have entertained the crowds who watched it. It was hardly a militaristic display and was described as more of a carnival than a march. Blower's analysis of it is first-rate, though she comes to the conclusion that "the Legion's superficial lightheartedness and the group's potential as a dangerous political force were really two sides of the same coin." Americans who took part in the Legion's activities in Paris "acted out many Americans' growing belief that Europe was stagnant and inefficient, a region weighed down by cumbersome tradition, spent by the war, and burdened by out-of-control radicalism."

I mentioned at the start of this review that the expatriates (those usually identified with Paris in the 1920s and 1930s) were only one element in the American association with the city. And they were often condemned by other Americans for having, it was alleged, abandoned their native land and its problems and sought refuge in Paris where they could avoid involvement with anything other than the purely personal. According to Blower, since the publication of Hemingway's *The Sun Also Rises*, "expatriates have been stereotyped as escapists who selfishly renounced civic responsibilities, watching unscathed from afar the social conflicts of the post-war United States while at the same time maintaining distance from the vagaries of European affairs." And she proposes that the expatriates themselves helped perpetuate this myth when they wrote about their experiences in Paris after they'd returned to the United States and often were involved in radical politics.

The fact is, though, that people like Hemingway, John Dos Passos, William Shirer, and Josephine Herbst, frequently travelled far beyond Paris and were aware of what was happening in the world generally. Hemingway, working as a journalist, covered events in Italy, Greece, and elsewhere, while Dos Passos also went to Greece and Turkey and into parts of the Soviet Union. As Blower says: "Casting themselves as radical sympathisers or noble partisans of democracy ready to take on the burdens and moral choices demanded by the period's popular politics, they modelled a deeply social and cosmopolitan sense of the engaged world participants Americans could be, an alternative to the bellicose versions of worldliness displayed in Paris by the veterans, casual tourists, or the Chamber of Commerce crowd." The journalist William Shirer covered wars and political turmoil in many countries, the black writer Langston Hughes visited Russia, as did Josephine Herbst and her husband, John Herrmann. I'm pulling just a few names out of the text to emphasise the point Blower makes, that the expatriates were much more aware of, and sometimes involved with, wider social and political matters than some accounts of their activities would have us believe.

Blower sums up by telling how, following the end of the Second World War, a kind of depoliticisation of Paris began to take over in depictions of the city. The 1951 film, *An American in Paris*, "showcased a Paris of timeless appeal and stock clichés: boulevard cafes, neighbourhood bistros, and - now the most important icon of the city for Americans - the Eiffel Tower." She also says that, in various films, "Impressionist and Post-Impressionist masterpieces by Manet, Degas, or Toulouse-Lautrec became crowd-pleasing vehicles for celebrating the city in purely aesthetic terms," probably because such paintings did not seem related to any kind of art (surrealism, for example) that "smacked of the factious interwar political scene." Blower mentions a "depoliticised epilogue" in a reprint of Malcolm Cowley's *Exile's Return*, originally published in 1934, and she adds that Hemingway's *A Moveable Feast* "stripped the city of its shrill newspaper headlines, its refugees, its rampaging policemen." According to her: "This sanitised version of Americans' place in the capital appealed at mid-century because it resonated so well with the intellectual and social preoccupations of the age." Disillusionment with communism and the rise of McCarthyism meant that "many quietly buried their past associations of their more adventurous days of youth." The real Paris of the 1920s and 1930s was forgotten and in its place appeared the mythical one that it suited later generations to believe in.

Becoming Americans in Paris is an important book and adds an extra dimension to what we know about the city and the Americans who spent time there. It's well-researched, has a good bibliography, and is written in a style that never bogs down in jargon.

BECOMING AMERICANS IN PARIS: TRANSATLANTIC POLITICS AND CULTURE BETWEEN THE WORLD WARS by Brooke L.Blower
Oxford University Press. 354 pages. £22.50. ISBN 978-0-19-973781-9

THE PARIS MAGAZINE : ITS EARLY HISTORY

I ought to explain why this article refers to the "early history" of *The Paris Magazine*. In June, 2010, the fourth issue was published from Shakespeare and Company, the famous Parisian bookshop. With over 160 pages, and successful writers like Tariq Ali, Jeanette Winterson, Luc Sante, and Michel Houellebecq listed on the contents page, it was well-produced and obviously aiming to reach a wide audience. Or at least an audience wider than little magazines usually attract. There's nothing wrong with a magazine wanting to go beyond a small circle of writers and their friends, though it's probably true that a lot of little magazines, including some we now think of as famous, didn't do much more than that. How many people in the 1920s read magazines like *This Quarter* or *Transatlantic Review*? Or how many read *The Black Mountain Review* in the 1950s? Margaret Anderson said that the influential *The Little Review,* famous for its advocacy of James Joyce's *Ulysses*, never had a circulation of more than a few hundred. Who those few hundred people were was what counted.

I suppose it's also debatable about what the purpose of a little magazine is? Is it to promote the work of new, unknown, experimental writers, or to attract wider attention by printing material by established novelists and poets? The editor (Fatema Ahmed) and publisher (Sylvia Whitman) of *The Paris Magazine* in 2010 may have thought that little magazines, in the old sense of them, were no longer viable or necessary, and that's why they produced a publication that might have some commercial appeal. Little magazines were always linked to bohemia and some would argue that they faded away as bohemia lost its definition and character. To be fair, the magazine did have a fairly large selection of work (mostly prose – poetry was noticeable by its absence) by relatively unknown writers. And who would want to complain about a bookshop that published a magazine? You can't imagine the big chains doing it, other than to advertise the latest best-sellers.

If the fourth issue of *The Paris Magazine* appeared in 2010 there had obviously been three earlier ones, and it's those that interest me. They were all published from Shakespeare and Company and edited by George Whitman, who had established the bookshop in 1951, though it was then called Le Mistral. It was still using that name when I first visited it in 1962, and changed to Shakespeare and Company in 1964. There had, of course, been an earlier bookshop in Paris with that title, owned by Sylvia Beach, and noted as somewhere where Ernest Hemingway, Ezra Pound, Robert McAlmon, Kay Boyle, and many others, could be found in the 1920s.

It's not my intention to provide a history of how George Whitman arrived in Paris, opened a bookshop, and developed Shakespeare and Company. All that has been written about elsewhere, most recently in *Shakespeare and Company: A History of the Rag and Bone Shop of the Heart*, edited by Krista Salverson, published by Shakespeare and Company in 2016. And there's Jeremy Mercer's *Books, Baguettes and Bedbugs: The Left Bank World of Shakespeare and Company* (Weidenfeld & Nicolson, 2005). It's the issues of *The Paris Magazine* that George Whitman got out, albeit on a sporadic basis, that I want to look at.

The first issue appeared in October, 1967. The 1960s had been an active period for little magazines, with the Beat explosion inspiring numerous editors to bring out publications in the United States, the United Kingdom, and across the Continent. Some were large, some small, and they varied in quality, both in terms of their production and their contents. Most were short-lived and survived for only a few issues, if that. Was Whitman inspired by all this activity? As I recall his somewhat untidy but fascinating shop, he stocked little magazines and small-press publications, and it had become a venue for young writers to gather. The Beats had been in Paris since the late-1950s, of course, so their books, and the magazines that featured people like Ginsberg and Corso, were on display. It was not a surprise to see Ginsberg's name on the cover of *The Paris Magazine* and his poem, "Kansas City to Saint Louis", inside.

That was the only concession to the Beats, however, and more space was allocated to a selection of letters from Lawrence Durrell, author of *The Black Book,* and other novels, and an interview (in French) with Marguerite Duras. There was also a long letter in French to André Malraux, who was then the Minister of Culture. George Whitman had more than his share of problems with French bureaucracy over the years. Contacting Malraux may have been an appeal for understanding of Whitman's situation as a foreigner trying to run a bookshop in France.

There was a useful article by Edward Lucie-Smith, an English poet and art-critic, about "The Little Presses of England," in which he discussed *Migrant, Wild Hawthorn, Matrix, Goliard, Trigram, Fulcrum a*nd other small presses that were then helping to circulate the work of new British and American poets. There were poets besides Ginsberg in this issue of *The Paris Magazine*, among them the strange Piero Heliczer, who *Matrix* had published.

Anyone familiar with little magazines will know that frequency and regularity of appearance were never guaranteed, but the gap between the first and second issues of *The Paris Magazine* may well be something of a record. It was the Autumn of 1984 when the second came out, with the *The* dropped from the title and the magazine optimistically described as a quarterly. A lot had happened since 1967, and it was possibly a sign of how Paris, and Shakespeare and Company, were beginning to become more than ever tourist attractions that one of the articles listed on the cover was about "Hemingway's Paris", and another was an extract from William Wiser's book, *The Crazy Years*, his lively celebration of the Paris of the 1920s.

There was, also, an article about the birth of *The Paris Review* in the early-1950s. It's now a famous magazine, having continued to appear on time for sixty or so years. It was an interesting piece and informative about the problems, financial and otherwise, of getting a little magazine off the ground. The author, John Train, had firm views about the poetry published in *The Paris Review*, being of the opinion that "Many American poets run in packs, so with any particular poetry editor you tend to find yourself printing the works of his particular coterie". Train's view of most modern poetry was that very little of it is memorable and memorability is the "touchstone of real poetry". As he said, the other editors accepted the poems chosen by the Poetry Editor, but rarely liked them.

The poems that *Paris Magazine* printed were mostly unmemorable, and several short stories were readable (it's usually easier to tolerate a second-rate prose piece than a second-rate poem) if hardly exciting. I don't think George Whitman had any great ideas about printing work that broke new ground and preferred stories that were often set in Paris. I'm guessing that they were written by mainly young men living in the city and writing near-autobiographical pieces. Did Whitman select the stories, or was David Applefield, then active in Paris and himself editor of *Frank,* a publication designed to feature new writers, assisting him in some ways? Applefield was in *Paris Magazine* with a poem and an excerpt from a novel.

The reference to being "published quarterly" in the second issue may have raised a smile or two when the third made an appearance in the Summer of 1989. Again, the magazine seemed designed to appeal to those who viewed Paris as almost a museum piece, with Shakespeare and Company at its centre. I'm perhaps being unfair, and it was just the expatriate Paris that was seen that way, alongside an awareness that it wasn't ever likely to match up to what had happened in the 1920s. David Applefield contributed an article, "The Paris Expatriate Today," in which he worked hard to make a case for the contemporary. He pointed out that there were good writers living in Paris, though "the need to be here is no longer essential". Easier communications, the growth of publishing outlets elsewhere, and other factors, had lessened the idea of being an expatriate, at least in Paris, a city in which, unlike in the 1920s, it was no longer easy to live cheaply.

So, with more from William Wiser about Paris in the 1920s, a short piece about Gertrude Stein's ramblings around the city, and a piece by Noel Riley Fitch about Sylvia Beach and the Lost Generation, plus something on Henry Miller, it was inevitable that the past dominated the *Paris Magazine.* There was a short interview with Lawrence Ferlinghetti, and contributions from Edouard Roditi and Edmund White. Roditi had lived permanently in Paris since 1951. There's an interesting interview with him in the fourth issue of *The Expatriate Review* (Winter/Spring, 1973-74) in which he discusses the "expatriate problem".

Personally, being interested in what American and some British writers got up to in Paris from the 1920s through to the 1960s, I found the three issues of *Paris Magazine* of value when I picked them up during various trips to the city. But I can understand why, when the magazine was revived in 2010, there was clearly an intention not to fall into the trap of nostalgia. If the magazine, like Shakespeare and Company, was to have a continued vital existence it was obviously necessary for it to relate to the present and not just the past.

I have fond memories of seeing George Whitman behind the counter in the shop, of meeting Ted Joans again (I'd known him in Berlin some years before), there one day, and of an encounter with a couple of slightly tipsy English poets which led to us adjourning to a nearby bar. One of the poets, Jim Greenhalf, later commemorated the occasion in a poem in his book, *Following the Seine*. The last time I visited Shakespeare and Company it was crowded with what seemed to me mostly American and other tourists perhaps trying to imagine they're sampling the bohemian experience by being there. Everything was tidier, too. No doubt it's all good for business, as is the cafe where you can buy "Flapjack Kerouacs," but I can't help wondering if any intoxicated poets would be welcome?

Obviously, the three early issues of *Paris Magazine* (thc new series starting in 2010 reinstated the "The") were not major contributions to literature. They were very much aligned to George Whitman's love of bohemian Paris. From that point of view, and as an extension of what Shakespeare and Company had stood for in the 1950s and through to Whitman's death in 2011, they have relevance. They were an expression of a bohemia that no longer exists.

NOTES:

Three books that may be of interest in connection with Paris and writers are:

Paris Interzone: Richard Wright, Lolita, Boris Vian and others on the Left Bank, 1946-1960 by James Campbell. Secker & Warburg, 1994.

The Continual Pilgrimage: American Writers in Paris 1944-1960 by Christopher Sawyer-Laucanno. Bloomsbury Publishing, 1992.

The Beat Hotel: Ginsberg, Burroughs, and Corso in Paris, 1957-1963 by Barry Miles. Grove Press, 2000.

TROTSKYISM IN THE U.S.A.

There's a story, "The Party", by Isaac Rosenfeld which satirises the members and activities of a small, left-wing political group that is, "the movement to which, when the false directions have been taken and all the mistakes made, the working class will of necessity turn". I was reminded of it when I read George Breitman reminiscing about the 1938 founding of the Socialist Workers Party: "I am sure most of the delegates shared my conviction that we had participated in something truly significant: the launching – at last! – of the party that would lead the American workers in their coming socialist revolution". You have to admire the spirit and tenacity of someone who, despite all the evidence to the contrary, thinks that they have the answer to a major problem, i.e. how to radicalise the masses. I must admit that I was also tempted to reflect on the man (Debs, I think, though my memory may be faulty) who, when asked to lead the workers into a better world, declined because if he could lead them in, someone else could lead them out.

It is, admittedly, sometimes easy to satirise Trotskyists. Their tendency to split into factions – Rosenfeld's story comments on it – and to often appear as if they're debating about how many angels can dance on the head of a pin, was (is?) likely to dissuade anyone, other than those with minds inclined to such things, from joining them. Like any similar party composed largely of middle-class intellectuals, they were (are?) desperate to enrol workers in their ranks. If they did attract someone from the factories they rarely managed to keep them involved. There's a telling quote from a memoir by Ed Mann, a Youngstown steel worker: "In the 1950s the Socialist Workers Party started splitting. It was like the Protestant Church. When there are splits and you don't understand why, you become disillusioned".

But where did the Socialist Workers Party (SWP) emerge from? From a split, inevitably, and it's necessary to go back further than 1938 to find its origins. The leading lights – James P. Cannon, Max Shachtman, and others – had been members of the American Communist Party, but were expelled in 1928 because of their support for Trotsky, and their opposition to the rising tide of Stalinism. They then formed what was, in Paul Le Blanc's words, "the Communist League of America, Left Opposition of the Communist Party

(CLA)......with about a hundred members in twelve cities". According to Shachtman, membership was still below five hundred even after six years. But the Trotskyists did make something of a mark for themselves with their participation in the 1934 Minneapolis general strike. Farrell Dobbs, and some of the other members of the Minneapolis Teamster local, and leading members of the SWP, were some years later charged under the Smith Act, which made it an offence to advocate the overthrow of the American government, and were sent to prison.

It wasn't all smooth sailing and B.J. Field, who was secretary of the New York hotel workers' union, was expelled from the CLA because he wouldn't accept the leadership's criticisms of the way he was running a strike. Needless to say, Field started his own short-lived group, The League for a Revolutionary Workers Party. The CLA then combined with an equally small party, the American Workers Party, led by A.J Muste, to form the Workers Party of the United States (WPUS). Divisions erupted over policy about whether or not Trotskyists should "seek to join mass social democratic parties," with the result that a number of people described as "destructively factional" were expelled and started "the Revolutionary Workers League, which soon suffered splits of its own and eventually faded away".

There was a split in the Socialist Party (SP) in 1935 and its leader, Norman Thomas, then invited other radicals to join it. The Trotskyists did so, and George Novack, a lifelong Trotskyist, said that their "goal was to win the more militant of its left-wing and youth movement to revolutionary ideas". But by 1938 they had been expelled from the SP and it was at this point that the decision was made to form the SWP. It might be encouraging to say that the SWP consequently became a kind of permanent home for Trotskyists, and in some cases it did, but it wasn't long before rifts developed, and a faction led by Max Shachtman and James Burnham broke away to launch the Workers Party (WP). The oncoming Second World War, preceded by the Nazi-Soviet Pact, had persuaded Shachtman and Burnham that an automatic defence of the Soviet Union was not necessarily the correct policy. And they disagreed with "the Trotskyist analysis of the Soviet Union as a degenerated workers' state". Needless to say, Shachtman's new party had its own magazine, as did most of the other splinter groups.

It's not unfair to think that Paul Le Blanc perhaps points to a factor in the continuous disagreements when he quotes Irving Howe as saying that Trotskyism was "marked by an abundance of intellectual pride". In some ways this could be a good thing in that the Trotskyists attracted support from a number of writers and intellectuals. If they didn't actually join the Party, they often offered forms of support, particularly when it came to defending Trotsky's right to live in safety and be allowed to express his opinions. There's a memoir of the 1930s by Max Shachtman in which he refers to James T. Farrell, Max Eastman, John Dos Passos, Dwight MacDonald, and others, as whole or partly sympathetic to at least some aspects of Trotskyism. Alan Wald's *James T. Farrell: The Revolutionary Socialist Years* is worth looking at in this connection, and some of Farrell's now unfairly-neglected novels and short-stories are also relevant.

The war years did bring some benefits to the SWP in terms of increased membership and a presence in factories and other workplaces. And the immediate post-war years saw a rise in union militancy as workers attempted to restore the imbalances in pay and working conditions that had developed because of no-strike agreements and other restrictions brought in under wartime conditions. The Party was still bedevilled by internal dissension, however, and in 1946 Albert Goldman and Felix Morrow, described by Paul Le Blanc as "among the party's most capable intellectuals", were expelled as arguments raged over the policies to adapt in the face of the developing situation in both America and Europe. Stalinism and social-democracy "were able to channel the post-war radical working-class ferment and energy away from revolutionary socialism", and "Trotskyists were unable to rally the masses to the banner of the Fourth International". I get a sinking feeling whenever I come across references to "the masses", and wonder just who they are? Or, perhaps, just who the person using such a term thinks "the masses" are?

The 1950s were fallow years for the SWP and, indeed, most radical parties, as a decline in militancy, and a Cold War-influenced rise in patriotism, together with repression (blacklists, etc.), and prosperity, combined to isolate the SWP even further than it may normally have been. It's probably not unexpected that more splits occurred, reducing the membership and leaving all control in the hands of an old guard anxious to preserve their own positions and what they saw as the purity of their ideas. Paul Le Blanc refers to various criticisms of

James P. Cannon, for example, as a "narrow-minded sect leader", and a "true believer" who constantly sought to purge "heretics" and "traitors". I should add that Le Blanc doesn't agree with these assessments.

Matters improved in the 1960s as students protested, there were large anti-Vietnam War demonstrations, the Civil Rights movement gathered pace, and there were other signs of increased militancy, though perhaps significantly not among most of the white working-class. By 1973 the SWP had 1,200 members, and its weekly publication, *Militant*, sold around 31,000 copies. Many of the new members were young and their concerns were often not those of the older generation of activists. They did seem to follow the veterans in some respects, and Le Blanc notes that while the new leadership was left "to make its own decisions, learn from its own mistakes, and develop its own orientation and style.......in some of the factional disputes that arose in the 1970s, however, this style could assume a harsh, at times even brutal, tone".

Alan Wald refers to the "human factors involved in movement building", and cites "problems of ego, arrogance and self-righteousness". He also suggests that "a crucial factor in many splits and disaffections has been the blockage of an individual's rise to a full-time leadership position". In other words, ambition. It's interesting that such factors can be applied to those who aspire to be leaders, but somehow can't be seen among "the masses" they want to lead. They're presumably all expected to think the same way and have similar interests and aims. The SWP under its new leadership eventually abandoned Trotskyism as its guiding philosophy.

Mentioning Alan Wald inclines me to say how much I admire his trilogy of books about the American literary left from the 1930s through to the 1950s, and his book on the New York Intellectuals. He's honest enough to ask some pointed questions about why should "revolutionary socialist political activists in the 1990s be concerned with the history and theory of U.S. Trotskyists?" He further adds: "Only those with a highly circumscribed reality can fail to see that, in a society where winning the support of the majority means the ability to influence millions, the balance sheet of the political accomplishments of Trotskyism after nearly seven decades tends towards the negative". Wald's comments were made in the 1990s, when this book was first published, but I doubt that they could be any different now, when Trotskyism might seem even more irrelevant. Or not, depending on your political views.

However, it's only fair to point to Wald's suggestions regarding the intellectual influence of Trotskyism, and he lists numerous noted writers and intellectuals who, at one time or another, and for one reason or another, had links to the Trotskyists. As he stresses, though, they all seem to be from the older generation. Few of those who came into the SWP in the 1960s are of a similar status: "Although a number of 1960s activists went on to become impressive scholars and professionals, none have at this date achieved the intellectual stature of Sidney Hook, Meyer Schapiro, Irving Howe, Leslie Fiedler, the *Partisan Review* editors, and so forth".

Another question that Wald asks is, "why are there so many splits, and what can be done about them?" He proposes that it should be possible to "foster a long-term commitment to constructing a serious and democratic organisation through collaboration with diverse individuals who are all pledged to a kind of collective political life, through which individuality is realised with, not against or apart from, one's co-thinkers".

It's an idealistic proposal, in my view, and not one likely to be adopted by many left-wingers as those factors referred to earlier – "ambition, ego, arrogance, and self-righteousness" – come into play. It may be that many left-wingers, like many religious people, are simply attuned to controversy. Years ago, I met Reg Groves, a one-time member of the Balham Group of early British Trotskyists. Reg died a little later, and friends told me that, at his funeral, his surviving old comrades gathered, and spent much of their time reviving the past and arguing about events and politics without coming to any kind of conclusion, or even an agreement to differ.

The earlier comment by Ed Mann regarding the 1950s factional fights and splits in the SWP being "like the Protestant Church", reminded me that where I grew up, in a mill town in the north of England, there was a group called The Strict and Particular Baptists who had a small chapel. They had been established in 1885 when twelve of them split from another group of Baptists in the town. I couldn't help thinking of them each time I met up with Percy, an old-time member of the Communist Party (no danger of him ever being a Trotskyist) who had been to Russia in the 1920s and was shocked to see women wearing lipstick and smoking in the street. Agreed, he wasn't a sectarian – the party line was good enough for him – but he struck me as having the capacity to be one, given the right circumstances. The intolerance was there, and the narrow-mindedness.

There seemed some similarities in both Percy's and the Baptists' basic attitudes, certainly about "heretics", and the like, but Percy's saving grace was that he enjoyed sitting in the pub, drinking beer, though still being dogmatic about party policy. The Baptists were never likely to be seen in a pub, as I know from my Baptist mother, though she wasn't one of the Strict and Particular variety. She had married my father, a hard-drinking lapsed Catholic. Percy is long-dead, and the Strict and Particular Baptists' chapel closed down around forty years ago when its last member passed on. They never had been all that successful at recruiting newer and younger members. I doubt that many people now think of Percy's politics or the Baptist's beliefs. The consumer society provides different distractions for many, and the less fortunate worry about how to make ends meet.

I'm not attempting to mock Trotskyists by equating them with communists and Baptists, simply wanting to point out that perhaps their tendencies towards doctrinal purity and factional disputes might have deterred a lot of people from joining them. The Isaac Rosenfeld story I referred to at the start of this review is most likely based on his own experiences of Max Shachtman and the Workers Party. In the end the party starts to split apart because a faction among its members are bored with the endless meetings and other activities that never seem to lead to any practical political reality. In Irving Howe's *A Margin of Hope: An Intellectual Autobiography* he reminiscences about his involvements with the Trotskyists in the post-1945 period, and recalls reading "The Party": "Like a finger pressing secret wounds, Rosenfeld's story hurt to the point of rage, perhaps because we knew that in its fantastic way it was scraping against the truth. Could we have dismissed him as an enemy it might all have been easy, but we knew he was not an enemy and that made the pain worse".

A longer, and less satirical fictional account of life in the Workers Party, can be found in Harvey Swados' excellent novel, *Standing Fast,* which traces the lives of a number of followers of Shachtman from the 1940s through to the 1960s. Using Swados' own experiences as a member of the Buffalo branch of the Workers Party, it does end on a somewhat disenchanted note resulting from the party's failure to achieve anything of significance.

It might also be worth referring to a review by Mark Shechner of Alan Wald's *The New York Intellectuals*. Shechner is less than enthusiastic about Wald's book, and at one point, writing about people who were members of the CLA or the SWP or the WP, or had some links to one or other of them, he says: "What the movement lacked in numbers and resources it made up for in words, and it is as a word factory and a school for writers, not a political movement, that American Trotskyism remains spellbinding. It has been said that for every member of the Abraham Lincoln Brigade that fought in Spain during the Civil War there would eventually be three books, either by or about. If so, then for American Trotskyism there would eventually be five books, one magazine, and two internal bulletins. They lived, it sometimes seems, in order to leave a record of their passing".

I must admit that reading the various pieces in *Trotskyism in the United States*, with their numerous notes and references, I was amazed at how much paperwork had been generated about a party, and its offshoots, that had frankly achieved very little in practical terms. Just about everybody had written a book or a memoir or some sort of record of their involvement in the debates and splits and other events. Or someone else had written an essay or book about them. And then there were all the little magazines, pamphlets, and other ephemera. It's easy to see why Trotskyism attracts attention from academics. There is a wealth of material to provide for a Ph.D. and essays and perhaps a book or two.

Despite my carpings and criticisms I found *Trotskyism in the United States* quite fascinating. It should be borne in mind that it was originally published in 1996, and some of its assumptions and conclusions need to be related to the situation twenty years ago. It is useful as a guide to many of the Trotskyist activists, not all of them necessarily well-known. In several ways the lives of the Trotskyists, known or obscure, are more interesting than the now-forgotten policies they endlessly debated and disagreed about. Their experiences, both in and out of "the movement", say a lot about what was happening in American society generally in the period concerned.

TROTSKYISM IN THE UNITED STATES: HISTORICAL ESSAYS AND RECONSIDERATIONS
by George Breitman, Paul Le Blanc, and Alan Wald
Haymarket Books. 384 pages. $22/£16.99 (paperback). ISBN 978-1-60846-685-6

I've mentioned several books and it may be useful to provide some details about them:

Isaac Rosenfeld, "The Party", in *Alpha and Omega* (MacGibbon and Kee, London, 1966)

Alan Wald, *James T.Farrell: The Revolutionary Socialist Years.* (New York University Press, New York, 1978) This is particularly valuable as a guide to Farrell's novels and stories which have fictional portraits of various left-wing writers and intellectuals.

Harvey Swados, *Standing Fast* (Doubleday, New York, 1970)

Alan Wald, *The New York Intellectuals: The Rise and Decline of the Anti-Stalinist Left from the 1930s to the 1980s* (The University of North Carolina Press, Chapel Hill, 1987)

Mark Shechner, "The Last Trotskyist", in *The Conversion of the Jews and Other Essays* (Macmillan London, 1990)

Alan Wald, *Exiles From a Future Time: The Forging of the Mid-Twentieth Century Literary Left* (University of North Carolina Press, Chapel Hill, 2002)

Alan Wald, *Trinity of Passion: The Literary Left and the Anti-Fascist Crusade* (University of North Carolina Press, Chapel Hill, 2007)

Alan Wald. *American Night: The Literary Left in the Era of the Cold War* (University of North Carolina Press, Chapel Hill, 2012)

Irving Howe, *A Margin of Hope: An Intellectual Autobiography* (Secker & Warburg, London, 1983)

Max Shachtman, "Radicalism in the Thirties: The Trotskyist View," in *As We Saw the Thirties*, edited by Rita James Simon (University of Illinois Press, Chicago, 1969)

NO PASARÁN!

The literature of the Spanish Civil War is voluminous. Histories, essays, novels, short-stories, memoirs, poetry, plays, and much more. I suppose most readers will be familiar with at least two books in English, Ernest Hemingway's *For Whom the Bell Tolls* and George Orwell's *Homage to Catalonia*, and the exploits of their writers. There are many others, some of which focus on the International Brigades, the units of foreign volunteers fighting for the legally-elected Republican Government against General Franco and his co-conspirators. They make for informative reading. On the other hand, all these books, and many pamphlets, articles, and other written sources, are largely concerned with what might be called the non-Spanish contributions to the narrative. And most of them are written from a pro-Republican point of view. We rarely get to read Spanish writers in general, and we're especially starved of work by those who supported Franco.

The difference between the material referred to above and *No Pasarán* is that the emphasis in the latter is on Spanish writers. There are, it's true, some well-known names – George Orwell, Arthur Koestler, Sartre, Laurie Lee, André Malraux. I was going to add John Dos Passos, but I wonder how many people read him these days? And some lesser-known writers – Muriel Rukeyser, Gamel Woolsey, Esmond Romilly – are among the English-speaking contributors. The rest, give or take a handful of writers from Italy, Poland, etc., are Spanish. It's perhaps worth noting at this point that there is little in *No Pasarán* about the International Brigades. I'm second to no-one in my admiration for the men and women who served in the Brigades and suffered, in more ways than one, because of that fact, but we do need to know much more about how Spaniards responded to events.

When the war started in 1936, the Republic was badly prepared to meet the threat from Franco. He had the support of what were some of the most effective fighting units in the Spanish Army. They were the Spanish Foreign Legion, and the regiments of the Army of Africa, which included Moorish troops. Both the Legion and the Moors were noted for their ferocity in battle. Franco was also soon supported by Hitler, who sent the Condor Legion, with crack airmen, to Spain, and Mussolini, who provided up to 80,000 troops, complete with tanks and artillery. There is an informative book, *Franco's Foreign Legions: Adventurers, Fascists, and Christian Crusaders in the Spanish Civil War* by Christopher Othen (Hurst & Co., 2013) which provides a great deal of information about who fought for Franco. Othen, for example, says that around 78,000 Moors served in the Nationalist army.

The Republic, by contrast, had to rely largely on some loyal soldiers and policemen, but also on militia units formed around political parties and trade unions. Initially, at least, the workers were denied arms, but when the Government realised the gravity of the situation, rifles and other armaments were issued to them. Further problems were caused by the hypocritical Non-Intervention policies practised by countries such as Britain, France, and the United States. The only two countries prepared to supply arms and ammunition to the Republic were Russia and Mexico, but at first the quality of what was provided was poor. Old rifles and machine guns, and defective ammunition, were common, and when added to the lack of training and discipline, the situation quickly became chaotic. It's frankly amazing that the Republic didn't completely collapse within a few months, if not weeks, of Franco launching his offensive.

The film director, Luis Buñuel, was in Spain when war was declared, and the excerpt from his autobiography, *My Last Breath*, describes what it was like: "The first three months were the worst, mostly because of the total absence of control.........No sooner had the people risen and seized power than they split into factions and began tearing one another to pieces. The insane and indiscriminate settling of accounts made everyone forget the essential reasons for the war."

Buñuel also recounts an encounter with border guards who refused to recognise documents issued by the Republican Government and said he had to have a visa from local anarchists. Just prior to that he had shared a railway carriage with a POUM officer who stated that the Government was "garbage and had to be wiped out at any cost". The POUM were non-communist Marxists and often referred to as Trotskyists, and like the anarchists would eventually fall foul of the communists. They were beginning to take over control of some key government positions, especially as Russian aid began to play a significant role in helping the Republican forces to continue holding back Franco's army.

I have to say that the anarchists do not come out well, on the whole, when reading through the various pieces in *No Pasarán*. Buñuel describes an incident in a town called Calanda. According to his account the anarchists executed eighty-two people: "Among the victims were nine Dominicans, most of the leading citizens on the council, some doctors and landowners, and even a few poor people whose only crime was a reputation for piety". And the Franco supporter José María Gironella's *The Cypresses Believe in God,* a novel described as "an ambitious attempt to capture the war on both sides", has a vivid description of mobs led by anarchists burning churches.

It's necessary to point out that anarchist excesses and atrocities were equalled on the Nationalist side, which doesn't make them any better or worse, but does indicate the high levels of hatred and bitterness that were an integral part of the war in Spain. Summary executions were a feature of the activities of both sides. The Basque, Bernardo Atxaga, was too young to participate in the war, but in his *De Gernika a Guernica,* he tells of reading in a newspaper the reminiscences of an old man from Fuenteguinaldo:

"Apparently, the Falangists asked the priest to draw up a list of all the reds and atheists in the village. On October 7th, 1936, they went from house to house looking for them. At nine o'clock at night they were taken to the prison in Cuidad Rodrigo, and at four o'clock in the morning, were told they were being released, but at the door of the prison a truck was waiting and, instead of taking them home, it brought them here to be killed".

There's a telling comment in a well-written and sympathetic (to the Republic) article, "The Villages are the Heart of Spain", that John Dos Passos wrote for *Esquire* in 1937: "How can they win, I was thinking? How can the new world full of confusion and crosspurposes and illusions and dazzled by the mirage of idealistic phrases win against the iron combination of men accustomed to run things who have only one idea binding them together, to hold on to what they've got".

Earlier Dos Passos had talked about a village he visited where the socialist U.G.T. was at odds with the syndicalist C.N.T. regarding the direction to take and the need for reform or revolution. The syndicalists, like the anarchists, believed that the war was an opportunity to push through a social revolution as well as defeat Franco. The Italian anarchist Antoine Gimenez, who fought with the Durutti Column, wrote a memoir, *Sons of the Night,* in which he described an anarchist giving a talk on "free love" to an audience of local people. One can imagine the "confusion" in the minds of people probably brought up in an atmosphere of strict social and moral control as they heard the idealistic statements of the speaker. And the "crosspurposes" his words might have induced as they wondered what defeating Franco had to do with looking favourably on one's wife having a lover.

The realities of war are described in more than one piece. Many soldiers have noted that war is often ninety-five percent boredom and five percent terror (the statistics may vary slightly, according to experience), and poor food, which was often in short supply, a lack of cigarettes, and lice, were fairly standard complaints. Mika Etchebéhere joined a POUM unit, where she soon became its commander, to the consternation of its soldiers. They liked and admired her, but were worried about being teased by other troops because they were led by a woman. Her account of being infested with lice is told with humour, though one can imagine that the experience wasn't a pleasant one. But neither was Esmond Romilly's experience of battle. His "At the End of the Alphabet", from his book, *Boadilla*, vividly describes the confusion and the fear, and the realisation that, though one has survived, several friends are dead.

There is, perhaps, some humour to be drawn from many situations, and Arturo Barea's "This War is a Lesson", from *The Clash*, part three of his *The Forging of a Rebel* trilogy, does have an element of black humour. Barea had a friend, a priest who, when the war started, remained loyal to the Republic. One night a car drew up and several anarchists got out and told the priest to come with them. Knowing the anarchists' reputation for killing priests, his friends protested and stressed that he was a loyal supporter of the Republic. The anarchists insisted that the priest had to accompany them, and eventually one of them said: "Oh hell, nothing will happen to him. If you must know, the old woman, my mother, is dying and doesn't want to go to the other world without confessing to one of these buzzards. It's a disgrace for me, but what else could I do but fetch him?"

It's worth noting that Barea's trilogy has been available in English translation for some years. Its three books – *The Forge, The Track, The Clash* – describe his childhood, his service in the Spanish Army in Morocco in the 1920s, and his adventures in the Spanish Civil War.

There may be some humour, too, to be derived from Curzio Malaparte's "The Traitor," which is about a group of young Spaniards who, having been sent to Russia as refugees during the Civil War, have grown up as staunch communists. They are captured by the Finns during the fighting beween Finland and Russia, but the Finns are at a loss as to what to do with them. They are offered the chance to return to Spain, but turn it down. One does eventually agree to return, and is turned on, and beaten up by the others. But he does go home and when he dies is buried as a Catholic.

There are many fascinating accounts in *No Pasarán.* Pierre Herbart went to Russia with André Gide, and when the latter wrote a book critical of some aspects of the Soviet system, Herbart was sent to Spain to ask André Malraux's advice about publication. While he was there, Gide, despite promises to the contrary, published the book. There was outrage in communist circles, and in the dangerous atmosphere in Spain Herbart came under suspicion for having played a part in getting the book into print while pretending to consult Malraux, a Party stalwart, about it. He did manage to get back safely to Paris, where Gide seemed more concerned about the favourable attention he was getting from the press and public than in what might have happened to Herbart.

There is also a short piece by Drieu La Rochelle which in a non-pedantic way presents his case for Fascism and support for Franco. He at one time associated with the Dadaists and Surrealists, but moved right and collaborated with the Germans when France was occupied. He went into hiding after the Liberation and committed suicide in 1945.

No Pasarán is a splendid collection and the fact of it having such a variety of writers, many of them Spanish, adds to its interest and usefulness. On my shelves is a book called *Cries From a Wounded Madrid: Poetry of the Spanish Civil War*, selected and translated by Carlos Bauer (Ohio University Press, 1984). *No Pasarán* will make a good prose companion for it.

NO PASARÁN!: WRITINGS FROM THE SPANISH CIVIL WAR
Chosen and introduced by Pete Ayrton
Serpent's Tail. 393 pages. £20. ISBN 978-1-84668-997-0

REVOLUTIONARY YIDDISHLAND

It might be useful to start this review by saying what is meant by "Yiddishland." In simple terms it refers to "the Jewish world of Eastern Europe," though in the introduction to this book it is mentioned that interviews were conducted with "former revolutionary Jewish militants from Eastern, Central and Southern Europe". So, Poland, Hungary, Yugoslavia, Bulgaria, Romania, the Ukraine, wherever there were concentrations of Jews, and the common language among them was Yiddish, was Yiddishland. As the authors stress: "It was a social and cultural space, a linguistic and religious world, rather than a territory in the strict sense." I don't think I need to labour the point that it was a world that largely came to an end with the Holocaust.

As for "Revolutionary Yiddishland," it was the society that essentially developed as industrialisation and urbanisation, and the consequent drawing of many Jews away from the shtetls and into towns and cities, began to break up traditional Jewish communities. As workers were concentrated in factories and other places of employment, they began to respond to the radical ideas that circulated in the late-19th century. Socialism, anarchism, communism were all in the air, and organising workers into unions was a priority. The Jewish General Workers' Union, or the Bund as it was known, was one of the leading organisations, but not the only one. Poale Zion and the Communist Party were also of importance: "In the period between the world wars, the Bund swung between communism and social democracy, while the trajectories of Poale Zion allegiance were also multiple, from Moscow to Tel Aviv". The authors also say that, "communist may mean Stalinist, but also Trotskyist or Brandlerite".

There was some separation from other proletarian groups due to the nature of the employment that Jews found in towns and cities: "they remained largely concentrated in the handicraft sector, a type of production with a low technological level at the end of the production chain: tailors, shoemakers, weavers, carpenters, locksmiths, etc". The Bund was founded in 1897, and initially, at least, the intention was to inaugurate the Jewish workers' movement into the general workers' movement, though specific Jewish matters, including the speaking of Yiddish, did require special attention. Bolsheviks like Trotsky and

Rosa Luxemburg spoke out against Jews being seen as a group apart, and were in favour of a "universalist current that wagered on the extinction of the Jewish question" as the "great current of the revolution" brought about assimilation. This was effectively saying that whatever differences there might be between groups of workers, they were of far less importance than the concerns they all shared as members of the proletariat.

"Militancy was the key word in the existence of our witnesses" in the years between the two World Wars, say Brossat and Klingberg when beginning to look at the lives of the people they interviewed. And though each party's "utopia" had its "particular colouration," they all "sprang from the same root: the great utopia of a new world, the New Covenant that was prefigured by the writings of the socialist thinkers of the second half of the nineteenth century, that was consolidated with the growth of the workers' movement in the early 1900s, and that stormed the heavens with the Russian Revolution".

The 1930s, however, tended to see the ending of the dreams that had inspired so many radicals. The rise of Stalinism in Russia, the collapse of the Left in Germany, and the eventual defeat of the Republic in the Spanish Civil War, all took their toll. People still believed, of course, especially in the notion that communism would eventually provide the answers so many people sought for. Looking back at an incident when she was young, one of the witnesses says: "At that time, things were simpler than they are today; that kind of simple humanity was more or less synonymous with communism." The problem was that, as the Communist Party in Russia became increasingly bureaucratised and wanted to control every action by communists world wide, activists began to question the level of their commitment. As Isaac Deutscher put it: "Bureaucratic uniformity and revolutionary enthusiasm are a contradiction in terms". Not all communists had doubts about the Party line, or if they did they kept their thoughts to themselves. One old radical, reflecting on what had happened in the late-1930s when the Polish Communist Party was dissolved on orders from Moscow, admitted that he was "naïve", and accepted the decision "without demur".

The Spanish Civil War was a key experience for more than one of the individuals described in *Revolutionary Yiddishland*: "In the revolutionary commitment of the former militants we interviewed in Israel, as for so many thousands of others, the Spanish war was a strong and special moment, both in itself and as a turning point". The reasons are fairly obvious. Fascism was on the march. Germany and Italy had already succumbed to it, and though there had appeared to be some signs of a growing opposition with the election of Popular Front governments in France and Spain, the events in Spain as Franco launched his offensive clearly indicated that decisive action was needed. Some Jews were already there, having left their homelands as anti-semitic feeling increased, but it took the formation of the International Brigades to provide the main source of Jewish recruitment to the fight against Franco.

The anti-Franco opposition was always riven with arguments about the purpose of the struggle against attempts to overthrow the democratically-elected government. The Communist Party, along with the "moderate" socialists, and the bourgeois who had committed to the Republic, said that the aim was simply to defeat the fascists. But many others saw it as an opportunity to push through a social and political revolution. The anarchists and anarcho-syndicalists of the FAI-CNT, and the alleged Trotskyists of the POUM militia, therefore had to be suppressed. As with earlier events, doubts were raised in some people's minds, but others were inclined to think that the Party must be right: "I was one of the fanatics. The party pointed out the way and we followed. Our motto could be summed up as this: `The party said so, the party is right. Stalin said so. Stalin is right'."

When the International Brigades were withdrawn from Spain in 1938, and the war ended with Franco's victory in 1939, many volunteers found themselves imprisoned in what were effectively concentration camps in France. And although the policy of the French Communist Party was not to offer armed opposition to the occupying Germans until June, 1941, when Hitler attacked Russia, Jews were quickly active with the Resistance. They knew from years of bitter experience how to survive in a hostile environment. Their experiences in Germany, Spain, and elsewhere, gave them a "realistic perception of German fascism". And being in the Resistance provided the possibility of survival, whereas doing nothing was almost certainly likely to lead to their deaths.

The post-war years did not bring the Utopia that had seemed to be promised. The anti-semitic nature of the communist authorities in Russia and their satellite countries such as Czechoslovakia and Hungary, became obvious when the show trials began in Prague and Budapest in the early 1950s. Jews were prominent in the ranks of the accused. Artur London, a veteran of the International Brigades, was among them. The fact that he survived the purges, though spending years in prison, meant that he could later tell his story, but others were not as lucky and were executed after trials that were farcical in their allegations of Trotskyism, Titoism, spying, sabotage, and other "crimes". Even those militants who had managed to suspend their disbelief about earlier purges began to think that something was terribly wrong.

"The USSR holds a central place in the experience and thought of Yiddishland", according to Brossat and Klingberg. And they suggest that this can partly be ascribed to the fact that the Soviet Union opened its borders to the "flow of Jewish refugees from Poland" in 1939 and 1940. As one of the people they interviewed stated: "Stalin was a criminal, but it was the Soviet Union that saved my life, while my whole family, who stayed in Poland, were exterminated by the Nazis". For a time, until around 1948, Jewish cultural activities were encouraged in Russia, that is until Stalin embarked on a campaign against "cosmopolitans", who were defined as individuals "deprived of patriotic sentiment, detached from the interests of his homeland, a stranger to his own people with a disdainful attitude towards its culture". It's not hard to detect the undertone of anti-semitism in that, and as noted earlier, Jews were often a majority among the accused when show trials were held.

The interviews with one-time militants that provide a basis for this book took place in Israel, where they had gone to live despite whatever their earlier political involvements had been. It would, however, seem that little respect was given them for their activities. Brossat and Klingberg say that there is, a "gaping, radical break between the world that they lost and the arrogant new Sparta within whose walls they have chosen to live". It would seem that few people know or care about "Revolutionary Yiddishland", and the official view is that the Jews of the Diaspora, which is where the militants came from, are not relevant or at least not to be acknowledged as ancestors worthy of attention: "As taught in Israeli primary schools, thousands of these Jews, degraded by the spirit of the diaspora were led to the gas chambers like cattle to the slaughter". "Yiddishland" not only ceased to exist in reality because of communist ideology and repression and fascist brutality, but also in memory because its history has largely been blotted out by many Jews.

The account that Brossat and Klingberg provide uses a great deal of personal testimony from the one-time activists, and I should point out that the original edition of their book was published in France in 1983. I'd guess that all of the people they refer to are now long dead. I've used only a few phrases from their testimonies when writing this review, partly because to do more would take up too much of the available space. The testimonies are essential, because through them one gets an idea of the levels of commitment and suffering that were experienced. It is sobering to read about people who survived Nazi concentration camps and the Stalinist gulags, who fought in the Spanish Civil War and the French Resistance, who were beaten by the police and imprisoned in various countries, and retained their political convictions despite what happened to them. It is reasonable, of course, to wonder how and why some of them sustained a belief in communism when the evidence pointed to its corruption.

There was, also, a reluctance on the part of some of those interviewed to speak too much about their roles in the communist states that were established after the Second World War. Brossat and Klingberg say that "the blue heaven of utopia gave way to a reality with far more varied colours." The new regimes in Poland, Hungary, Czechoslovakia, Romania, Bulgaria and Yugoslavia "needed" these experienced Jewish militants, who thus turned from revolutionaries into officials, privileged people in countries that had a hard time rising from their ruins." They became a part of the bureaucracies they would have scorned in their younger days. But that, perhaps, was inevitable.

Brossat and Klingberg added a great deal of information about the various factions and intrigues in The Bund, Poale Zion, and the communist parties in various countries, to their history of "Revolutionary Yiddishland", and so rounded out this fascinating and essential story.

REVOLUTIONARY YIDDISHLAND: A HISTORY OF JEWISH RADICALISM
by Alain Brossat and Sylvie Klingberg (translated by David Fernbach)
Verso. 304 pages. £16.99. ISBN 13: 978-1-78478-606-9

JACK KEROUAC

Most readers will think of Jack Kerouac's literary career as having started with the publication in 1957 of his now-famous *On the Road.* But he had been active for some years prior to that, and his first novel, *The Town and the City,* appeared in 1950. It has now been reissued, and it thus becomes available, in an English edition, at least, for the first time in more than twenty years.

It was probably the most formal of Kerouac's books. He himself remarked that it was written "according to what they told me at Columbia University", and the marks of a young writer's initial attempts to shape something out of his experiences are stamped all over the text. He was, in the 1940s, still much influenced by Thomas Wolfe, and some of the tone of that writer's attempts to capture the movement of American life comes through in Kerouac's work. And, like Wolfe, he sometimes forces the pace a bit too much, with the result that his enthusiasm sometimes overtakes his technique.

On the whole, though, he is immensely readable, and his story of family life, and the effects on it of the war years, rolls along in fine fashion. In it one can see signs of the later Kerouac, the inspired chronicler of his times.

The last hundred or so pages are especially interesting, with their references to the "underground" life-style of the New York hipsters, and their descriptions of the characters Kerouac found increasingly fascinating. *The Town and the City* was one of the first novels to put into print fictional portraits of such notable figures as Allen Ginsberg and William Burroughs.

Incidentally, Quartet Books seem to be cornering the market in reissues of Beat-related material, and I wonder if there is any chance they will give us the full text of John Clellon Holmes's *Go*? An edited paperback version is the only one to have been published here. And how about George Mandel's *Flee the Angry Strangers*, a little-known but valuable document in the "underground".

Maggie Cassidy was first published here in 1960, in paperback form only, and I doubt that many people took much notice of it among the plethora of cheap paperbacks then in the shops. It is certainly one of the lesser-known items in the Kerouac catalogue, partly because of its previously limited availability, but also I suspect because it is somewhat removed from the Beat myths surrounding the man and his work. A quiet, easy-paced book, it deals with adolescent life in a small American town just prior to the Second World War, and vividly captures the mood of the period. It's good to see it in print again.

Jack Kerouac's expansive talents were largely destroyed towards the end of his life by a combination of bitterness and drink, and he wrote little of consequence in his final years. A sudden burst of inspiration just a few weeks before his death did result in one short novel, however, and it is this which is now available, together with an earlier book.

The later work, *Pic*, has all the virtues and faults of most of Kerouac's writing. It centres on the adventures of a young black boy as he moves from North Carolina to New York and then California. Although occasionally sentimental in both style and tone, it nonetheless looks at people in a sympathetic and warm-hearted way. And if its black characters are too often portrayed as happy-go-lucky swingers, living only for the moment, there are hints of the harshness of the cities in which they struggle to survive.

In general, what comes through is that, although Kerouac's vision largely eschewed political realities, his appreciation of people as individuals was genuine enough.

The main strength of *Pic* perhaps lies in its set scenes. A session in a jazz club, a crazy old man encountered on the road, a way-out soapboxer raging against television. All are painted with vivid strokes of the brush. The reader is caught up in the fast pace of the writing, and feels in its pulse the rhythm of each situation. The same is true of the dialogue. It ebbs and flows, and is full of excitement and wonder.

Pic is only a minor novel in the Kerouac canon, and its final passages suggest either a failure of energy on the writer's part, or edited versions of certain overwrought passages. But it has some of the charm which was always a hallmark of the best of his work.

The Subterraneans was first published in 1960, and deals with life and love among the Beats in San Francisco. It was, in fact, really about the New York scene, but the location was changed for legal reasons. It remains an engaging book, and is full of lively and evocative writing.

Jack Kerouac was once quoted as saying that *Visions of Cody* was his favourite of the various books he had written. Strange, then, that the complete manuscript only saw print after his death. A portion of it was published in 1959 in a limited-edition format, and other excerpts appeared in magazines and anthologies. But, for various reasons, various publishers were reluctant to take a chance with the full work.

Books like this invariably achieve an "underground" reputation, which is what happened to *Visions of Cody*, and it's always best to approach them from the point of view of whether or not they match up to the praises and promises.

I suppose it really all depends on one's liking, or otherwise, for Kerouac's vigorous but sometimes untidy style. I have to admit to being prepared to tolerate his occasional indulgences in order to get at the meat of his writing, which is his contagious and often-moving nostalgia.

His America can probably be compressed into the years 1935 to 1955. True, he wrote books which dealt with the post-1955 period, but I suspect he was always looking back wistfully to the earlier days.

They were, for Kerouac, at least, the days of roadside diners, Alan Ladd in *This Gun For Hire*, fabulous nomadic characters, Glenn Miller (and, on a more-intense musical plane, the great jazz saxophonist, Charlie Parker), old union organisers. It's an endless list and it all blends into a picture of the stimulating disarray of those years.

I can't see how anyone interested in pre-1955 social and cultural (in the popular sense) manifestations can fail to be fascinated by Kerouac. And if one is prepared to ride on his prose roller-coaster, it's possible to pick up more of the emotional atmosphere of the 1940s than any pure sociological documents can provide.

There is one weak section in the book, and it's the overlong transcript of a conversation between Kerouac and Neal Cassady, the "Cody" of the book's title. It may have some significance for Beat historians, but like any such documents it contains a fair amount of frankly dull cross-talk. Still, it's a minor fault in an otherwise entertaining work.

One final point. The American edition of *Visions of Cody* had a beautifully-evocative jacket – a collage of Forties images (a 78rpm disc, a pin-up of the Rita Hayworth/Betty Grable variety, typical cars of the times, Billie Holiday, and more), all of which abound in Kerouac's work. It's a shame that the British publisher dropped it in favour of their drab design.

THE TOWN AND THE CITY by Jack Kerouac. Quartet Books.

MAGGIE CASSIDY by Jack Kerouac. Deutsch.

PIC and THE SUBTERRANEANS by Jack Kerouac. Deutsch.

VISIONS OF CODY by Jack Kerouac. Deutsch.

LEW WELCH: THE LETTERS

Readers of Jack Kerouac's books, and of Beat Generation literature generally, will be familiar with a character called Dave Wain who appears in *Big Sur*, where he's described as "that lean rangy red headed Welchman". It doesn't take much stretching of the imagination to realise that Wain is Lew Welch, a poet who was a leading light of the Beat movement on the West Coast during the Sixties, and whose letters, along with correspondence from various friends like Kerouac, Gary Snyder, and Philip Whalen, comprise the contents of these two volumes.

Welch's life makes for an interesting comment on the America of the Fifties and Sixties. A student at Reed College in the late-Forties, along with Snyder and Whalen, he went into advertising in 1953, a career that seemed to both attract and repel him at one and the same time. Early letters to his mother find him falling over himself to convince her that work, marriage, material possessions (the whole bit that was to be looked on as "square") were what he really wanted. But, as the decade progressed, and Welch again came into contact with Whalen and Snyder, and heard about the burgeoning Beat scene, he indicated that he was unsettled, and he really thought that he ought to be writing.

After persuading his employers to transfer him to Oakland, he soon decided that the only way to live was to dedicate himself to poetry. Advertising and marriage went out of the window, and Welch settled down to hammer out his poems. He also took on a variety of odd jobs in order to eat, one of them as a cab-driver. He had a reputation for being able to handle cars as skilfully as the legendary Neal Cassady, and it was this skill as a driver that partly led to him accompanying Kerouac on a cross-country trip in 1959 that has gone down in Beat history.

Besides writing poetry and a little prose, Welch was clearly an inveterate correspondent, sometimes one suspects because he felt forgotten if letters didn't come and go with rapid regularity. There's a nervous energy in this that often betrays an uncertainty about life generally. Likewise, he alternated between considering himself a good poet, even a major one, and worrying about his position in the Beat pecking order. Other writers have had these kind of concerns, of course, but in Welch's case they were somewhat at odds with his often-stated desire to withdraw into a kind of Zen-influenced calmness and detachment. The letters are far more revealing than the poetry in this respect.

Welch had only gravitated to the Beat scene proper around the end of the Fifties, but as the Sixties developed he did have some success as a poet. He had several small collections published by prestigious presses, such as Auerhahn and Oyez, appeared in magazines and anthologies alongside his fellow-Beats, gave poetry readings, and ran workshops. Some poets might have been happy with this perhaps small-scale, but steady progress, whereas Welch worried constantly. As he said in a 1963 letter to Kirby Doyle, "I am world's welterweight worry champ". It didn't help, either, that his relationships with women were less than easy, and that he had a record of mental instability. And he drank heavily. The letters frequently refer to mishaps and mistakes resulting from excesses, and the problems caused by heavy hangovers.

The alcoholism, instability, and pressures to create, eventually wore Welch down, and by 1971 he was falling apart. He planned to build a cabin where he could withdraw to write, and even made some moves towards getting the scheme underway. But, in May, 1971, he wrote a farewell note and walked off, into the forest. His body was never found, despite extensive searching by friends, but it seems fairly certain that he did kill himself.

As I said earlier, Welch's life, with its movement from conformity to non-conformity, stretching over the Fifties and Sixties, does say a lot about society generally during those years. And not just American society, because parallel developments were noticeable elsewhere in that period. His dichotomy of purpose perhaps also says a great deal about general attitudes, too, because like a lot of people, Welch couldn't settle down on either side of the fence. He gave up a career in advertising, and yet his letters constantly point to a preoccupation with money. Everyone needs it, that's true, but Welch seemingly worried about it more than many others, and not only because he didn't have a regular supply coming in. His upbringing, and the impetus of the society he lived in, were always there to remind him that he had to prove himself by linking his talents to material success.

But leaving aside the general themes in Welch's life and letters, there is much in both that illuminates the man himself. If we forget the

Beat Generation tag, and the social situation in the Fifties and Sixties, we will have the struggle of a sensitive, talented individual trying to come to terms with a world he found alien in many ways. In this the experience is fairly typical of the artist in many places and at many times. I think that Welch himself realised that, despite his occasionally obvious concerns to earn a place in the Beat pantheon. In some programme notes for a poetry reading that he enclosed with a letter to James Schevill, he talked about the casualties of the Beat movement, but added, "It has been no different for me than for any generation".

Welch's letters seem to me to work on several levels. They're clearly of major importance for those specifically interested in the Beats, tracing as they do one poet's activities during a key period in the history of the movement. The opinions offered, and the personalities referred to, provide fascinating material for the researcher. Social historians should also find Welch's words of value as they show, in their idiosyncratic way, one man's responses to the social pressures and events of his time. And, as I've already suggested, the letters have importance as a record of a poet's struggle to survive which steps out of period and place.

It's good to have these two volumes available. They clarify a lot about Welch and his world. They're very readable, and Welch, for all his problems, comes across as quite a sympathetic character.

It should be noted that Volume One has a brief chronology of Welch's life,and a preface by Donald Allen. Volume Two has four pages of photographs and an index to both volumes.

I REMAIN: THE LETTERS OF LEW WELCH & THE CORRESPONDENCE OF HIS FRIENDS

Volume One: 1949-1960

Volume Two: 1960-1971

Edited by Donald Allen. Published by Grey Fox Press, Bolinas, California, 1980

FIRST THOUGHT

I'm not sure how many interviews Allen Ginsberg gave over the years. Some of them probably never made it into print, or may have appeared in ephemeral publications that no-one now remembers. Michael Schumacher says that: "Ginsberg considered interviews to be a vital part of his work, as one might surmise from the titles of two previously published anthologies of interviews: *Composed on the Tongue,* a relatively slender collection edited by Don Allen and issued by Grey Fox Press in 1980, and *Spontaneous Mind*, a hefty volume edited by David Carter and published by HarperCollins three years after Ginsberg's death in 1997".

That Ginsberg was a good interviewee, both happily responsive to questions and informative, I can testify to myself. I interviewed him for *Beat Scene* magazine in 1990 when he was in London for readings. I have a recollection that someone from *The Daily Telegraph* also interviewed him around the same time. Probably, like other interviews, they've disappeared from view unless an earnest researcher finds them. But I did try to give my own encounter with Ginsberg a degree of extra life by including it in my book, *Beats, Bohemians and Intellectuals*, published by Trent Books in 2000. This wasn't so much to enhance my own reputation as to give some of Ginsberg's comments a little more permanency. I had been particularly intrigued by what he'd said about the influence of Ben Maddow's 1930s poem, *The City*, on the writing of *Howl*. If nothing else, my interview with Ginsberg had highlighted that fact.

Michael Schumacher's selection of interviews uses material that wasn't in either of the collections referred to earlier. And the first one in his book is particularly interesting. The journalist, Al Aranowitz, had written a series of articles about Beat Generation writers for *The New York Post*, and expanded one of them into the longer "Portrait of a Beat" that was published in 1960 in *Nugget*, one of the slick "men's magazines" then cashing in on the interest in the Beats. Aranowitz, to give him his due, was generally sympathetic towards what Ginsberg, Gary Snyder, and others, were doing, and generally managed to balance journalistic needs to appeal to a broad readership with some intelligent comments about Beat aims and achievements in their writings.

It's a personal reminiscence that, in order to find copies of *Nugget* and other similar magazines (*Swank*, for example, which around 1960 published several sections of Beat-related writing), I had to prowl around various sleazy, back-street bookshops which stocked them. Respectable shops didn't sell publications like those in early-1960s England. My forays into the nether world of mild titillation on display (*Nugget* and *Swank* each had a few fairly innocuous photos scattered around their pages), and pornography under the counter, paid off, and I got to read things like the Aranowitz interview with Ginsberg in *Nugget* which were probably overlooked by most people.

It was in his conversation with Aranowitz that Ginsberg claimed that the Beats were "prophets howling in the wilderness against a crazy civilisation". It was a typical Ginsberg statement, and very much in line with his need to propagate a cause and indulge in generous promotions of his fellow writers, such as Jack Kerouac, William Burroughs, and Gregory Corso. And it makes one realise that, had it not been for Ginsberg, there may well never have been a Beat Generation, or at least not in a way that, for a time attracted a great deal of attention from journalists, intellectuals, and some parts of the general public. He was the man who, in a sense, sold the idea to other people. Had it not been for him some writers may never have been published, and those that were may have been just passing fancies on the bohemian fringes of the literary scene.

Ginsberg combined the enthusiasms of an old-style radical organiser with those of a talented and skilled poet. He would never have got away with being simply a publicist for the others had he not created some striking poetry himself. Long Poems such as "Howl", "Kaddish", and relatively shorter ones like "America" and "A Supermarket in California", gave him a credibility that allowed him to speak authoritatively about writing generally. Some writers prefer not to talk about writing in any great detail, but Ginsberg wasn't one of them. There is an interview, conducted by Kenneth Koch, himself a poet, in the 1970s, and it's useful to read (hear?) Ginsberg explaining about what influences him and how he writes a poem: "On the other hand, I write a little bit every other day. I just write when I have a thought. Sometimes I have big thoughts, sometimes little thoughts. The deal is to accept whatever comes. Or work with whatever comes. Leave yourself open".

Music was something that Ginsberg liked to evoke as influential on his work, and in the interview that is headed, "Words, and Music, Music, Music", he talks about the various forms of music that he heard and found interesting. I have to admit to a personal prejudice in favour of his comments on the jazz of the 1940s, and his introduction to bebop through Jack Kerouac and Seymour Wyse. Ginsberg often said that he was influenced by tenor-saxophonist Lester Young's playing, and in the interview he also mentions another tenorman, Illinois Jacquet, and claims him as an additional influence.

I'm always intrigued by Ginsberg's capacity to name people – musicians, writers, philosophers, etc. – as influences, almost at the drop of a hat, and I can't help wondering whether or not there wasn't an element of myth-making in what he was doing, and that he was, in a sense, laying the ground for future scholars to carry out research into those he named. And their possible presence in his poems. And, in this case, to pursue the supposed connection between words and music.

As Ginsberg moved on he involved himself more and more with pop music, associating with Bob Dylan, the Beatles, and others. I've always been curious about the motives for his activities in that line. Did he genuinely believe that it was a way to draw attention to poetry (not necessarily just his own), and take it to a younger audience, or was there a degree of opportunism in the way he seemed to enjoy mixing with celebrities? I'm probably risking incurring the wrath of those to whom Ginsberg was something of a guru by asking such a question, but if I dare suggest that his poetry mostly declined in quality after his productive days in the 1950s and early 1960s, it may be that he needed to find ways to stay in the limelight.

That Ginsberg liked to ramble around matters that he was concerned about, such as censorship, legalisation of drugs, sexual repression, anti-Vietnam protests, etc., is obvious from this assembly of interviews. And the usefulness of the material may depend very much on what a reader's interests happen to be. From my own point of view, it's handy to read him reminiscing about San Francisco in the 1950s, before the Beat boom drew in more people, not all of them necessarily with a deep involvement with poetry. Asked if there were a lot of people who were a part of the scene, he replied: "No, just thirty to forty people. But they all knew each other so that seemed like a lot. They were all poets. Robert Duncan would come out and give a reading, and whenever there was a reading afterwards everybody would go to the same place. 'The Place'. That's back in the mid-50s. There was a kind of camaraderie, and then, later, around 1958-59, there were a lot of music, poetry places.....jazz poetry places. But originally it was just straight poetry".

I find that valuable, more so than Ginsberg pontificating about drugs, and it helps towards an understanding of what was taking place on the West Coast in the 1950s. But I suppose it will be argued that Ginsberg wasn't just a poet, he was a poet with a wider social and political purpose, hence his need to give numerous interviews and have opinions on just about everything.

To be fair, there is much of interest to be found in the interviews. He talks about his experiences when he was expelled from both Cuba and Czechoslovakia. There is a joint interview with Ginsberg, William Burroughs, and Norman Mailer, that has things to say about writers and writing, and another when Ginsberg was interviewed alongside his father, Louis Ginsberg, himself a poet, though of a very different kind to his son. He was a different sort of personality, too, and was much quieter, both in person and as a writer. But in his day Louis Ginsberg had appeared in anthologies such as *May Days: An Anthology of Verse from Masses-Liberator,* and Louis Untermeyer's *Modern American Poetry.*

There was something about Allen Ginsberg which, whatever one thought of his poetry, was quite appealing. He seemed generous in his appraisals of other poets' work, and he had the gift of loyalty to his old friends of the Beat Generation. When asked about the "philosophies" of the Beats, he replied: "We didn't have what you could call a philosophy. I would say that there was an ethos, that there were ideas, and there were themes, and there were preoccupations". It was a good way of summing up what the Beats were about.

First Thought is a fascinating book in many ways. As I said earlier, what Ginsberg talks about may be of interest according to one's inclinations towards various subjects. I certainly got a great deal out of it.

FIRST THOUGHT : CONVERSATIONS WITH ALLEN GINSBERG
Edited by Michael Schumacher
University of Minnesota Press. 264 pages. $19.95. ISBN 978-0-8166-9917-9

BURROUGHS AND BAX

William Burroughs has something of an esoteric reputation, his work usually being associated with experimental methods, his aims generally thought of as bizarre and depending more on shock value than anything else.

But throughout his books runs a common thread which may be best described as a theory of a grand conspiracy in which we are all involved, and which has grown so vast that it is now impossible to control. *Exterminator!* is probably Burroughs' clearest exposition of this theory since *Naked Lunch* appeared fifteen or so years ago.

It is essentially a series of vignettes, and the references to "novel" on the jacket should be taken with a pinch of salt. Many of the pieces have been published as stories and articles, and they stand as such even when collected together. This doesn't lessen their impact, nor does it alter the fact that the common thread referred to earlier runs through them all. However, the reader shouldn't bother to look for a story line in the accepted sense. There isn't one.

The vignettes range over a fairly wide area, from a racy memoir of a period spent working as a pest exterminator, to a semi-surreal account of the 1968 Chicago Democratic Convention when demonstrators experienced what can only be described as a "police riot". There's also a slightly chilling – because of its paranoiac compulsiveness – sketch cast in the style of a slick detective story. In this a man is watched, becomes the watcher, then finds he is being watched. And so it goes on.

What is remarkable about almost all the pieces is their sheer readability. Burroughs has a good ear for the right rhythms to catch the mood of his stories, and the writing often has the kind of tight-lipped assertiveness associated with authors like Dashiell Hammett and Raymond Chandler. Add to that, Burroughs' habit of piling up images like old snapshots, and the total effect is of a fast-moving intensity which jabs and slices at the reader's mind until he begins to wonder if the world outside the window really is as mad as Burroughs says it is.

Exterminator! is an awesome forecast of a future which could be as outlandish as Burroughs suggests. After all, can anyone look at American politics and not admit that they are approaching the realms of fiction? And how far are we behind them? The reader who chooses to treat Burroughs as an oddball is being unfair. His message, and it is one that needs to be listened to, is that writers needn't fantasise in a world where reality is so extreme.

William Burroughs is a one-man band. By that I mean he plays several different parts – novelist, essayist, occasional journalist, social critic – and yet they all blend into one performance. His main vision is peculiarly his own, and a Burroughs idea, and the way it is expressed, is always instantly recognisable, if not immediately understandable. Burroughs may like to think of himself as intending clarity at all times, but he can be difficult to follow.

Still, he has created a body of work worthy of close attention, and it's valuable to have something to hand which, in effect, explains the "aims" of his writing, and clears up some of its idiosyncrasies. *The Job*, in which the Swiss critic, Daniel Odier, interviews Burroughs at length, is an intriguing document. Apart from various sub-concerns (drugs, sex, etc.), Burroughs has a theory of a grand conspiracy, and occasionally his paranoiac (or so it will seem to many people) vision seems shockingly clear.

This is not the place to doubt the validity of Burroughs' views, though I'm inclined to sympathise with his analysis of a conspiracy. Not that it is a contrived conspiracy, but rather an accumulation of attitudes and events stemming from various forms of conditioning. This doesn't make it any less dangerous, but the question arises of how to combat it. Burroughs puts forward some suggestions, not all of them ("there should be more riots and more violence") acceptable. But you can't deny he's trying to find a solution, and you also can't deny the power with which he expresses his theories, especially in his creative works.

The latest of these has been published recently and makes a useful addition to the Burroughs catalogue. I'd better explain that Dutch Schultz was an American gangster, gunned down by a rival in 1935. As he was dying, the police made a complete transcript of his disjointed ramblings. Burroughs is not the first creative writer to have been fascinated by this document (Bernard Wolfe's novel, *The Late Risers,* makes references to it), but he is, perhaps, the first to use it as the basis for an original work.

The Last Words of Dutch Schulz is a film-script by Burroughs, based on the Schultz transcript, which is printed in full at the end of the book, but freely using images and characters from the period in general.

Not being familiar with cinematic techniques, I wouldn't like to hazard a guess as to how successfully it would work on screen. At this point, though, it doesn't matter. The script reads well in itself. Burroughs has always been a visual writer, in that he often builds up a story by a series of prose "snapshots", and consequently the fast-moving sequence of scenes has an impressive effect.

Burroughs may milk a certain milieu of sleazy hotel rooms, faded pornographic photos, sick junkies, greasy-spoon cafes, and so on, for all its worth, but he convinces the reader of its reality. I'm inclined to think *The Last Words of Dutch Schultz* represents some of his best work since *The Naked Lunch.*

William Burroughs is not a social realist as a writer, and yet his books are critiques of contemporary society. *The Wild Boys* is one of his more-readable works, the narrative style being relatively direct and the story line at least traceable. And the paranoiac vision of the breakdown of values is disturbingly real. Other than that, it is typical Burroughs, with the scenes thrown up like a series of snapshots, and the flickering images nagging at the reader's mind until he's almost weary of their continued joylessness and swelling violence. A Burroughs trip is not a pleasant affair, and whether you can complete it will depend on your taste for his repetitious view of things. But he does have something to say.

Terrible things happen in the world. Continents erupt into wholesale warfare, nations slide into disaster. Casualties (mental as well as physical) mount, and a weird new dimension is added to the chaos as a grey-suited army moves around crucifying the male population.

The hospital ship, fitted out to deal with major problems and staffed by teams of doctors and nurses, sails through this horrifying tale of woe, picking up survivors where and when it can, the crew and passengers increasingly conscious of the fact that they may be the last chance for civilisation to survive.

That's the basis of Martin Bax's semi-surreal novel, but a bald description of the outline of plot does little to put across the lively and provocative nature of the writing. Bax uses anything he can lay his hands on to build up his picture of a sick and crumbling world. Excerpts from other people's poems, medical texts, references to the war in Vietnam, satirical comments on contemporary manners and morals.

The whole lot is skilfully woven into what at first sight seems to be a rambling and discursive account, but is actually a carefully organised and controlled document.

Shades of William Burroughs might be brought to mind, but Bax is much more lucid, his page-to-page writing easier to digest than the American novelist. And the overall tone is different. There's a sense of decency about *The Hospital Ship*, and a suggestion that things aren't better when people give up and stop loving each other. I was inclined to think more of Richard "Lord" Buckley than Burroughs: "My Lords, Ladies, Beloveds. Would it embarrass you very much if I were to tell you that I love you?" You can't imagine Burroughs ever expressing a sentiment along those lines.

The Hospital Ship is an intriguing book, all the more so because it's written by a doctor with literary leanings and a social conscience. Left-wing historians will be interested in the author's associations with Ernest Belfort Bax, early socialist and friend of Marx and Engels. True, it has an edge of desperation, a kind of constant awareness of the fact that the hospital ship is not totally immune from the prevailing madness, but it's positive in its own way. It asserts some sort of hopeful face for the future. And you can't say that about a lot of contemporary writing.

EXTERMINATOR! by William Burroughs. Calder & Boyars.

THE WILD BOYS by William Burroughs. Calder & Boyars.

THE JOB: AN INTERVIEW WITH WILLIAM BURROUGHS by Daniel Odier. Cape.

THE LAST WORDS OF DUTCH SCHULTZ by William Burroughs. Cape Goliard.

THE HOSPITAL SHIP by Martin Bax. Cape.

W.H. MANVILLE : COOL, HIP AND SOBER

Cool, Hip and Sober was the title of one of W.H. (Bill) Manville's books, written some years after he'd given up drinking and was living in relative obscurity in California, advising fellow-alcoholics on how to cope with their addiction, and running creative writing workshops for local people. His earlier experiences, however, were a little more colourful, and included a brief link to the Beat scene around Greenwich Village in the late-1950s and early-1960s.

Manville was born in New York in 1926 or 1927. He was in the army around the end of the Second World War. He studied at universities in America and France, and later worked in advertising on Madison Avenue. By the late-1950s he was part of the Greenwich Village crowd and contributing his lively "Saloon Society" columns to *The Village Voice.* They were entertaining and other publications, such as the slick magazines, *Gentleman* and *Swank,* also featured some of the pieces. They were ideal for the kind of format those magazines favoured, with short stories, articles and other odds and ends, tucked in between the photographs of the girls they spotlighted.

Swank, for a short period, in 1960/61, got Seymour Krim to edit a special section called "The Swinging Modern Scene" which, surprisingly, included Lawrence Ferlinghetti, Ray Bremser, Kerouac, Ginsberg and Frank O'Hara. Manville seems to have acted with Krim as co-editor, and contributed some work of his own to the magazine. Obviously, the people at *Swank,* Krim apart, didn't have any real interest in the Beats. They were simply concerned to sell copies, and were happy to jump on whatever bandwagon came along. The Beats were in the limelight for a little while, but once the interest among the general public waned, they were dropped by newspapers and magazines.

Manville's satirical "Saloon Society" sketches were popular enough for a major New York publisher to invite him to collect some of them together for a book. Using the same title, *Saloon Society* (Duell, Sloan and Pearce, 1960), and published as by Bill Manville, it gave him a degree of fame, at least for a short time. With references to the Cedar Street Tavern, the White Horse, and other locations, and its anecdotal accounts of the adventures of A.E. Kugelman, as he meets up with a variety of oddballs in his wanderings around Greenwich Village, the book no doubt appealed to those who saw the bohemian life as something romantic and entertaining.

I think his book's success was due to the fact that it just managed to be in the bookshops when publicity about Beats, bohemians, and other outsiders was riding high. Some might suggest that 1960 was the peak year (the anthologies, *The New American Poetry, The Beat Scene, Beatitude Anthology, The Beats,* and *Beat Coast East*, all appeared in 1960), so Manville's book was published around the right time to cash in on the curiosity. A year or two later and tastes among journalists and the public would probably have moved on to something else.

It's difficult to pin down Manville's movements accurately. After *Saloon Society* appeared he spent time in Europe (Paris, Rome, London, elsewhere), had a short-lived marriage to the feminist writer, Nancy Friday, and worked for *Cosmopolitan* magazine, and for *Nugget* in the early-1960s when Seymour Krim had an editorial post there, and the magazine published Chandler Brossard, John Clellon Holmes, Gregory Corso, and Kenneth Rexroth. I don't know in what sort of sequence these involvements occurred. According to an obituary in a local newspaper, *The Union Democrat,* when he died in California, Manville always refused to be interviewed and was reluctant to talk about his life in the 1950s and 1960s, so it's difficult to check on his activities with any conviction.

I'm always of the opinion that what matters in the long run is what a writer wrote, not what he did outside writing. I can see that the facts of someone's life can throw light on what he or she wrote, but the sort of biographies that insist on telling us everything in detail seem to me to be unnecessary. A lot of the minor information is often irrelevant.

Manville, whatever else he did, was reasonably productive as a writer. His novel, *Breaking Up* (Simon & Schuster, New York, 1962) attracted some favourable reviews, though without becoming a bestseller. It was competently written and had a "hero" (if he can be called that) who is a would-be sculptor but makes a living as a writer in an advertising agency. The sections of the book that take place in the agency do sound convincing, and Manville was presumably drawing on personal experience when he described the people and how they dealt with each other and their job.

He denied that there were any autobiographical factors in the novel, or rather he said that the emotions were autobiographical but the events described weren't. It seems, in retrospect, very much of its time and place – late-50s and early-60s, New York – and is compulsive in its way, though the central character is hardly likeable. And it has a melodramatic ending. One review described the book as "uninhibited and modern", and others said that it showed the influence of writers like Ernest Hemingway, J.D. Salinger, and even the pulp crime-writer Mickey Spillane!

It's interesting to note that, whereas *Saloon Society* was published as by Bill Manville, *Breaking Up* came out under the name of W.H. Manville. Two later novels, *The Palace of Money* (Delacorte, New York, 1966) and *Goodbye* (Simon & Schuster, New York, 1977) also had W.H. Manville on their covers, but something called *The Man Who Left His Wife and Then Had a Nifty Time* (Dell, 1966) was by Bill. Presumably, Manville thought of it as a minor production (it appears to have been published directly in paperback form) when compared to his novels?

Not much seems to have happened after *Goodbye* appeared in 1977 (alcoholic writer wakes up and finds a dead woman in his bed, is the start of the story). Manville lived in Florida for a time before moving to California. According to his obituary an old flame had persuaded him to make the move. He had been drinking heavily, which probably explains why his literary activities seemed to have tailed off. His book, *Cool, Hip and Sober: 80 Ways to Beat Booze and Drugs* (Forge Press, 2004), was praised by people involved with dealing with addicts and alcoholics, and Manville wrote an advice column in his local newspaper. He had managed to master his own alcoholism, not having had a drink for twenty years, and the fact of his dying at the age of 90 perhaps points to the beneficial effects of giving up alcohol.

W.H. Manville (Bill) Manville wasn't a major writer, and if he is remembered it will probably be for *Saloon Society*, something that might not have pleased him. I would guess that he would have most likely seen his three novels as of more importance. And he may have a minor place in a history of Beat bohemianism around Greenwich Village in the late-1950s and early-1960s period when it seemed to be thriving. *Saloon Society* might ensure that, if only in passing.

It's a sign of how much Manville was a part of the "scene" for a short time that his photograph appears several times in Fred McDarrah's *Kerouac & Friends: A Beat Generation Album* (William Morrow, New York, 1985) and *Beat Generation: Glory Days in Greenwich Village* (Schirmer Books, New York, 1996). The fact of his inclusion in both books also demonstrates how wide the definition of "Beat" had become. By 1960 it encompassed any kind of activity that would once have been simply referred to as "bohemian."

Bill Manville died on the 14th February, 2017. His passing deserves to be noted.

THE HIPPIES

It all seems so long ago now, and I suppose it is. It's fifty years since the so-called "Summer of Love", when people were advised to wear some flowers in their hair if they were going to San Francisco. I can recall talking in a pub in London with a young American who had left his country to avoid being drafted. Someone slid a coin into the jukebox and Scott Mckenzie's voice came out of the loudspeakers. The young man smiled wryly and said that a steel helmet might be a better choice as protection against the police batons that were being freely applied to heads, especially those with long hair on the streets of San Francisco.

There is, perhaps, a surge of nostalgia for the 1960s, even if those feeling it weren't actually around then, or at least were too young to be fully aware of what was happening. San Francisco in 1967, Paris in 1968. "Bliss was it in that dawn to be alive,/But to be young was very heaven!". Viewed from today's perspective, with uncertainty, unemployment, and the seeming unshakeable domination of international capitalism, the 1960s might well appear to have been a decade that offered the opportunity for radical change.

John Anthony Moretta seems to think so, though to be fair his exhaustive account of the rise and fall of the hippies does point to the many pitfalls they encountered along the way. And he's sharply critical of the self-indulgences that, as much as anything, held back the possibility of altering situations. A revolution based on drugs and rock music was never going to be more than a pipe dream.

Moretta takes the conventional route when he says that the Beats laid the foundations of the hippie rebellion, providing "the template and inspiration for the most important countercultural phenomenon in post-World War 2 America, the hippies". The snag with this argument is that the Beats were essentially a literary movement, and perhaps the last movement of an old-style bohemia of little magazines and small-press publishers, whereas the hippies produced nothing of value in terms of novels, poems, or any other form of written expression. It may well be true that most of the original hippies had read Ginsberg, Kerouac, Burroughs, but the later hordes invading Haight-Ashbury in San Francisco probably read very little. Some of them may have clutched a copy of *Howl* or *On the Road*, but I wonder if they ever got beyond the surface of what the writing represented?

It was the 1950s, with its combination of increasing affluence (for some) and corresponding increasing conformity that caused the rise of the hippies. That's a simple way of putting it, of course, but it may well sum up Moretta's argument, which he admittedly develops with a fair amount of evidence. Things did get better for many people, and for those who had lived through the hard times of the 1930s, and the dangers and austerities of the 1940s, the fact of being able to work at a steady, decently-paid job, and afford to take out a mortgage on one of the new, mass-produced houses that sprang up, was no mean factor in how they felt about life in general and in the United States in particular.

Moretta quotes an ex-G.I. who had "been living in a one-room apartment with his wife and a relative before he moved to Levittown", and who said that his new home and its surroundings were wonderful in comparison. Intellectuals might have been bothered by the seeming uniformity of life in the suburbs (read Galbraith or Marcuse) and folk singers like Pete Seeger may have sneered that the houses and the people "all looked just the same", but not everybody felt that way. Moretta has the good sense to say, "Suburbia was far from utopia, but it was not the social disaster some claimed".

By the time the 1960s got under way, probably around 1963 in terms of beginning to take on a definite form that distinguished it from the previous decade, teenagers who had grown up discontented with life in the suburbs were ripe for being influenced by the hype that both the media, and the proponents of pop culture, were beginning to peddle. Most of those who headed for San Francisco were the children of middle-class parents. Very few working-class teenagers left home to let their hair grow long and smoke marijuana. When they did leave home it was more often than not to look for work, escape from an overcrowded environment, or enlist in the armed forces, willingly or otherwise. The same was true of blacks. There were few black hippies. Or Indian hippies. When counter-cultural ambassadors, hooked on romantic notions of "tribes", approached tribal leaders among the Indians, they were promptly brushed off.

For San Francisco the influx of thousands of young people with nowhere to live, and little idea of how to survive on the streets, led to major problems. Drug use was rife, sexual promiscuity widespread, and crime on the increase. Malnutrition, hepatitis, venereal diseases, and much more, were almost out-of-control. While the "underground" papers that began to publish in the 1960s referred to "love" as a guiding light, women were just as much exploited in the hippie communities as they were anywhere else. There may have been some genuine concerns to develop new ideas about living among hippies with a settled commitment to an "alternative" society, but they were over-ridden by the desires of the many who simply wanted to take drugs, have sex, and get by without working or doing anything of value for themselves or the "alternative" community.

Some genuine seekers after fresh ways of outwitting the capitalist system set up communes, and Moretta has interesting things to say about them. Not many of the communes survived very long, and they differed in their policies, but certain common problems often afflicted them. Not all of the people who participated in commune living were suited to it. They were idealistic, but hadn't allowed for the lack of basic amenities, nor had they realised how much hard work would be required to construct buildings, when necessary, and grow enough food to sustain themselves.

Although a commune might appear to be based on an idea of shared responsibility and requirements, a dominant personality might soon emerge and take control. Sexual exploitation of women could be a cause of dissent. And communes often attracted misfits of various kinds who were unwilling to contribute in productive ways to what was needed to keep the place going. A knowledge of the nineteenth-century communes in America might have alerted the well-meaning to the likely problems they would experience.

Even among the dedicated members of a commune there were differences of opinion and personality clashes. It was a mistake to assume that people would necessarily like each other. Moretta looks at a commune in Pennington, Minnesota, that petered out after two years as those involved bickered about minor matters. He also suggests that, without financial support from middle-class parents, plus Government "largesse" ("welfare, unemployment compensation, government surplus foods, and food stamps"), many communes would have quickly collapsed. The kind of discipline found in older, established communities like the Shakers didn't exist among the hippies.

It's a personal recollection, and based on a British experience, but I can remember visiting in the 1960s what was a kind of commune set up in a large house in the country, and supported financially by an idealistic local businessman and politician. The middle-class people living there were, among other things, supposed to be studying the causes of friction and the lack of co-operation between nations, organisations, and individuals. I sat in on their weekly meeting and listened to them fall out about whose turn it was to sweep the stairs and clean the windows. As someone who came from a working-class home where six people lived in a small house without electric lighting, hot water, indoor toilet, etc., and who had spent three years in the army to get away from it, I might have been forgiven for being less than impressed by what I heard.

The supposed idealism, what there was of it, of the 1960s soon degenerated. And there were moves towards a more-confrontational approach to and from the authorities. Having a slight personal involvement, I was intrigued by Moretta's account of John Sinclair's experiences in Detroit. He ran the Artists' Workshop, and Trans Love Energies, and published a magazine called *Work.* I still have my copies of the second issue, dated Fall, 1965, and the fifth, dated 1968, in which I had poems published. Tucked inside the latter is a notice from Trans Love Energies which apologises for the late-arrival of the magazine, and refers to "much police hassel, fire bombings" as among the problems Sinclair had been faced with. I recall also that, at some point, he returned one of the envelopes from letters I'd sent to him to let me know that my mail was being opened by the U.S. Postal Service on the grounds that it might contain subversive material. I was amused.

John Sinclair was additionally involved in the music scene in Detroit. Moretta largely looks at his promotion of the band, MC5, but there was a magazine called *Change* which I think was mostly devoted to jazz and especially the free-form music of the 1960s. I have a memory of contributing some material to it, probably relating to what was happening in Britain on that front, but I no longer have the magazines so can't check.

Later in the 1960s a number of events occurred that might be said to have brought the hippie dream to an end. The chaotic scenes in San Francisco could have forecast it, anyway, but the 1968 Chicago "police riot" (against the yippies, but not many policemen or politicians were inclined to distinguish between them and hippies), the killing by Hell's Angels of a black spectator at a Rolling Stones concert at

Altamont, and the murders committed by Charles Manson's devotees, when taken together, seemed to suggest that "the times they are a-changing". The tide had turned against the hippies, and the winding down of the Vietnam War, and a slowing down of the economy as the 1970s started, saw them disappearing, at least from the point of view of mass turnouts of long-haired young people. There was a brief revival at Woodstock in 1969, but it was just that, brief, and though now legendary from a music point of view, it didn't lead to much else. Everyone just went home in the end.

It's only fair to ask if the hippie rebellion (was it even that?) added up to anything significant? Moretta thinks it did in terms of helping to end American involvement in Vietnam. But others, such as the New Left, the Old Left, and student activists, equally contributed to that. Likewise with Civil Rights, which was a cause largely fought by blacks with support from white liberals and left-wingers. Hippie attitudes towards women and homosexuals were hardly open-minded. So they can take little credit for improvements there. It can perhaps be argued that personal attitudes were changed in terms of the way people dress, etc., though that might not be thought a great achievement. A pot-smoking, jeans-wearing capitalist is still a capitalist. Immediate self-gratification is not likely to lead to changes in the power structure.

Christopher Lasch wrote a book called *The Culture of Narcissism* which could describe what developed from the 1960s, though he traced it back much further and developed a complex discussion around his theories. A simpler way of summing up what the 1960s may have led to is to refer to the "me-ism" that pop culture and technology have combined to encourage. And even the briefest consideration of how society functions will show that little has altered when it comes to who controls what. In fact, a strong case can be made for saying that things are even worse now.

The other point is the one made earlier, that the hippies achieved little or nothing when it came to the arts, unless one takes rock music into consideration. That might be the only success they can claim. But did the music arise from the hippie experience, such as it was? There had been rock'n'roll in the 1950s and, some might argue, it was a less-pretentious music. Musicians and singers weren't looked on as if they had the answer to the world's difficulties. But I'll let that pass.

With regard to the visual arts, there was little, apart from the psychedelic posters, underground newspaper illustrations, etc., which were colourful and imaginative, though sometimes stereotyped.

And literature? I can't think of a novelist or poet who can be said to have come from the hippies. A writer like Richard Brautigan might be considered, in that his winsome stories and poems seemed to be tied in with the drug culture. Moretta refers to Lenore Kandel, largely because her sexually explicit *Love Book* caused something of a scandal, but she was more-related to the Beats. Poets like Allen Ginsberg, Gary Snyder, and Michael McClure, who sometimes appeared at hippie events, were likewise directly linked to the Beats. They were writers, even if they did like to sound off about how society should be organised.

I have to admit, too, that sometimes reading their pronouncements in the underground newspapers and elsewhere in the 1960s, I began to wonder just how much they related to the wider society they lived in and preferred to pontificate for the benefit of an audience who, they imagined, thought like themselves. Moretta says that "Snyder wanted to turn Chicago into a centre for cybernetic technology and the rest of the country into buffalo pasture". Perhaps he had his tongue firmly in his cheek, but I doubt it. After all, he talked enthusiastically about "living simply but beautifully and wholesomely off the land", which may have been fine for a small number of dedicated people, but was never going to be practical for most, and especially not for the kind who were making a mess in Haight-Ashbury.

John Anthony Moretta has written a very thorough study of the hippie phenomenon, and on the whole manages to be fair-minded in his descriptions and judgements of personalities and events. He doesn't attempt to hide the misdemeanours and mistakes made by many hippies, nor does he fight shy of all the problems resulting from their excesses. The prevalence of drugs was a sure way for something to end in disaster. The fact of a few writers and intellectuals experimenting with various narcotics and, in some cases, turning their experiences into literature, doesn't mean that every spaced-out teenager is ever going to be imaginative or creative.

I did spot a few misprints in the text, and a couple of factual errors that were noticeable to an old veteran of the bebop into Beat experience. Moretta refers to Gregory Corso as a "San Francisco poet", which he certainly wasn't. Born in Greenwich Village, though not of bohemian parents, Corso was usually firmly based in New York. His book, *Gasoline*, was published by Lawrence Ferlinghetti's City Lights Press in San Francisco, and he did spend time in the city. Corso, as befits his bad boy image, later became notorious for stealing books from City Lights Bookshop and even allegedly once burgling it. Corso could be an entertaining poet, but he wasn't a pleasant person.

As for bebop, Moretta places Lester Young and John Coltrane among the originators of bebop, along with Thelonious Monk, Dizzy Gillespie, and Charlie Parker. I suspect that Moretta, like a lot of younger (than me) enthusiasts for rock music, doesn't know much about jazz. And old beboppers like myself are sticklers for accuracy. Young was an influence on some young musicians, especially saxophone players, and was respected by Parker and Gillespie. But he didn't play bop. Coltrane was influenced by what Gillespie and Parker were creating in the 1940s, but didn't have anything to do with the development of bebop. His own major contributions to jazz came a decade or so later. Yes, I know, I'm being pedantic, but subjects like bebop and the Beats are close to my heart.

THE HIPPIES: A 1960s HISTORY
by John Anthony Moretta
McFarland & Co. 430 pages. £47.50. ISBN 978-0-7864-9949-6

POETS IN TRANSLATION

Most British and American readers will think of the poetry of the Spanish Civil War as written by Auden, Spender, Edwin Rolfe, and others like them. They'll tend to overlook poems written by Spaniards, though to be fair this will be because few of them have been easily available in English translations. A handful were included in Valentine Cunningham's *The Penguin Book of Spanish Civil War Verse* (1980), but they were mere drops from a torrent of an estimated 20,000 poems written by approximately 5,000 poets. Around three-quarters of the poems were produced by people sympathetic to the Republican cause.

Carlos Bauer's bi-lingual book is the first to give English-language readers an opportunity to study a sustained and varied selection of Spanish poetry of the Civil War period. His guides have been three anthologies published in Spain between 1936 and 1938 which, he considers, contained some of the best and most representative poems of those years. There is always a debate about whether or not such work, with its high level of political commitment, has value outside its context, and Bauer does quote Luis Cernuda, one of the poets in his anthology, as stating that little, if any, of the poetry written by Spaniards survived the war years. There may, of course, have been a variety of reasons for this, including censorship and repression once Franco triumphed. It's also true that very little poetry of any kind does survive from any period in history. Most poets are fated to be forgotten.

That some of the poems were purely functional, designed to comment on a specific situation, is obvious, but it would be incorrect to say that all of them have become mere historical documents. León Felipe's long "The Insignia", with its anarchist inclinations and passionate statements, still reads well, and brings to mind Lawrence Ferlinghetti's populist poems, which is no bad thing. Many of the sentiments expressed in it are as relevant today as when they were first written almost fifty years ago. It is, perhaps inevitably, the sentiments behind the poems generally which will amuse, anger, or amaze some readers, especially those whose politics incline to the right. In this respect it should be noted that the poems and their politics are all of the Left.

It seems to me that this anthology serves several useful purposes. Carlos Bauer's sound English versions of the poems make available material which would otherwise be unknown in this country. Also, as mentioned earlier, the content of the poems raises the perennial, though fascinating question of how committed, in political terms, poets ought to be. And from a historical point of view, the book helps explain why passions ran so high in Spain. It has been fashionable in recent years to suggest that both sides in the Spanish Civil War were at fault, and that those who supported the Republic were naïve, at best, and chose to overlook the depth of communist infiltration of the government, army, etc. Historians can argue about that. This fine collection may help us to understand how those involved at the time saw the situation, and why they did what they did.

I don't think all that much contemporary French poetry is published in translation in this country, and what little I have seen has frankly never excited me. So, it's good to have this anthology, though it doesn't claim to be a wide-ranging survey of what French poets are doing these days. Its sub-title, *French Countercultural Poetry*, sums up where its priorities are – with the Left, and in particular, with a group of poets who cluster around Francis Combes and his publishing house, *Les Temps des Cerises*. You can read all about them in the excellent introduction that Alan Dent provides, and in which he places the poets in context, emphasising the radical bohemian tradition in French poetry.

Now I don't doubt that some people, seeing the reference to the Left and a radical line of writing, may back away, thinking that what they'll read is a parade of poems that wave flags or shout slogans demanding revolution. And, yes, it's true that the poets make no apologies for their political leanings. But it's refreshing to hear poets speaking directly. In Francis Combes' poem, "The Achievements of Capitalism", there's a list of obvious contradictions ("the development of media/under-information", and "the unification of the world markets/the division of workers and people"), and the poem ends on a bleak note: "as for artists/all that remains for them/is to produce commodities/and to cultivate ugliness".

A spirit of pessimism pervades Combes' poem, but there's a more-hopeful aspect to Jacques Gaucheron's "From the Cliff-Tops": "Wave after wave/You can see the tide remaking/The sea front/There are eddies/whirlpools/But like the sea/Freedom knows no rest".

Interestingly, Gaucheron seems to be the oldest contributor (born 1910, and at one time involved with legends of the Left like Aragon and Eluard) but his poems are lively and optimistic. His "A Cock-stride into Town" is a wonderful chant of praise to Paris. David Dumortier's "Metro Sketches" are just that, short statements about the kind of characters and scenes you see on the Paris underground (literally so when "sitting on the folding seats/You can look at the backsides/Of the folk standing/Without meaning to"). They appear fairly slight individually, but add up to an amusing sequence which also says something about the transient nature of urban life. Georges Hassomeris is probably the most experimental of the group in terms of technique, with his poems ranging across the page and drawing on the Dadaist and surrealist movements for inspiration.

I haven't mentioned all the poets in the anthology (there are eight) but the unnamed ones are equally energetic and alert to their surroundings. I've no way of comparing the translations to the originals, but the English versions seem to me good in their own right. Have I any criticisms to make? Just one, and it's that it's far too short a book. I wanted another hundred pages. Still, what there is can be highly recommended.

CRIES FROM A WOUNDED MADRID: POETRY OF THE SPANISH CIVIL WAR selected and translated by Carlos Bauer. Swallow Press.

WHEN THE METRO IS FREE: AN ANTHOLOGY OF CONTEMPORARY FRENCH COUNTER-CULTURAL POETRY edited and translated by Alan Dent. Smokestack Books.

A FEW GOOD POETS

It was John Ashbery who said, "Lee Harwood is one of Britain's best poets and best kept secrets", and it's true that Harwood, despite a writing life that now stretches over forty years, has never received the recognition he deserves. Most of his work has been published by small presses, and too little of it has been noticed outside the world of little magazines and the like. And that's a pity because he can be a very readable and entertaining poet. He's quiet, and he doesn't have the kind of poems that become favourites for anthologies, but taken as a whole his writing is subtle and provocative, nudging at the reader's sensibilities in a way that leaves lasting impressions in the mind. It isn't that one remembers a specific line or phrase, but rather that the overall mood and movement of the poems creates a kind of other world that one is invited to enter.

I've seen the term "surrealist" sometimes applied to Harwood's work, and he has always shown an interest in the literature associated with that area of activity. He has quite extensively translated Tristan Tzara, who had links to both dada and surrealist writing. But Harwood has always been his own man in terms of how he writes, and an identifiable world is often the basis for what he does: "Alone in an upstairs room -/the sound of the wind,/a train in the distance,/and, faintly, the sea breaking/on the shingle beach".

To be honest, I've been very selective in using those lines, and I'm perhaps doing Harwood a disservice because, as I suggested earlier, it's the totality of his work that counts. It needs to be read in bulk, and with consideration for the mixture of prose and poetry that he so easily handles.

The earliest piece in the book is "Cable Street", a reflection on an area of London where he lived in the Sixties which brings in references to the General Strike and the "battle" of Cable Street in 1936 when the local population and political militants stopped a march by Mosley's fascists. And short prose pieces crop up elsewhere, showing that Harwood has always liked to have the freedom to move from one form to another.

A short review can't offer a guide to everything in a book of over 500 pages. There is too much variety, too much playfulness, and too much depth to explore, and readers need to do that for themselves.

Suffice to say that this book is highly recommended.

In 1933 Olive Dehn, then 19 and visiting an aunt in Germany, sent a satirical poem about Aryan notions of racial purity to *Punch*. The letter was intercepted in the post, and Dehn was arrested by the Gestapo and deported to England. The poem in question is included in this small collection (Olive Dehn's only book of poetry and covering 1929 to 1995) and it still reads amusingly and pertinently. Dictatorships, whether of the Fascist or Communist kind, never did like to be mocked. It's worth noting that, forty years after her encounter with the Gestapo, Dehn was arrested by the KGB when visiting Russia. Not a bad record, falling foul of both tyrannies.

Most of Dehn's writing was for children, and she published several novels and collections of stories. She also ran a small farm, and wrote for a trade magazine, *The Pig Producer*. Her book has a poem called "Death of a Pig", and another about milking cows. Both are effectively descriptive. "A muffled whistle/Sounds in the pail" captures the situation for this townie. And the lines that end the poem about the pig ("And sheep like tears/Are running down the face of the hill") introduce a note of human sentimentality to the bleak fact of the animal's throat being slit.

What I like about the poems is that they're direct, and with the words kept to a minimum: "In Victoria Street/When the lamps were lit/She danced, she danced/For love of it".

There's a kind of folk-song /poetry quality to writing such as that, and it can sound both old and new at the same time. Simplicity can often provide a continuity that spans the ages. But being simple is not easy. It's a gift and Olive Dehn has it. A poem entitled "October, 1941" evokes the mood of the war years with an image of autumn: "By Etchel's Farm/In the long rank grass/I saw the feet of/October pass".

Thirty-two poems from over sixty years. It doesn't seem a lot but, to me, it adds up to a worthwhile achievement. I should add that the book has a useful introduction which gives an account of Olive Dehn's life and the background to her poems.

Let me first of all say that I'm not going to pretend this review is objective. I met Gael Turnbull here and there over the years, corresponded with him, and published his poems in a couple of little magazines I edited in the Sixties and Seventies. And I admired what he did with *Migrant*, both the magazine and the press, and I wrote articles about his activities. He was, as some notes in the book say, "central to the early transatlantic poetic contacts which were to have a transforming effect on many poets in Britain in the 1950s and 1960s". One day someone will write a full account of what might be called the non-establishment history of British poetry, and Gael Turnbull will have a major role in it.

But what of his own poetry? He was an individualist, and though he knew a variety of poets, and welcomed a variety of styles, he held firmly to his own idiosyncratic voice. He moved cheerfully from short, simple rhyming poems to longer sequences in free verse which aimed to incorporate his everyday activities into reflections on the way the world works. I think it's true to say that he didn't think of poetry as something separate from what he did (he was a doctor, practising as a GP and an anaesthetist) or the routines of his daily life.

There is a fascinating piece, *Twenty Words, Twenty Days*, which almost sums up many of his concerns, with references ranging through films, books, art, family life, writing poetry, and other things. What intrigues me, as it did when I first read it, is that it slots neatly into place among all Turnbull's other writings. It may be a sequence that was once published as a small book, but it convinces me that he was, in fact, writing one long sequence all his life. The individual poems he wrote have a continuity that leads the reader from one to another without a sense of complete separateness, even if they can be read in that way. Turnbull did what a lot of poets never really do, he established his own voice on the page.

What I also value in Turnbull's poetry is the ease with which he wrote. His technique was always unobtrusive, which is the way it should be, and he clearly thought that a poem ought to say something. He didn't use technique as a means of pretending to a substance that wasn't there.

I'm conscious that I haven't quoted from any poems, and there is good reason for this. An excerpt simply wouldn't give the flavour of the complete work. Read the book in its entirety. It's well worth it.

How much of the ordinary is significant? And, writing poems, how much of the ordinary and everyday do you need to put in them? How much can you employ in a poem before readers begin to think that something extraordinary ought to happen? Do we need the extraordinary in a poem?

I was pushed into asking these questions by reading John Freeman's book. He isn't afraid to build on the ordinary and everyday. In a poem called "My Job", he says: "I put on my tidy clothes and go to work/I mean the place where I have a room/with my name on the door on a corridor/with other rooms like mine. I work hard/shifting things about inside/reading stuff, talking to people/who come and see me. Typing too/documents, answers to messages".

A description of a routine that many might identify with? Well, yes, and that's part of its strength. It draws the reader in, inclining him to think that the poet will have something to say to him. And if nothing extraordinary happens in the poem, that can be another strength because the reader will accept that nothing significant needs to happen for something to have value. The poem is about life, as lived by the poet and lived generally by most people.

I'm being a little unfair to John Freeman by suggesting that his poems may be largely concerned with direct descriptions of the obvious. They're not at all like that, and within the framework of what he does there's room for reflections, contemplation, and commentary. The poems refer to rising "out of the murk of every day into sunny air,/where we can bask in the eternal without/leaving our familiar surroundings". In other words, it's all there if you want to find it. The ordinary and the everyday needn't be limiting factors in anyone's life. They have the potential for wonder.

There are also nostalgic poems, remembering lost loves, family matters, trips to foreign lands: "Visiting a museum in France./Summer certainly, maybe that first/trip to unfamiliar heat further south./A shady courtyard. Tall open doors,/lofty glass-walled orangery perhaps?/Sparse antique furniture. No crowd".

It's clear writing, the language never ornate, the technique relaxed and unobtrusive, the loose rhythm helping to push the energy from line to line. It looks easy, but it's carefully crafted to ensure maximum use of the words and their impact. Quiet poetry, telling interesting stories, and impressing with its sincerity.

Julia Casterton, who died last year (2005) was well-known to *Ambit* readers, having published poetry and reviews in the magazine for several years. She was also a highly-respected teacher of creative writing and her book on the subject went through a number of editions. *Night Lightning* is a posthumously-published selection of her poems, and the long list of subscribers at the back of the book points to the affection with which she was regarded by many people.

She was essentially a calm, relaxed poet, often dealing with what are referred to as domestic subjects: "My daughter is six./She swims like a collie dog/hands smacking the ruffled surface/neck straining backward".

However, this focus on the family, the personal, and what I suppose some people would call the interior life, doesn't say it all about the poetry. The following lines should indicate how alert Julia Casterton was to the outer world: "Sandpipers, gulls, the first silent/on their little legs, the second/a late-August symphony of complaint/above the silvery baby shoals that now run/more alive in a stream that's opening slowly/over an unwatched mystery of glowing sand". I like the way the lines appear to lengthen to match the widening out of the water.

There are also passing references to politics in some poems ("This is the mysterious time/that capitalism knows nothing whatever about") and history, with the Levellers mentioned and Chernobyl brought into one poem. I'm not suggesting that she was, in any way, a political poet, just simply someone who didn't want to live in an ivory tower, even if it is the lyrical and the personal tone of the poems that comes to the fore.

Night Lightning mixes early and late poems, and also has a group of provocative prose poems. It was sad that Julia Casterton died when she was so young, and seemed to be approaching a creative peak in her writing, but this final collection is a tribute to her skill and humanity.

I like poems which seem simple, but which lead me to the depths of feeling that something longer and more contrived might not achieve. Consider this short poem: "You've just shaved and you smell of cream./I'm watching you press the metal point/Between buttons, over a collar, into a seam/When you've left, I open the wardrobe quietly -/I want to climb in and hang there with your shirts/With my creases, waiting for you to iron them out".

It's direct and the language is clear and without pretensions, but it manages to suggest a great deal in terms of a relationship and, perhaps, the vulnerability of the narrator. The idea of "waiting" for the other person to "iron out" the "creases" indicates a degree of reliance on that person.

I think it's one of the strengths of Olivia McCannon's poems that she can write about powerful emotions without sliding into sentimentality, or overdoing the descriptive aspects of a poem. It's enough to outline the situation and then add a few well-chosen words, as she does in several pieces about her mother's final days. One of them is a sort of catalogue, listing a series of actions ("I have fiddled with your pillows. Adjusted the angle of the bed/Stroked your head") but framing them with first and last lines which say, "There is nothing I can do". The effect is to stress the inevitability of death, and the fact that, no matter how many small practical things are done, there is truly nothing that can be done. It's quite a visual poem, and I could see the scene in the sick room.

These are essentially unobtrusive poems. They don't attempt to deal with more than there is in a situation, nor do they force the pace as they work through the ideas implicit in the carefully controlled narratives. Even so, they are often quite memorable in their way. And I'm always impressed when a poet can make an impact with just a few lines, as Olivia McCannon does in "All Saint's Day": "I stand here in the ruins of your garden/In the dark/Searching for a late flower in bloom/To fill my empty hand/To fit the space between your fingers./Wet leaves coat my shoes".

That final line seems to me absolutely right from the point of view of evoking autumn in the heart.

COLLECTED POEMS by Lee Harwood. Shearsman Books.

OUT OF MY MIND by Olive Dehn. Happenstance.

THERE ARE WORDS: COLLECTED POEMS by Gael Turnbull. Shearsman Books.

A SUITE FOR SUMMER by John Freeman. Worple Press.

NIGHT LIGHTNING by Julia Casterton. The Rialto.

EXACTLY MY OWN LENGTH by Olivia McCannon. Carcanet Press.

THE RED AND THE BLACK

It's often assumed that film noir was largely a product of the 1940s, and that, by the early-1950s, it was petering out as a genre, with perhaps a few late-arrivals still set in the world of "an extreme use of shadow, constant rain, paranoid voice-over, threatening camera angles, and jarring close-ups". I'm not sure that even many of the earlier films usually listed in books on film-noir necessarily used all those characteristics, but the general idea is accurate enough. They caught a mood. And their black-and-white photography emphasised the often-downbeat and gritty environments where the action took place.

Problems arise when determining which films fall into the film noir category, and just when did the genre start (or, more likely, become obvious), and when did it end, if it did. An earlier book, *Kiss the Blood off My Hands: On Classic Film Noir* (University of Illinois Press, 2014), edited by Robert Miklitsch, raised these questions (see my review, *Northern Review of Books,* May, 2016), though without really answering them. There probably aren't any answers, or at least not definitive ones. My own feeling is that there may be only a handful of films from the 1940s which can truly be classified as film noir, and that most of the others will include certain aspects of the style, as categorised above, in their general approach, but are not necessarily film noir in the strict sense of the term.

In *The Red and the Black,* Miklitsch mentions a 1940s film called *Leave Her to Heaven,* and refers to it as an example of what he calls, "colour noir", a film in technicolour (most, if not all, film noir used black-and-white photography) that otherwise might easily slot into a noir pigeon-hole. Personally, I'm inclined to the view that *Leave Her to Heaven* is best described as melodrama. All film noir may be melodramas, but not all melodramas are film noir. I watched *Leave Her to Heaven* again just to refresh my memories of it, and frankly couldn't for the life of me grasp how it can be described as film noir. It has a central female character who might be seen as something of a femme fatale in the way she has a negative effect on the main male character. But her personality and actions have more to do with neurotic obsessions than anything, and are not necessarily only noir characteristics.

The main thrust of Miklitsch's survey of 1950s film noir is in the direction of films which exploited the rise of anti-communism in the United States. The House Un-American Activities Committee (HUAC) had arrived in Hollywood in 1947 to investigate supposed communist infiltration of the film industry, and events in America and the world generally helped to build up a situation of near-paranoia about what communists were supposedly doing. There were dedicated anti-communists, as well as opportunists, in Hollywood, and a number of films began to appear which played on the fears of the subversion that the media, and various politicians, claimed to be prevalent in the country. Senator Joseph McCarthy didn't get to Hollywood, but he wasn't alone in allegations of spies and agitators at work in branches of the civil service, industry, politics, the arts, education, and just about everywhere in American life. That there were spies and agitators wasn't in dispute. Whether or not they were as widespread as someone like McCarthy suggested might be another matter. But people believed they were.

One of the films that worked on the susceptibilities of the public was *The Woman on Pier 13*, which had initially been titled, *I Married a Communist.* The switch of titles points to the appeal that a thriller, or similar sort of production, would have over something that might be thought of as a documentary. Its story was fairly simple. A newly married, successful businessman comes face to face with his radical past when Communist Party members try to draw him back into their activities. The film noir links are obvious. There's a glamorous, communist femme fatale, several gangster-like Party members, and a plot that, with a few changes of names, etc., and with criminal aims substituted for communism, could have been taken from any number of "B" movies of the 1940s. And the lighting, camerawork, and settings (down by the docks, and along dark streets) were all designed to emphasise the noir atmosphere. It's interesting that the communists, as in other films of the period which focused on their activities, are portrayed as akin to gangsters and not averse to killing to protect their interests.

A 1949 film not analysed by Miklitsch, *The Red Menace,* shows communist thugs beating a man to death when he dissents at a party meeting, and driving a sensitive young poet to commit suicide when his work is savagely criticised and he is ostracised by all his former comrades. The idea of writers being attacked did have a great deal of validity, as witness the treatment of Albert Maltz by the American

Communist Party when he suggested that writers should be true to their own consciences rather than to a Party line. He was abused extensively, both in person and in print.

Among other anti-communist films which utilised the trappings of film noir, and are dissected by Miklitsch, were *Walk East on Beacon, I Was a Communist for the FBI,* and *Big Jim McClain.* The latter was the most successful, in commercial terms, of the genre, probably because it starred John Wayne. It didn't help it rise much beyond the level of a "B" movie. It is a fact that few, if any, of the films that Miklitsch discusses, were of a quality that could push them into being classed above the "B" movie rating. An exception might be made for *Pickup on South Street,* directed by the maverick Samuel Fuller and starring Richard Widmark and Jean Peters. It does portray the communists as being no better than gangsters, and ready to murder to achieve their objectives, as when they eliminate an old woman who defies them, but other factors helped to give it greater interest as a film.

Jean Peters plays the part of a one-time prostitute who is unwittingly acting as a courier carrying a microfilm with atomic secrets for the Party. Widmark is a small-time crook, a pickpocket who steals the purse with the film from Peters' handbag. His attitude when he finds out that what he's got is worth something is to ask a high price for it. He has no compunctions about dealing with communists. When he's taken in by the authorities (an FBI agent had been tailing Peters and had seen Widmark stealing the microfilm), and his patriotism is appealed to, he sneers and tells his interrogators to stop waving the flag at him. The demands of the Hollywood system required a suitably positive ending, but the body of the film allowed Fuller to be idiosyncratic and raise questions about both communism and capitalism. The authorities are shown to be just as ruthless as the communists in their disregard for the individual in order to get what they want.

A number of other films employed film noir characteristics to play on fears of atomic espionage. One of them was the ludicrous *Shack Out on 101*, in which Lee Marvin (appropriately nicknamed "Slob") played a short-order cook at a roadside diner who also happens to be the head of the local branch of the Communist Party. A nuclear scientist frequents the diner, and is romancing the waitress (a nubile young woman with aspirations to pass the Civil Service entrance exams) while she is being lusted after by Slob. The scientist is supposedly passing secrets to Slob, though he's in fact working for the government. It's hard to take the whole thing seriously, and the film doesn't even have the benefits of good photography or imaginative lighting, as do, for example, *Pickup on South Street* and *The Woman on Pier 13*.

A much more provocative film dealing with the passing of secrets is *The Thief*, starring Ray Milland as a nuclear scientist who is involved in stealing information and handing it over to the communists. In fact, it's never overtly stated that they are communists, though the period and the nuclear aspect inevitably lead viewers to assume they are. What makes the film of great interest in cinematic terms is that it contains no dialogue. The usual extraneous noises – footsteps, doors, telephones, etc. – are heard, but no-one ever speaks. It adds tension to the narrative and also lays emphasis on the increasingly paranoid actions of the professor.

It's true that, to a degree, the communists are viewed somewhat stereotypically. A small, bespectacled man peers ominously from behind a desk in the reading room of the Library of Congress, as the professor hides information on a shelf of books. A female communist carries three books under her arm at the top of the Empire State Building as a sign that she is the professor's contact. Perhaps that was how it was? The way the professor seems to be caught in a web of spying that he can't escape from, puts one in mind of the words of the communist boss in *The Red Menace* who, speaking of a possible recruit, says, "when we get him into the Party he'll find out that it's not so easy to get out".

A film that continues to attract attention is *Kiss Me Deadly,* written by A.I. Bezzerides from Mickey Spillane's novel. Spillane, a pulp writer if ever there was one, described his work as "the chewing gum of American literature". The novel referred to a stolen canister that contained drugs, but the film changed it to radioactive material that would, should the canister be opened, bring death and destruction. Miklitsch says that it's not an anti-communist film, but rather "an atomic or apocalyptic noir". It certainly uses all the stylistic aspects of film noir, and has been described as probably the final film in what might be called the classic tradition of the genre. It's definitely an example of a film improving on a book.

It's worth noting that another 1950s film, *City of Fear*, also used the idea of a stolen deadly canister of radioactive material being carried around by someone who doesn't realise what it contains. In this case, it's an escaped prisoner who believes that he's holding a can of narcotics worth a million dollars. In the meantime, the authorities, alert to the fact that, if opened, the contents could decimate the city and its surroundings, are trying to track him down. There is no anti-communist theme to the film, and it simply emphasises the fear of what an atomic mishap could result in. People were aware of the possibility of atomic warfare and its consequences, but both *Kiss Me Deadly* and *City of Fear* appeared to suggest that an accidental release of radioactivity was just as much of a threat.

It's a fascinating side-issue in relation to *City of Fear* that its director, Irving Lerner, who had been active in the left-wing Workers Film and Photo League and Frontier Films in the 1930s, may have been linked in some way to espionage activity in the 1940s when he worked with the Office of War Information (OWI). He was caught trying to photograph some highly-secret equipment located at the University of California which was linked to the development of the atom bomb at Los Alamos. Lerner wasn't prosecuted, but he did resign from his position at the OWI, and went to work for Keynote Records whose owner, Eric Bernay, was reputed to have been involved in espionage, as was Arthur Adams, a Keynote employee, who moved to Russia in 1946. Keynote Records initially specialised in folk music and protest songs, but also became known for some excellent jazz records, including examples of early bebop. As for Lerner, he was, not surprisingly, blacklisted when the anti-communist hysteria hit Hollywood.

Miklitsch looks at several 1950s films which, he says, can be classified as examples of late-film noir. He cites *Black Widow, A Kiss Before Dying*, and particularly *Niagara*, as among them. I'm not convinced of his arguments, persuasive though they seem to be. As with my earlier comments about *Leave Her to Heaven*, I find that the use of technicolour, and the wide screen, work against the elements of darkness, dreary settings, and paranoia that were highlights of film noir. Agreed that the stories may be similar to those in many of the earlier films, but it's how the stories are interpreted that makes the difference. And the early noirs made imaginative use of often limited resources.

Despite my occasional challenges to Miklitsch's ideas and opinions, I thoroughly enjoyed his book. He's an astute critic and a rigorous analyst of the plots and contents of screenplays. He also rightly gives a lot of credit to the technicians who worked on the films, in particular cameramen like John Alton, Lucien Ballard, Joseph MacDonald, and others. Without them the all-important visual aspects of film noir would have been much reduced. *The Red and the Black* is a book for all those who love to read about the Hollywood films of the 1940s and 1950s, and especially those that fall into the film noir category. We can argue all day about exactly what that term entails, but the subject will never fail to fascinate.

THE RED AND THE BLACK: AMERICAN FILM NOIR IN THE 1950s
by Robert Miklitsch
University of Illinois Press. 312 pages. $28. ISBN 978-0-252-08219-1 (paperback)

FINKS

I'm looking at a couple of copies of *The Paris Review* from around 1954/55, along with some issues of *Partisan Review* and *Encounter* from the same period. And I can't help being impressed by the range of writers appearing in them: Ralph Ellison, Albert Moravia, Isaac Bashevis Singer, Delmore Schwartz, Hannah Arendt, Robert Penn Warren, John Berryman, Elizabeth Hardwick, Leslie Fiedler, Daniel Bell, Raymond Aron, Dwight Macdonald, Albert Camus, Stuart Hampshire, Philip Toynbee. I've selected only a few names from those appearing on the contents pages of the magazines, and there are many more. It's like a roll-call of the literary and intellectual fraternity of the period.

The question that comes to mind when I pull these old magazines from my bookshelves is how many of the writers mentioned knew, or even suspected, that the publications concerned were in receipt of funding from the CIA? And if they did know, or suspected, did it bother them? After all, they could have perhaps justifiably taken the view that their work wasn't censored in any way, nor were they required to tailor it to suit an overt anti-Russian programme or an overt pro-Western (and especially pro-American) point of view. In other words, they weren't being asked to write propaganda. And most of the writers and others like them, were no doubt firmly opposed to communism and conditions in the Soviet Union, even if some had leaned to the Left in earlier years.

When the fact of CIA support for cultural activities became public in the early-1960s there were many expressions of denial and dismay, some of which were probably feigned. It's difficult to believe that the people named above, and others like them, didn't sometimes pause to wonder just how the publications they wrote for managed to survive. It's true that the CIA didn't directly subsidise them and money was channelled through seemingly reputable individuals and organisations.

The Congress for Cultural Freedom (CCF) attracted what many people might describe as the great and the good. Bertrand Russell, Benedetto Croce, Arthur Koestler, Arthur Schlesinger, and others like them. Frances Stone Saunders' *Who Paid the Piper? The CIA and the Cultural Cold War* (Granta Books, London, 1999) provides an excellent account of the founding and activities of the CCF. Saunders quotes the CIA's Tom Braden as saying, "Of course they knew", when, in 1967, *Partisan Review* published a statement, signed by a number of noted intellectuals and writers, claiming that they didn't know about CIA funding of "literary and intellectual publications and organisations".

Joel Whitney's purpose in *Finks* is to look at how the CIA used literature to further its efforts to promote a programme of activities that would demonstrate how the West was superior to the Soviet Union, and its satellites, when it came to cultural matters. As well as providing funds for magazines like *Paris Review, Partisan Review, Encounter,* which would have otherwise most likely closed down due to distribution difficulties and their relatively small circulations, the organisation financed the publication of books. A classic example was the English-language editions of Boris Pasternak's *Doctor Zhivago.* It was considered something of a coup for the CIA to have had a hand in getting the book into print in America and Britain.

One of the cases of CIA funding that Whitney deals with in some detail concerns *The Paris Review*, a little magazine that was started, as its title suggests, in the French capital by a group of young Americans living there in the early-1950s. What is especially intriguing is that one of the group, the novelist, Peter Matthiessen, was a CIA agent, though the others involved (among them, George Plimpton and H.L. Humes) claimed not to have known this, or at least not until much later.

Matthiessen wrote a novel, *Partisans*, while in Paris, though Whitney doesn't mention it, and it demonstrated a knowledge of the workings of the French Communist Party, which at that time (the book was published in 1955) was a particularly powerful force in French politics. But Matthiessen wasn't in Paris to check on the local communists, and it's more than probable that his brief was to keep an eye on the American expatriate community which included more than a few writers who had left America when their radical involvements were brought to light. There were others, such as the black writers, James Baldwin, Richard Wright, Ralph Ellison, and Chester Himes, who also thought that they would encounter less racism in France.

Humes wasn't black, nor was he then a political militant. He wrote a large and very good novel, *The Underground City* (1958), which was about the French resistance in the war years, and the Communist Party in the post-war period. One of the characters in the book was an American "former secret agent". It's unlikely that Humes was aware in the 1950s that one of his colleagues at *The Paris Review* worked for the CIA, though he may well have known that it was rumoured among the expatriate community that embassy employees kept track of what they were doing.

It was in the 1960s that Humes was told that Matthiessen had been a CIA agent, and the information, he claimed, came from Matthiessen himself. Humes, then living in London, wrote to George Plimpton to try to persuade him to make the information public, and threatened to resign from any connection to the magazine. There was an amusing exchange during which Plimpton said that he could understand someone resigning because of the poetry that the magazine published, but not because of the alleged CIA links.

Plimpton wasn't the only one to seemingly dislike the poetry editors' choices. John Train. one-time managing editor and almost certainly a CIA agent (he later cropped up in Afghanistan and elsewhere), was on record as claiming that a lot of the poems in *The Paris Review* were not to the taste of most of its editorial staff: "with any particular poetry editor you tend to find yourself printing the works of his particular coterie" and very little of it was "memorable". I bought *The Paris Review* regularly throughout the 1960s and rarely found the poetry in its pages all that interesting.

It has to be said that Humes, by the mid-1960s, was not in good shape, as witness his behaviour when he returned to New York. He was paranoiac, though, as has been pointed out, some of his suspicions about being followed and spied on were not without foundations in fact. The FBI had an extensive file on him.

The FBI also kept files on many of the New York Intellectuals and their magazine, *Partisan Review*. It would be valuable to know exactly who J. Edgar Hoover's boys trailed and tracked. John Rodden, in *Of G-Men and Eggheads,* deals with just three, Lionel Trilling, Irving Howe, and Dwight Macdonald, but I would guess that most, if not all, of the others (Philip Rahv, Harold Rosenberg, to name just two) associated with *Partisan Review*, came to the attention of the FBI at one time or another. The magazine was suspect in its eyes, which raises a question about relations between the CIA and the FBI. Although the long-standing editor, William Phillips, always denied that the magazine received any CIA money, it's more than likely that some funding was channelled to it through the CCF or similar organisations. So, there may be some humour to be derived from a situation where the FBI was compiling reports on a publication and its writers financed, in part at least, by the CIA.

The FBI's interest in Lionel Trilling came about because of his early contacts with Whittaker Chambers. Trillling's novel, *The Middle of the Journey*, had a character clearly based on Chambers, who had left the Communist Party in the late-1930s and by the late-1940s was openly confessing to his misdemeanours as an operative in the communist "underground" in America. His court confrontations with Alger Hiss put both their names in the headlines. And Chambers' autobiography, *Witness*, got praise and condemnation in equal measure. Trilling's early encounters with left-wing organisations (he was never a member of the Communist Party) were long behind him, and by the late-1940s he was a highly-respectable professor at Columbia University. This didn't stop the FBI from compiling a dossier on him, though Rodden suggests that he was never formally investigated. Most pages in the dossier relate to the Chambers/Hiss case, and the fact that Trilling had known Chambers during their student days together.

Something that does become clear, not only from Trilling's experiences with the FBI but from what Rodden says generally, is that FBI operatives appeared to have little or no awareness of the nuances of left-wing politics. Trotskyists and Stalinists were all communists, and it was probably impossible to explain to an FBI agent just how many varieties of Trotskyists there were. Rodden also points out that no-one belonging to the FBI seems to have bothered to read anything that Trilling wrote, other than, perhaps, *The Middle of the Journey*. They may not even have read that in any systematic way, and simply wanted to know if it said anything about Chambers they could use.

There was quite a difference between the FBI and the CIA, in that the latter could boast more than a few agents or associates who were also writers of some reputation. Peter Matthiessen has already been mentioned, but what about Sol Stein, author of *The Touch of Treason*, among other novels, and E. Howard Hunt, notorious for his part in the Watergate conspiracy, who wrote several novels and was awarded a Guggenheim Fellowship? He also produced a few pulp novels for Gold Medal Books including the aptly-titled *House Dick*, "a twisty tale of burglary and murder, of skulduggery under cover of darkness, of deception and loyalties – and of the price you pay when you trust the wrong people".

If the FBI thought that dealing with Lionel Trilling was fairly straightforward, they must have been less than happy with Dwight Macdonald. A born maverick, he was noted for being argumentative and contradictory. He also had a record of radical involvements. In the 1950s he wrote a long, two-part essay for *Encounter* which gleefully recounted his adventures among the Trotskyists, his time with the *Partisan Review* people, his departure from their ranks, and the founding of his own publication, *Politics*. It was later used as the introduction to his *Memoirs of a Revolutionist*.

Macdonald wasn't likely to be anyone's servant when it came to what he wrote. He worked for *Encounter* in London for a year, and on his return to the United States wrote an essay, "America! America!", which took a fairly jaundiced view of his native country. It was accepted for publication by *Encounter*, then rejected, and it was only later, with disclosure of CIA involvement in the CCF and, by extension, the financing of the magazine, that Macdonald could put two and two together and reason that worries about the withdrawal of the subsidy might have played a part in the decision not to use the essay. It could have provided ammunition for those with an anti-American agenda.

The essay was eventually published in Britain in a magazine called *Twentieth Century*, and in America in *Dissent*, the publication started by Irving Howe when he thought that *Partisan Review* was moving too far from politics in its choice of material. Howe had been associated with the Trotskyists for some years in the 1930s and 1940s, so was on the FBI's list of "persons of interest". Like Trilling and Macdonald, had the FBI bothered to read what Howe wrote they would have easily seen that he was an obvious anti-communist, though more than the others, he retained a greater degree of socialist commitment. That was probably enough to arouse suspicions, and the launching of *Dissent*, clearly a publication with a leftist slant, in 1954, a time when McCarthyism was still rampant, no doubt suggested to the authorities that Howe was someone to be watched. He was questioned, as were people he worked with, and lectures he gave were monitored, his mail was opened, and his movements recorded.

Rodden notes that Howe's FBI file was bigger than either Trilling's or Macdonald's, but says that he would have been well aware that what he experienced was "an annoying pinprick" compared to what others in America had to deal with. University professors and schoolteachers lost their jobs, screenwriters were blacklisted, union activists fired, many others were harassed and forced to testify against colleagues and friends. If they refused to do so, they faced being sent to prison. Needless to say, the situation for writers and intellectuals behind the Iron Curtain was even worse. Howe, on the other hand, was free to come and go as he pleased, and had no problems getting published in established magazines, his books came out from well-known publishers, and he obtained teaching posts at prestigious universities. Saying this does not in any way diminish Howe's determination to court unpopularity by launching *Dissent* as an outlet for dissident voices in America.

The point that Rodden is making when he describes how the FBI kept track of what Trilling, Macdonald, and Howe had done in the 1930s and what they were doing in the 1940s and 1950s, is that it was unnecessary and unproductive. There was no evidence that any of them had ever engaged in the kind of subversive activities that could arouse suspicion. They were simply dissenting and, in the cases of Macdonald and Howe, asking legitimate questions about what was going on in their country. Trilling's was mostly a quieter voice, and largely devoted to academic literary questions after his initial dabblings with left-wing politics in the 1930s.

Taken together these two books offer an informative view of a time when writers and intellectuals were probably in the limelight more than they are now. And thought sufficiently influential to warrant being checked on by the FBI, and subsidised by the CIA. Were they compromised by publishing in magazines that received money from government sources? Tom Braden's view of *Encounter*, as quoted in *Who Paid the Piper?* was "Let them publish what they want", though he did admit to pulling the plug on one article attacking American policy. Was that Macdonald's piece?

The question of any kind of government funding, openly or secretly, for publications is always subject to suspicions of possible censorship, of one kind or another. But writers and editors of magazines happily, in my experience, take money from the Arts Council and similar organisations in Britain. They probably couldn't survive otherwise. And who knows on what basis the decisions regarding which writers or publications to subsidise are made? Do politics play a part in them?

The Cold War period, and in particular the years between 1945 and roughly 1965, was one of intense political activity when old certainties were fading fast, and it seemed important to present a united front in the West to the threat of communism. At the same time, the loyalties of many people were still in doubt owing to their earlier involvements. That doesn't excuse the way in which the FBI hounded people for no reason other than that they had once been a member of a tiny Trotskyist group, or had signed a petition or two. Nor does it excuse the machinations of the CIA when it came to secretly financing cultural activities because of their usefulness in showing how the West was superior to Russia and its allies. But the atmosphere of the time, and the doubts in many minds about the sincerity of those on the left claiming to be working for peace, might explain why some writers and intellectuals thought that they ought to come out clearly about their commitments, and in doing so take CIA money (assuming they knew about it). But, again, who knows?

FINKS : HOW THE CIA TRICKED THE WORLD'S BEST WRITERS
By Joel Whitney
OR Books. 329 pages. £20/$25. ISBN 978-1-68219-024-1

OF G-MEN AND EGGHEADS : THE FBI AND THE NEW YORK INTELLECTUALS
By John Rodden
University of Illinois Press. 132 pages. $19.95.
ISBN 978-0-252-08194-1

HARD-BOILED NOIR

Pulp fiction. What exactly is it? And what is the difference between "hardboiled" and "noir?" I'm not sure that Rick Ollerman ever really clarifies what it is that distinguishes the two genres, though in a way it doesn't really matter. A hardboiled novel can often have a hero who, in the end, turns out to be bigger than expected and reaches a satisfactory conclusion, whether of a problem he has to resolve or a relationship with a woman he has fallen for. The noir "hero", on the other hand, may start off thinking himself big but is likely to fall prey to a variety of temptations that will break down his resistance in various ways, The femme fatale is usually the main one. It's little wonder that pulp fiction paperback covers often featured a semi-clothed female vamping a worried-looking man. But that's a loose distinction I'm making and easily shown to be not all that accurate. Things are often not as they seem

I'm not sure that, over the years, I've ever bothered too much about whether or not a book falls into the hardboiled or noir category. Likewise with the question of its "pulp" status. Pulp usually suggests something printed on cheap paper and sold mainly in small shops, or on newsstands, as opposed to big bookstores. Many pulp writers only ever went directly into paperbacks, but some others did make a breakthrough to hardbacks with major publishers. It perhaps gave them a status never likely to accrue to the hard-pressed novelists who turned out twenty or thirty paperback books in as many years, and often even less time. Their books rarely, if ever, got reviewed, and few, if any, critics bothered to even acknowledge their existence, let alone wrote about them. Anthony Boucher may have been a rare exception.

Ollerman reminisces about the time when he could browse through the paperback racks in the local store and decide which of the latest novels he could afford. I had similar experiences myself, albeit in Britain rather than America, but I'd guess the results were much the same. Without any kind of guide as to which writers might be worth reading it was a case of trial and error. Sometimes a book would attract not because the cover featured a beautiful blonde posed seductively, but when the subject-matter might seem interesting. I recall picking up Malcolm Braly's *Shake Him Till He Rattles* because it appeared to have some jazz connections. Ollerman is informative about Braly, who had spent years in prison before he became a reformed character and wrote several novels. His *On the Yard* is considered a brilliant portrayal of prison life.

I suppose there is some irony in the fact that all those paperbacks which were looked down on by the literary establishment, and were often condemned by moralists, sometimes on the basis of their covers rather than their contents, are now collectors' material. At one time it was possible to still find them (I'm talking about the original editions) in odd places at low prices. They weren't always in good condition, but that didn't matter too much if all the pages were there. Pulp publications weren't meant to last. The rise of the Internet, coupled with re-assessments of their qualities, has meant that it's now difficult to easily obtain them without paying too much. And they're often more difficult to find. Nostalgia can take over when I think about the books I picked up from market-stalls and second-hand bookshops.

This is where the reprint houses have stepped in to save the day. Stark House is probably the key player in the field, but others, such as Hard Case Crime, are also active. The problem is that reprints aren't always reviewed widely, and bookshops don't always stock them unless the writer has a name the public will recognise. Jim Thompson's books, or certain of them, at least, sometimes creep onto the shelves of Waterstone's. There's occasionally a chance that David Goodis will be seen. And there's a major snag. In most British cities and towns these days there is only a Waterstone's.

There used to be a very good crime bookshop on Charing Cross Road in London, but it went under some years ago. I miss it because I could always find both new and old editions of books by Gil Brewer, William P. McGivern, Benjamin Appel, Steve Fisher, Ed Lacy, and many others, on its packed shelves. It was always a pleasure to come across an old book in the Gold Medal series. Or a reprint from Stark House. I'm talking about writers from the 1940s and 1950s, which is where my personal interests are, but more-contemporary writers that I read, such as John Harvey and Lawrence Block, were also very much in evidence.

Rick Ollerman clearly has his favourites among the older pulp, hard-boiled, noir, call them what you will, writers. Charles Williams is one of them, and Ollerman writes at length about him. It's only fair to say that he's fully aware that the kind of writing life that pulp authors often led didn't always make for consistency in the quality of their work. Even the best writers produced books that were routinely plotted and showed evidence of haste in their composition. Reading them I sometimes have the feeling that publishers may have been applying the, "We don't want a masterpiece, we want it Tuesday", maxim to their demands for manuscripts to be delivered with speed. The writers themselves also needed to turn out books regularly in order to maintain some sort of steady income. It's easy to see why a writer like Jada M. Davies, who wrote the classic (of its type), *One for Hell,* preferred to make a living as a businessman. He had known extreme poverty as a child, had a family to support, and published only two novels in his lifetime.

Discussing Charles Williams, Ollerman rightly refers to his *Hell Hath No Fury* as one of his best books. It was made into a film, *The Hot Spot,* starring Don Johnson and Virginia Madsen, and directed by Dennis Hopper, and perhaps was an example of how sometimes a cinematic version of a book can be its equal in terms of effectiveness. Quite a few pulp novels provided the inspiration for noir films, usually in the "B" category, but they didn't necessarily always turn out for the best. I recently caught *Guilty Bystander,* featuring Zachary Scott as the alcoholic private detective, Max Thursday, on YouTube, and thought it a poor version of the novel of the same name by Wade Miller. That was the pen-name of Bill Miller and Robert Wade, two writers who had a successful partnership for many years. On the other hand, Whit Masterson's *Badge of Evil* became the highly-rated (by the critics) *Touch of Evil,* though with some substantial changes. But that's Hollywood. Fans enthuse about the famous long tracking shot that opens the film. And about the performance by Orson Welles as the corrupt policeman.

Mentioning Max Thursday points to the fact that more than a few pulp writers created a character who was the centre of attention in a series of books. There were, perhaps, practical reasons for this. People who read crime novels like to follow the adventures of a detective, usually a private investigator but sometimes an official policeman. Need I say more than Sherlock Holmes? Publishers have a useful selling point when they advertise the latest novel featuring a specifically named person. And it may be that the writer knows that readers will be drawn into the story automatically when they recognise the name. That's the "hook", the device which creative writing tutors will tell you is essential to interest readers enough to make them want to carry on. Did any of those early pulp writers ever attend a creative writing class? Or teach one? Somehow I doubt it, though I'm more than ready to be corrected. Ollerman says that when it was suggested that Charles Williams write about a "series character" he "thought that would be boring for him".

Peter Rabe is another writer who Ollerman favours. And I want to use something that he says when writing about Rabe, though it's not necessarily directly in connection with him: "The point is anyone can write a bad review just like anyone can repeat a dirty joke. Both can make you laugh. But how many critics or reviewers can make you see the good in something that may not be wholly good? Or the good in spite of the overall bad". Reading that I thought of lots of critics and reviewers I've read who just haven't done what Ollerman suggests and I've wondered whether it's worth taking the trouble to ever read them again. Lots of people condemning pulp fiction simply fail to note its virtues and see only its faults. I prefer to read reviewers who respond rather than ridicule.

Writing about Rabe, Ollerman refers to his *Kill the Boss Good-by* (a title I like alongside Fredric Brown's *We All Killed Grandma*, but a whole essay could be written about the titles of pulp novels, which can admittedly vary from the interesting to the ridiculous). Rabe "never wrote the same book twice.........He didn't follow the same formula book after book, he didn't use the same plot over and over again". He did write novels which had "series characters", in one case a gangster named Daniel Port, in another a lawyer who gets involved In espionage.

Ollerman's focus is mostly on crime, but the pulp writers often turned their hands to other genres, like westerns. Not all pulp was about murders and mayhem, though the most popular books largely concerned themselves with those subjects. And sex, but it had to be inferred or hinted at in the 1940s and 1950s. Was that necessarily a bad thing? I hate to think what Steve Fisher's *Sheltering Night*, originally published by Gold Medal in 1952, might have been like had it been written twenty years later. Fisher had to suggest rather than state in his story of a girl who likes sex too much.

I referred earlier to some films based on pulp novels, and Ollerman has a good chapter on Lionel White who wrote a book called *Clean*

Break. This was turned into *The Killing*, a film beloved of fans of film noir. It starred, among others, Sterling Hayden, playing the "muscle man" taking part in a robbery. He played a somewhat similar role in *The Asphalt Jungle*, based on W.R. Burnett's novel of the same name. Ollerman writes about Burnett in a useful essay.

It's when writing about Lionel White that Ollerman tries to clarify the difference between "hardboiled" and "noir". He makes a distinction between "most of Chandler's and Hammett's novels", which he says are "examples of hardboiled writing", and James M. Cain's *The Postman Always Rings Twice*, which he thinks is "as good an example of noir that's ever been written". The private eyes in Chandler and Hammett survive, whereas the poor drifter who falls for the femme fatale in Cain's book is certain to end badly.

Just going back to titles, there may be a case for claiming that *You Play the Black and the Red Comes Up* (a 1938 novel by Richard Hallas, or Eric Knight, to give him his real name), is the classic noir title, though some might argue that it more likely fits into the hardboiled category. The roots of the hardboiled, and perhaps of noir also, can be located in Depression America. And corruption and crime could be found in small towns and rural areas as much as in the big cities. As well as writers like Chandler, Hammett, Cain, and the *Black Mask* bunch, think of Erskine Caldwell, Horace McCoy, James T. Farrell, Nelson Algren, and James Ross. The latter's *They Don't Dance Much*, a "sleazy, corrupt but completely believable story of a North Carolina town" (Raymond Chandler's words) is little-known but well worth reading.

Eric Knight was English, but moved to America and worked in Hollywood, and it's interesting that Ollerman has a chapter about James Hadley Chase, author of *No Orchids for Miss Blandish*, a book considered quite scandalous in its day. It was George Orwell who described it as not "the product of an illiterate hack, but a brilliant piece of writing, with hardly a wasted word or a jarring note anywhere". But Ollerman does note that Orwell also described it as "American" fiction and consequently not really acceptable from a British writer. Chase's proper name was René Brabazon Raymond and he was born in London in 1906. He wrote ninety books, but sometimes had problems when he "borrowed" plots from other writers' novels. Ollerman says that *No Orchids for Miss Blandish* obviously took a great deal from William Faulkner's *Sanctuary*, with details about the "kidnapping, holding and corruption of a society girl".

Ollerman is good when analysing various novels, and he can be thought-provoking, as when he says that Lionel White, unlike other writers, doesn't often describe people "through dialogue". Instead, he "defines his characters mostly through exposition". It may seem that Ollerman is sometimes repetitious because he has more than one piece each about Charles Williams, Peter Rabe, Ed Gorman, and James Hadley Chase. But he usually manages to come up with fresh information and insights in each short or long essay.

Hardboiled, Noir and Gold Medals ought to be read by anyone wanting to know more about the world of pulp writers, and can be usefully placed alongside another Stark House publication, Brian Ritt's *Paperback Confidential: Crime Writers of the Paperback Era*, as a guide to what is brightest in the world of hardboiled and noir writing. No sensible claim can be made for every pulp writer being of interest. There were hundreds of forgotten paperback novels produced during the heyday of the pulps, and many don't deserve to be revived or reprinted, but a discerning reader can find some worthwhile writing in the best of them.

HARDBOILED, NOIR AND GOLD MEDALS : ESSAYS ON CRIME FICTION WRITERS FROM THE 50s THROUGH THE 90s
By Rick Ollerman
Stark House Press. 295 pages. $17.95. ISBN 978-1-94452-0-328

WEIMAR IN EXILE

"Already in 1933, the number of intellectuals, writers and poets who fled the Nazi dictatorship rose into the thousands".

Those opening words of Jean-Michel Palmier's massive study of the diaspora created by Hitler's take-over of Germany do not exaggerate the numbers involved in the "blood-letting of its cultural life". The effect on theatre, cinema, music, literature, and intellectual activities generally was enormous and, some might argue, could still be felt for many years after the Nazis had been defeated. The division of Germany into East and West regimes as a result of the war was, in itself, a devastating blow in terms of not allowing a return to any sort of pre-1933 normality.

It is a fact that Germany's loss possibly benefited other countries as refugees from Fascism took up residence elsewhere. It wasn't quite that simple, of course, because the émigrés often met some opposition from local people, or had difficulty adjusting to conditions dissimilar to the ones they were used to in their homeland. Initially, they tended to move to France, Austria, and Czechoslovakia, but all those countries would eventually fall to Nazi domination, so settling into long-term situations was impossible. They had to move on or become victims of the Nazis.

In some interesting comments, Palmier says that, in certain ways, the seeds of the Nazi persecution of writers and others who had expressed radical ideas in their work, had been sown during the time of the Weimar Republic. There is a popular idea of the 1920s, perhaps largely based on portrayals of a decadent life-style in Berlin in films and novels, which dominates our understanding of the period. But according to Palmier :

"The Weimar Germany we have mythologised was extremely repressive towards its intellectuals, and the artistic upsurge which immortalised the period developed despite the state and often against its laws. A number of the Third Reich's repressive measures had their origin under Weimar. The struggle against `left-wing art' and `cultural Bolshevism' started well before Hitler, and the intellectual freedom that the Nazis suppressed for more than a decade had already been considerably restricted by the Republic. The treatment inflicted on writers between 1919 and 1933 already showed certain aspects of Hitler's cultural policy, without its barbarity".

It was the Nazi barbarity – books burned, apartments ransacked, libraries and manuscripts thrown into the streets, people assaulted, arrested, even killed – which convinced many people that it was time to leave Germany. Many of them probably hoped that the Nazi ascendancy was an aberration that would soon pass. They didn't realise that, for some of them, it would be a permanent exile, and that, even for those who did eventually return, the world they had known would be lost forever.

Palmier looks at most of the countries that offered at least some sort of hospitality, even if of a grudging kind. It's worth noting what he says about a few of them. Britain, for example, wasn't the first destination that large numbers of refugees headed for. He says that "It was only with the annexation of Austria that it became a real land of asylum, especially for many Jews". But he adds that because Britain was suffering from the effects of the Depression, would-be immigrants could be turned away if they had insufficient funds to support themselves. And efforts were made to weed out those "suspected of Communist sympathies". But he adds that: "By 1937, more than 4,500 refugees had reached Britain, including major scientific and literary figures", and "After 1938, many refugees of Jewish origin were accepted, as well as Socialists from Vienna and Prague. A thousand scholarships were granted to exiled students, while British universities and colleges took on about fifteen hundred teachers".

Christopher Isherwood's novel, *Prater Violet*, about an émigré Austrian film director arousing "boredom and scepticism" among people in London when he talks about "his worry for his country and his friends" sums up some of the problems facing those fleeing Hitler. For the record, Isherwood's novel was based on his experiences working in England with Austrian director, Berthold Viertel on a 1934 film, *Little Friend*. Viertel had gone to Hollywood in the late-1920s, but wasn't happy there, though he stayed in America when he saw how events in Europe were developing.

Some émigrés did go to Spain, where they struggled for a time, but when the Civil War started they soon found roles in either the International Brigades or working for the Republican government. The difficulty was that, when Franco was victorious in 1939, they had to escape into France, where they were interned in squalid conditions. Later, those who had been unable to get out of the internment camps (some were given the opportunity to join the French Foreign Legion) were often handed over to the Gestapo when the Germans overran France.

For members of the Communist Party who left Germany, the obvious country to head for was Russia, where, they naturally assumed, they would be welcomed. For a time they were, and Palmier refers to some historians who claim that "the USSR differed radically from other countries of asylum in the generosity of its welcome, the immediate application of proletarian internationalism in favour of the émigrés, and the readiness with which these were entrusted with tasks that were important".

Palmier isn't convinced that the USSR was all that welcoming. Stalin's paranoia about foreigners and the purges among Party members soon meant that the émigrés were caught up in tragic events. Palmier refers to the case of Heinz Neumann who was arrested and his room searched. It was claimed that in it were books not only "of a Trotsykist character", but also "Zinovievist, Kamenevist, and Bukharinite" material. Neumann disappeared into a Siberian camp. Later, his wife was arrested and sent to a labour camp for five years as a "socially dangerous element". Some other refugees were accused of Trotskyism because they had received catalogues from émigré publishers. These are just a few of the examples that Palmier mentions. And when the Nazi-Soviet Pact was signed in 1939, Stalin, as a gesture of goodwill, handed over a number of German communists to the Gestapo.

A long section deals with the experiences of German writers, artists, intellectuals, and others in France, a country with a tradition of offering hospitality to political refugees. The problem was one of numbers, and it's estimated that between 30,000 and 35,000 may have been in France, at one time or another. Some of them were only passing through on their way to different places, but others were there on an almost-permanent basis, which inevitably caused problems relating to work and accommodation. When France went to war in 1939 foreigners were interned. Some managed to arrange to obtain papers and passages to America and elsewhere. The unlucky ones were left behind and were either rounded up by the Germans or went into hiding.

America not surprisingly receives a great deal of attention in *Weimar in Exile*. In many ways, the culture clash was much greater than that experienced by émigrés arriving in other countries. Palmier says that: "Whatever their degree of politicization, the exiles almost all found America repellent. Walter Benjamin saw scarcely a difference between the United States and Kafka's nightmare world. Franz Werfel preferred to risk his life in Europe than to cross the Atlantic". The émigrés, mostly writers, intellectuals, and others used to the high culture of Europe, and especially Germany, often simply couldn't cope with the mass culture that was typical of cities like New York and Los Angeles. There were obviously fine art galleries and great universities in America, but authors and philosophers weren't likely to receive the respect that had been accorded them in Berlin, Paris, and other major cities in Europe. The musician Arnold Schoenberg was of the opinion that: "No serious composer in this country is capable of living from his art. Only popular composers earn enough to support oneself and one's family, and then it is not *art*." He had to teach to make any money.

Palmier points out that "America possibly left a stronger mark on the German emigration than did any other country. Avant-garde artists whose names were known all over Europe were often unknown here, and their styles failed to arouse any interest. To make a living, to work and continue to create, they had to adapt, discover mass culture and the laws of the market. American cinema, and the way it was organised, was the radical negation of everything that had made the grandest of German cinema. Fritz Lang and many others learned this lesson painfully and had to modify their aesthetic".

Palmier obviously thinks that Lang perhaps compromised too quickly and too easily when he began to work in Hollywood: "There can certainly be no question of the interest, value and beauty of several of the films Fritz Lang made in America, but it has to be admitted that a gulf separates them from his German productions". It's not an opinion necessarily shared by supporters of Lang's American career.

In the same way, some criticised Kurt Weill for adapting to the demands of the Broadway musical, but he had already shown an interest in jazz, blues, and the music of an American composer like George Gershwin before moving to New York. In any case, who can doubt the grace and excellence of many of the popular songs, such as "September Song", "Speak Low", and "My Ship", that he wrote in America?

Numerous émigrés – teachers, scientists, doctors, etc. – did manage to eventually adapt to the American way of life, despite what initial misgivings they may have had, and their contributions to academic learning, art, and other subjects were beneficial. Writers found it more difficult to adjust, and even someone as famous in Europe as Bertolt Brecht , who lived in California, struggled to earn enough to support himself and his family. He tried to find employment in Hollywood by writing screenplays and selling stories to the studios, but was never all that successful at it. Thomas Mann managed to survive, probably because his work was known in the United States, but Heinrich Mann, who had written the novel on which the famous Marlene Dietrich film, *The Blue Angel*, was based, lived in near-poverty.

Brecht had problems, too, when the post-war years saw the rise of anti-communism in America, and he was called to appear before HUAC (the House Un-American Activities Committee). His testimony was a masterpiece of evasion, and after making it he immediately left for East Germany. Other émigrés also decided to move back to Europe, though not necessarily for political reasons. Some had just never really settled in America.

Palmier looks at the witch-hunts in Hollywood and suggests that the "left intelligentsia of the 1920s and 1930s certainly contributed to the greatness of the Hollywood cinema". When the HUAC hearings led to many writers being fired and blacklisted, Palmier thinks it "explains how uninteresting so much of the output of the 1950s was". I do wonder if that was true? In Alan Casty's *Communism in Hollywood* (Scarecrow Press, 2009) there are lists of many excellent films made in the 1950s and early-1960s which easily refute the argument that the 1950s was an "uninteresting" period in Hollywood.

I've referred to Spain, France, Britain, Russia and America as countries where exiles from Hitler moved to, but Palmier also looks at their experiences in the Netherlands, Scandinavia, Turkey, Palestine, and even China. Palmier refers to "more than 18,000 German, Austrian, Czech and Romanian refugees" having arrived in Shanghai, where they joined White Russians who had left after the Bolshevik Revolution, and some Sephardic Jews from Baghdad. And he adds that "an important centre of Yiddish culture developed in Shanghai".

There is some black humour to be gained from the fact that the city also hosted Walter Stennes, one-time officer in the German Army who fought with the notorious Freikorps in the street battles against communists, joined the SA, and narrowly survived a falling-out with Hitler. He left Germany, travelled to China, and became a military advisor to Chiang Kai-Shek. Palmier adds the ironic comment that, "It goes without saying that there was no connection between left-wing émigrés and the SA".

There is so much information packed into *Weimar in Exile* that, writing a review, I feel I've only skimmed over its surface. It was originally published in 1987, with the first English translation in 2006, and it's good to see it available again.

WEIMAR IN EXILE: THE ANTIFASCIST EMIGRATION IN EUROPE AND AMERICA
By Jean-Michel Palmier (translated by David Fernbach)
Verso. 852 pages. £25/$34.95. ISBN 978-1-78478-644-1

COAL MINE DISASTERS

My mother was born in Whitehaven in the early 1900s, and her father was a miner. When I was young I was sometimes sent to stay with my grandmother in Whitehaven, though I never got to meet my grandfather, He had been killed in 1915 in France, and though my grandmother had married again to another miner, her second husband had died before I started visiting her. One of my uncles was still working in the mines in the late-1940s and early-1950s, and I have a faint memory of seeing him in his working clothes.

Spending time in Whitehaven, I picked up an awareness of how much a disaster in the mines could affect the local community. Whitehaven wasn't a big town, so any problem which caused a large number of deaths could have a serious impact. There had been several mine disasters in the area, and the one I mainly knew a little about happened in 1910, when an explosion at the Wellington Pit resulted in the deaths of 136 miners. I suspect I heard more about it because my mother would have been around five in 1910, so she no doubt had memories of the atmosphere in Whitehaven at the time. And my grandmother's house was not far from the pithead, and I could see it when I went to play on the beach. The mine workings had extended out, under the Irish Sea, and I tried to imagine what it must have been like to have been trapped down there.

Brian Elliott's survey of mine disasters excludes any when under five men lost their lives. But he gives some figures for deaths in total and says that over 1,000 a year were being killed in the early-1900s, with the figure rising to 1,453 in 1909. Mines in Wales were notoriously dangerous because of the "gaseous and highly inflammable steam coal" that they produced. But mining everywhere was a precarious job, and not made any safer by the fact that coal owners frequently cut corners when it came to safety. There were rules but they were often ignored, and a total of 30 mine inspectors were supposed to cover 2,700 collieries.

Explosions were the most frequent causes of disasters, and occurred when some sort of ignition took place as a spark or other sort of naked light came into contact with the gases that were an ever-present danger in mines. When the National pit at Wattsdown in Glamorganshire exploded in 1905, and the West Stanley in Durham in 1909,

119 and 168 men died respectively. It may be better to say men and boys. At Wattsdown, 33 of the dead were under the age of 15. Before those disasters 81 miners were killed in an explosion at the Universal mine at Senghenydd in Wales in 1901.

I've just picked out a few of the larger disasters from a list of 44 that Elliott compiles for the 1900-1909 period. The other 41 involved explosions, roof falls, winding occurrences when the cages taking miners up and down the mine-shaft crashed to the bottom, accidents when new shafts were being sunk, and inrushes of water when it burst through from old seams and drowned all those who couldn't scramble to safely quickly enough. In one such incident at a mine in the Forest of Dean, several miners died and three were trapped for five days before being rescued. As I said earlier, Elliott generally excludes any disaster with less than five dead, and there were plenty of those.

I mentioned the disaster at the Wellington Pit in Whitehaven, and later that same year the Pretoria mine at Westhoughton in Lancashire experienced an explosion that killed 344 miners, making it the largest loss of life in English coalfields. It was thought to have been caused by a build-up of gas that was then ignited by a faulty lamp. A reporter from *The Times* noted the effect on surrounding districts, where "every other house at Chequerbent and Wingates had its blinds drawn today, and few families have escaped losing one or more members. A Wingates family has lost the father and five sons".

If the Pretoria tragedy was the worst in England, the events at the Universal Colliery at Senghenydd in Glamorganshire in 1913 established the record, if that's the right word, for the most serious in Britain. 440 men and boys died. Elliott says that "the most astonishing and annoying feature of the worst disaster in British coalmining history was that the Universal Colliery Company, in its greed for profit, had blatantly ignored safety legislation in the new (1911) Coal Mines Act. A fine of only £24 was imposed on the manager whilst the owners got away with `compensation' of just £10 and £5.5s.0d in costs following legal challenges in the courts".

It's difficult to know exactly how families that had lost a father or son, perhaps both, and possibly other relatives, got by when money stopped coming in. Welfare provisions were scanty, if they existed at all, and writing about the Podmore Hall (Minnie Pit) disaster in Staffordshire, where 155 miners and a member of the rescue team died,

Bennett tells us that, "Despite what could be done by the miners' union and contributions from a public relief fund, many families were reduced to a subsistence existence alongside their great personal distress". He also notes that about a third of the fatalities were `boy miners', teenagers with so much life ahead of them". Bennett quotes from a poem, "The Miners," written by Wilfred Owen about the Minnie Pit disaster.

Going back to Whitehaven, I see that 39 died at the Haig Pit in 1922 and another 13 in 1927. The same pit had 27 deaths in 1931, and the William Pit in Whitehaven registered 12 killed in 1941 and another 104 in 1947. But it wasn't just Whitehaven, and looking down Bennett's lists of disasters can make for painful reading. 266 miners died at Gresford Colliery near Wrexham in 1934, another 58 at Wharncliffe Woodmoor, Barnsley, 79 at Markham (Blackshale Pit), Chesterfield and 35 at Valleyfield, Culross, Fife. Again, I'm being selective and picking out the higher numbers of casualties. There were many others where six or eight or ten were killed, and no doubt quite a few below that cut-off point of five deaths that Bennett has established.

Following nationalisation of the mines in 1947 the situation seemed to improve, which isn't to say that disasters stopped occurring. 80 men died at Creswell, Derbyshire in 1950, another 83 at Easington, West Hartlepool in 1951, and 47 at Auchengeich, Lanarkshire in 1959. And there were the handfuls of others at a variety of locations across the country. But the list for 1950 to 1959 is shorter than earlier ones. And the list for 1960 to 1969 is likewise comparatively short, though it still includes 45 killed at Six Bells (Arrael Griffin), Abertillery in 1960, and 31 at the Cambrian mine at Clydach in the Rhondda in 1965.

Reading about all these disasters, the deaths, and all the heartaches they must have produced for the families of those killed and badly injured, can be a somewhat depressing experience. The only light comes from reading about the heroism and self-sacrifice of many of the miners, especially those in the rescue teams.

The arrogance and indifference of the mine owners is often shocking. Many of the accidents could have been avoided had proper safety precautions been in place. It's true that there were occasions where the actions of a miner may have been the cause of a problem. The 1947 explosion at the Louisa (Morrison) Pit at Stanley, County

Durham, was the result of someone lighting a cigarette. More than twenty men died, and what was referred to as "contraband", materials like cigarettes and matches that they weren't supposed to take into the mine, were found on the bodies of some of the victims.

There are tales of survival that lighten the narrative, and some anecdotes that bring out the tragedies of men trapped and aware that they're going to die. Rescuers found a message, "Farewell Fanny old pet", chalked on a rock when there was an explosion at the North Gawber pit, Barnsley, in 1935. And returning to Whitehaven and the Wellington Pit disaster of 1910, "chalked messages inscribed on doors and pieces of timber" showed that some of the miners were probably still alive when rescue operations were called off because it was deemed too dangerous to carry on.

The extensive illustrations in this book add to the poignancy of the situations described. There are photographs of crowds gathered outside various pits, anxiously waiting for news of survivors. Others show rescue workers bringing out bodies or assisting injured miners. Clippings of reports from old newspapers add a touch of authenticity in terms of the contemporary nature of the writing. In some cases photographic lists of those killed were produced by local firms and gave their names. Monuments erected in later years also listed the names of the dead. I couldn't help remembering a couple of lines from Idris Davies's long poem, *The Angry Summer: A Poem of 1926*: "For those who toil without a name/And pass into the night". Some names have been remembered, though it often took their deaths for it to happen.

And as I finished it and thought of the numbers of the dead, not to mention the maimed, and the families mourning their lost fathers and sons and brothers, I couldn't help turning to an old poem, "We have fed you all for a thousand years", credited to "an unknown proletarian", and first published in radical magazines and newspapers in America in the early-1900s. It includes the lines, "Then if blood be the price of all your wealth,/Good God! We have paid it in full". Those are words that could truthfully have been spoken by the people in all the mining towns and villages across Britain.

COAL MINE DISASTERS IN THE MODERN ERA c. 1900-1980
By Brian Elliott
Pen & Sword History. 175 pages. £14.95/$24.95. ISBN 978-1-47385-884-8

ANGEL MEADOW

In Benjamin Disraeli's 1844 novel, *Coningsby*, there is a chance meeting between Coningsby and Sidonia. They talk about travel, and Coningsby wistfully expresses a desire to visit Athens to see the glories that were Greece. Sidonia responds by saying that he has been there, and dismisses Coningsby's longings by adding: "Phantoms and Spectres. The Age of Ruins is past. Have you seen Manchester?"

There's no doubt about the fact that, at the time Disraeli was writing, Manchester was indeed attracting attention from across Europe and America. Its rapid development as an industrial centre, with, in its case, particular emphasis on the cotton trade, meant that it was being seen as a forerunner of the industrialised future for British society, and for other countries. The old phrase about what Manchester does today, the rest of the world does tomorrow, had some meaning. The problem was that as the mills and factories opened they needed large numbers of workers to operate them. Manchester's population quickly expanded to meet the demand for labour. People poured in from adjoining rural areas, and especially from Ireland where the Famines of the mid-19th Century had left thousands destitute.

People require accommodation and they also often inevitably gravitate towards parts of a town or city that can offer cheap lodgings, and perhaps already has an existing network of those from a similar background. The pleasant-sounding Angel Meadow (close to where the present-day Victoria Railway Station stands) had once been the home of members of Manchester's business class, and many of its houses were quite large. But Dean Kirby records that the popularity of Angel Meadow "faded overnight," as the centre of Manchester became dominated by factories. The middle-classes soon deserted Angel Meadow and moved out to what were then the suburbs of Ardwick Green and Broughton.

As the middle-classes left the working-classes, and those that Marx would have called the lumpenproletariat, took over. The houses were divided up and rooms rented out to single men and women, and to families. Even the cellars were seen as suitable for housing the ever-increasing hordes of men, women, and children, arriving in Manchester, attracted by the possibility of work, or in some cases, by the likelihood of opportunities for crime of one kind or another. Overcrowding became a concern and sanitation, or the lack of it, caused health problems. New houses were built, after a fashion, but soon became slum properties. Angel Meadow almost immediately lost its reputation for gentility, and became notorious for its poverty and criminality.

Many of those gravitating to Angel Meadow were Irish and they often brought with them a proclivity for drinking and fighting. Kirby doesn't necessarily single out the Irish for special attention in that respect, but they crop up often enough in his narrative to acknowledge the fact of their waywardness. But the British residents of Angel Meadow could be just as violent or drunken. It's perhaps significant that, when later in the 19th Century, Jewish and some other immigrants came to Red Bank, which was just across the River Irk from Angel Meadow, and suffered from some of the same problems with regard to deprivation in terms of housing and steady work, they were noticeably less inclined to drink heavily and fight each other.

There's no doubt that a lot of the violence in Angel Meadow was caused by drink, and the area had numerous beer houses, drinking dens, and other places where anyone could seek oblivion. The quickest way out of Manchester was, as they said, through the pub door. And both men and women could be found in drunken stupors or brawling in the streets. The domestic violence practised against women was shocking in its familiarity and no-one, including sometimes the police, took much notice of it. One resident, when asked if he'd paid any attention to hearing a woman screaming as she was assaulted, replied: "I didn't think it worthwhile to interfere. It's such a common occurrence." Even if the police got involved and took a man to court they found that the woman concerned was often reluctant to testify against him. They were fearful of what would happen later. Or of being cast adrift alone if they lost their man, no matter how brutal he was.

Angel Meadow was not a good place for a woman, whether alone or with a family to look after, and many turned to prostitution to earn enough money to get by on. Kirby notes that in Mrs Gaskell's 1848 novel, *Mary Barton,* one of her female characters who falls into prostitution after being abandoned by her lover, ends up in Nicholas Street, an actual location in Angel Meadow. And he refers to the 800 prostitutes believed to be operating in the Manchester area in 1894.

Many were street-walkers, others worked in brothels, of which there were numerous in Angel Meadow. Kirby provides some figures for a couple of the streets: "Prostitutes operated from 46 out of 54 houses in Angel Street and 58 out of 79 houses in Charter Street." Needless to say, sexual diseases were rife among both prostitutes and their clients. Prostitutes were also involved in crime, and often used by gangs to lure prospective customers to a lonely spot where they could be beaten and robbed.

The lodging houses that proliferated in Angel Meadow attracted "a mixture of vagabonds, wayfarers, workmen and harvestmen who arrived and departed like swallows, following the seasons. Tradesmen, labourers and hawkers also occupied rooms." But there were additionally better-educated men who had made a fateful slip that plunged them into the abyss that the Victorian middle-classes feared so much. A reporter who visited one lodging-house in Angel Meadow wrote: "In this very house are to be found broken down clergymen, demoralised doctors, shoeless solicitors, and penniless as well as briefless barristers." Once in the abyss it was frequently difficult to climb out of it. The name Angel Meadow stuck and no respectable person wanted to be associated with it.

Gangs were a feature of Angel Meadow, and a particular problem arose when "scuttlers" began to appear in the late 19th century. These were groups of young men and women who frequently wore distinctive dress, as described by Kirby: "Scuttlers wore tight-fitting punchers' caps, loose jackets and white, black or brightly coloured silk scarves. They also adopted the flared trousers known as `bells` or `narrow-go-wides` worn by sailors." And they had "narrow-tied, brass-tipped clogs and broad leather belts with brass buckles." Both clogs and belts were useful implements in a fight. Their girls had "distinctive uniforms of black and grey shawls, short skirts, pink stockings and clogs. They did their hair in a knot with a low fringe." They also used their clogs as weapons.

The scuttlers roamed their respective areas, looking for opponents to fight and sometimes they invaded enemy territory. One night "the police were called to Holland Street near Angel Meadow following reports that 600 `roughs` were taking part in a pitched battle with belts and knives." The first policemen to arrive on the scene were driven away and had to send for reinforcements. In the end they made just three arrests, and the officers had to force their way back to Goulden Street because the crowd was so hostile. If scuttlers were sent to prison they were greeted as heroes when they were released. The police did eventually reduce scuttler activity to a manageable level after middle-class people expressed concern at what they saw as an "epidemic" of violence among the young that was seemingly seeping into the city generally. And magistrates imposed stiffer sentences to deter others from indulging in scuttler activities.

The police battled endlessly to keep some sort of order in Angel Meadow and were often badly injured as they went about their duties. And there were others who, in different ways, attempted to turn people away from drink, crime, prostitution, and general loose living. Kirby mentions more than one churchman, both Catholic and Protestant, who was willing to go into Angel Meadow and make contact with the inhabitants of the hovels. The founders of the ragged schools struggled manfully to teach children to read and write. And in hard times, when unemployment rose, churches set up soup kitchens to give people at least some sort of minimum diet. There were few provisions for welfare of any kind, with only the dreaded workhouses offering relief. And they were a last resort and the homeless often preferred to sleep on the streets rather than be admitted to a workhouse. Kirby's descriptions of what it took to get into one, and the conditions inside, make for grim reading.

Looking at the levels of violence (vast and vicious) that Kirby writes about it strikes me how little reference there is to the use of guns. They were, after all, relatively easy to obtain, though the cost may have been a deterrent factor. One of the few occasions when they played a significant role in Kirby's account is when, in 1867, several Irishmen, Fenians as they were called, attempted to free some prisoners who had been suspected of plotting to attack public buildings in Manchester. These armed supporters of what was known as the Fenian Brotherhood attacked a police van and during the ensuing fighting shot and killed a police sergeant. The police then combed Irish areas of Manchester, including Angel Meadow, and arrested several suspects. Three were eventually sentenced to death for the murder of the policeman, and were hanged at "New Bailey Prison on the banks of the Irwell."

Thousands gathered to watch the hangings, though Kirby says that there were few Irish among the crowds. Their priests had instructed them to stay away. It was perhaps as well. One of the men died immediately he dropped, but the other two required "assistance" from the executioner, and one seems to have lingered for some time before finally dying. Later in 1867 there was a procession to honour what had become known as the Fenian Martyrs. For many years Irish Republicans have come to Manchester to take part in a ceremony commemorating the three men at the monument erected in their honour in the graveyard at St Joseph' Cemetery in Moston. I recall being in a pub in Manchester many years ago when, at afternoon closing time, the landlord locked the door but allowed a group of Irishmen to continue drinking. For some reason I seemed to have been overlooked when other customers left, so I carried on drinking, too. It turned out that they had been over for the ceremony.

After years of investigations by journalists, churchmen, health inspectors, and others, plans got under way to do something about cleaning up the mess that was Angel Meadow. But not without opposition from those with an interest in keeping things as they were. A Councillor Ashmore, who sympathised with the landlords of the cellars that were rented out, claimed that people were much more comfortable in cellars than they would be in garrets. And, as proof that cellar living was healthy, he claimed to have known people who lived until they were 90 in such conditions. And Alderman Boardman, chairman of the Sanitary Committee, was also a member of an organisation that opposed closure of the cellars. Kirby mentions that he "owned 20 cellars in Back Style Street, two in Style Street, and eight in old Mount Street." I don't know if among Boardman's cellars was the one described by Kirby: "Sanitary inspectors found one 18ft-long cellar beneath Ludgate Street where the ceiling was just 3ft 3in high which was home to 18 men, women and children."

Kirby's brief is Angel Meadow as it existed in Victorian times, so he doesn't do more than sketch in how it was gradually cleared in the 20th Century, and finally by a combination of housing improvement schemes in the 1930s and the Luftwaffe during the great air raid on Manchester in 1940. His account of the history of Angel Meadow, and its surrounding areas, is colourful and anecdotal as it works its readable way through the stories of poverty, violence, and the continual endeavours of priests, policemen, local politicians, sanitary inspectors, schoolteachers, and others, to tame the area. There are heroes and villains, and of course the thousands of ordinary people who passed through Angel Meadow, and in some cases survived to go on to better and certainly cleaner (in all its meanings) lives. Some of the tales that Kirby tells can break your heart unless you have a heart of stone, as I suspect some of those opposing reform had.

I'm reminded of the story that Engels told about meeting a Manchester businessman and speaking to him about all the problems in Angel Meadow and elsewhere. The man listened patiently until Engels had finished and then said, "And yet there is a great deal of money to be made here. Good day to you, sir." Academic historians will, I hope, forgive me if I haven't quite got the words right (I'm working from memory) but I believe the substance of what was said is there.

Angel Meadow: Victorian Britain's Most Savage Slum is a vigorous book and is recommended to anyone with an interest in social history. It isn't an academic work, and none the worse for it, but has a useful bibliography. And it's written in good, tight prose.

ANGEL MEADOW: VICTORIAN BRITAIN'S MOST SAVAGE SLUM
By Dean Kirby
Pen & Sword Books Ltd. 196 pages. £14.99. ISBN 978-1783-831-524

1919

My father, who was in the Royal Navy from 1913 to 1925, served on the battleship, HMS Valiant, at one point. I don't know if he was on board when she sailed up the River Mersey and, with two escorting destroyers, acted as a deterrent to those who were thought to have been planning some sort of revolutionary activity. There was certainly a great deal of what might best be termed social unrest in the city in 1919, but was it in any way revolutionary?

From a government point of view, and bearing in mind what was happening across Europe and elsewhere at the time, it must have seemed that the potential for revolution was there. Following the Bolshevik takeover in Russia in 1917, and the ending of the First World War in 1918, there were attempts at communist coups in Hungary and Finland, and abortive risings in Germany and elsewhere. Strikes and other forms of militancy affected France and Italy. Australia was almost brought to a standstill by a massive strike of miners and seamen. The United States was hit by a major steel strike in 1919, in which left-wingers played a prominent part, and a general strike in Seattle on the West Coast also saw radicals actively involved. The IWW (Industrial Workers of the World) had a slogan, "every strike is a small revolution and a dress rehearsal for the big one", which was more than likely to convince conservatives that a revolution was imminent. I've mentioned a few examples of what was happening in 1919, and it's worth referring to Anthony Read's *The World on Fire: 1919 and the Battle with Bolshevism* (Jonathan Cape, 2008) for a much broader picture.

In Britain the ending of the war with Germany had brought problems relating to the slow demobilisation of the hundreds of thousands of conscripts who were idling in camps in France and across the United Kingdom. They were, naturally enough, of the opinion that there was no reason for them to be there now that the fighting had stopped. But the authorities were worried that the release of hordes of young men, often with no immediate prospects of obtaining work, into communities already affected by unemployment as the demand for labour declined when wartime production slowed, could create a situation similar to that experienced after the ending of the Napoleonic Wars. Then, the ex-soldiers had created a community of "sturdy beggars" and more who might use their military experience if they linked up with radicals in the working-class.

There were other reasons for not wanting to quickly demobilise, and indeed to continue with conscription, and they had to do with the military activities that Britain was involved with in Ireland, India, Iraq, and Palestine, not to mention Russia. We had intervened, ostensibly to stop guns and other supplies we had provided to the Czar's army from falling into the hands of either side in the Russian Civil War, but actually to try to influence the defeat of the Bolsheviks. Troops rebelled when they thought they might be sent to Russia, and there were mutinies on Royal Navy ships when sailors were faced with the same prospect. Dockers in London refused to load arms and ammunition onto ships bound for Russia.

Simon Webb does a good job of providing a wide survey of the general situation in Britain with regard to discontent among soldiers who no longer wanted to be in the army. There were numerous demonstrations and riots, sometimes involving Canadian troops who were anxious to return to their own country. Other soldiers, who were less likely to disobey orders, were often turned out to deal with the rioters who were sometimes armed. Did the storming of police stations to free fellow-soldiers, who had been arrested for drunkenness and other minor matters, constitute revolutionary activity? Not in itself, but in a country where industrial conflict was also causing concern, there were worries that a combination of incidents could lead to a wider situation in which the police, and even the army, might lose overall control.

In Britain. where the police were traditionally unarmed, it had always been legitimate for local magistrates to call for assistance from the army if it was considered that the police were unable to deal with rioters. There were times in the 19th century when this happened, and before the First World War troops had been involved with suppressing rioting and strikes in Liverpool and South Wales. They had been forced to open fire in both locations, with deaths resulting on each occasion. In 1919, however, there were doubts about the reliability of certain regiments, especially if it was thought that the soldiers could be from the same areas as strikers and/or rioters, and might refuse to fire on crowds if ordered to do so. Other units were brought in from different parts of the country when the situation necessitated such a decision.

It has to be said that some of the incidents that Webb describes had little or nothing to do with any sort of radical aims, though they could be ascribed to the particular social problems that were prevalent in 1919. There were major race riots in various places, including Liverpool, Cardiff, and Glasgow. These arose because of the number of Chinese, Asian, and Caribbean seamen and other workers who had come to the country during the war to replace local men who had been conscripted. When the war ended, and discharged soldiers returned home, they found that there were few jobs available, and they turned on those who they perceived as being "outsiders". These riots were especially nasty, with properties which housed the outsiders set alight and people badly injured and, in a few cases, killed. Again, this wasn't revolutionary in intent, but it's easy to understand how it was thought that the anger displayed by the rioters could be turned by agitators into something more serious.

Another example of violent activity, this time probably caused by the stupidity and arrogance of local officials, occurred in Luton. The Mayor decided to hold a large banquet, paid for out of Council funds, to celebrate Peace Day and invited councillors and local friends, but not any ex-servicemen. As Webb puts it: "This was especially galling, because neither the Mayor nor a single member of the council in Luton had actually served in the armed forces. All had belonged to what were known as `reserved occupations', jobs which were thought too important for a man to be conscripted into the army". Webb also points out that some of the councillors had been involved in operating the Luton Corporation Food Control Committee and were suspected of having profited from food shortages. They were, in the words of Stanley Baldwin, "Hard faced men who looked as if they had done very well out of the war".

An organisation representing ex-servicemen decided to arrange an alternative event, but their request for permission to hold it on a local recreational ground was rejected by the Council. A march on the Town Hall was then planned, and it inevitably turned into a riot which the police were unable to contain. The Town Hall was burned down, shops looted, and the army eventually called in to prevent further disturbances. Troops remained in Luton for a week. Again, it was hardly revolutionary in intent, but it demonstrated how close the country was to a situation where it was thought subversive elements could step in and take over.

The main cause for concern was probably the threat from organised labour. Unions that represented miners, dockers, and railway workers were particularly strong, and the Triple Alliance, as it was called, had the potential to bring the country to its knees if they decided to take joint action. They did get close to it on more than one occasion, but backed away when faced with the fact that, as Lloyd George put it to union leaders, they might have to take over running the country if their actions succeeded. Most union officials, certainly at higher levels, were less interested in revolution than in improving the pay and conditions of their members, and some sort of compromise could usually be worked out with them. That was the case when railwaymen threatened strikes, with the additional possibility of invoking the Triple Alliance, on being told that a wartime bonus would be withdrawn, with a consequent reduction in their wages. Lloyd George arranged a deal which assured them that the bonus would continue for another twelve months while a review took place. It was a classic British solution.

While it was true that the Government could usually work with the established union leaders, who were mostly quite patriotic and keen to be a part of the establishment, they were less certain about the activists in the rank and file. Glasgow presented a major problem, and there had been strikes among shipyard workers and others. There had also been rent strikes, and the city was reputed to be a hotbed of dissidents and revolutionaries. The area was known as Red Clydeside and had its own firebrands, among them David Kirkwood, Willie Gallacher, and Manny Shinwell. All three had fought the police and seen the inside of local prisons, but in due course would come to terms with the establishment. Gallacher was at least a communist MP, one of the few ever elected to Parliament. But Kirkwood was, eventually, an MP, a Privy Councillor, and Baron Kirkwood of Bearsden. And Shinwell had a distinguished career as a Labour politician, becoming Secretary of State for War and then Minister of Defence. He later became Baron Shinwell.

Their later involvements aside, they all participated in the troubles that erupted in Glasgow in 1919, and which led to a strike committee almost running the city. In response, the Government sent tanks to Glasgow and brought in troops to patrol the streets. Machine gun posts were set up at strategic points and for a time a system approaching martial law was in operation. When what were considered the ringleaders of the strikes and protests were arrested, the official unions stepped in to take charge and negotiate a pay and hours deal, which is what most strikers were interested in, just as most rioting soldiers were in being demobbed or protesting about a specific grievance.

It's Webb's contention that, "For all the talk of revolution which made the government and the middle classes so uneasy that year, there was no credible and organised revolutionary movement in the country". Riots, strikes, and mutinies enabled people to express their anger and dissatisfaction with existing circumstances, but none of the incidents involved were connected in a systematic way. The army and the police remained largely loyal to the State, though a police strike did lead to some disturbances in Liverpool, the only place where a substantial number of policemen walked out.

It's interesting that so little is ever said about the events of 1919. The General Strike of 1926 does get some attention, though it can be argued that it probably presented less of a problem to the Government than did the widespread social turmoil of 1919. Simon Webb calculates that between thirty and forty people may have lost their lives due to rioting, striking, or other forms of behaviour that lay outside the normal framework of social activities. That was certainly far more than the number who died during the General Strike, which was, on the whole, a relatively peaceful affair.

1919: Britain's Year of Revolution is a lively book, tidily written and covering a wide area of activity in a brisk but informative way. It manages to convey the mood of the period, including the paranoias of Winston Churchill and some other members of the establishment, in an entertaining manner. And it tells how Churchill and certain people in the armed forces got close to treason by plotting the overthrow of the Prime Minister, Lloyd George. Churchill had expressed admiration for Mussolini's rise in Italy, and it makes one wonder what this country may have been like had his conspiracies succeeded.

1919: BRITAIN'S YEAR OF REVOLUTION
By Simon Webb
Pen and Sword History. 170 pages. £19.99. ISBN 978-1-47386-286-9

RUNNING COMMENTARY

Keeping a magazine alive for 65 years is something of an achievement, especially when the magazine in question is devoted to intellectual evaluations of political, literary, and cultural matters. Many publications of this kind often close down when they think they've achieved whatever purpose they had in mind when they started, or when the energy runs out, or someone of key importance to their existence dies or moves on to other things. The noted New York publication, *Partisan Review*, ceased operations in 2003 when falling sales, the death of William Phillips, and changes in the social, political and intellectual mood in America combined to remove its relevance. One report said that it had "become obsolete."

I've mentioned *Partisan Review* because one of its major rivals was *Commentary*, currently still alive and the subject of the book under review. And it's a book that could be seen as contentious in its claims that the Jewish left has been transformed into the neoconservative right. You only need to read *Dissent* or the *New York Review of Books* to realise that a large number of Jewish intellectuals continue to adopt a liberal position on social and political matters.

But let me go back to the beginning. The American Jewish Committee in 1945 asked Elliott Cohen to edit their new monthly magazine, *Commentary*, which they envisaged as "a journal of significant thought and opinion on Jewish affairs and contemporary issues." Cohen had a good track record as editor of an earlier publication, *Menorah Journal*, and jumped at the opportunity to be in control of a magazine that he could shape to his liking. The only snag was that he "edited his authors exactingly, even intrusively, even if they happened to be Thomas Mann or John Dewey." Cohen himself was a blocked writer who fulfilled his needs by rewriting other peoplc's work. Not everyone reacted kindly to this and Balint quotes the art critic Harold Rosenberg as saying, "Listen Elliott, if you want to write, write under your own name".

Still, there's no doubt about the fact that, in its early days, *Commentary* was responsible for publishing some brilliant writing. And Cohen's staff included some talented young Jewish intellectuals who brought their own ideas to the magazine and helped shape its contents. Clement Greenberg, then just starting to make his name as an art critic, was one of them, and another was Robert Warshow, an early advocate of paying serious attention to aspects of popular culture. It's worth noting that, at this stage, contributors to *Commentary* also wrote for *Partisan Review* on a fairly regular basis.

Elliott Cohen, like many other Jewish New York intellectuals had been attracted to communism in the 1930s, with Trotskyism being of particular interest, but he later turned against it and closely inspected contributions to *Commentary* for anything that might be seen as soft on communists. He rejected Robert Warshow's essay on Charlie Chaplin because the famous film-star was "a fellow-traveller of Stalin." Warshow then gave it to *Partisan Review* where it was published and praised. As the Cold War developed *Commentary* frequently ran articles critical of Russia and its actions. By the early-1950s, with Senator McCarthy on the prowl and fear and suspicion rife in American society, there were attacks on liberal intellectuals because they seemed to be too sympathetic towards left-wingers who had fallen foul of blacklists and purges. Irving Kristol thought that the rise of McCarthyism was due to liberals not taking a firm enough anti-communist position. McCarthy may have been a "vulgar demagogue," but everyone knew where he stood in relation to communism, whereas the public were confused about whether or not many liberals were sincerely opposed to it.

To be fair to Cohen he did always aim for a high intellectual content in *Commentary* and its writers were prepared to say that they didn't care for the kind of populist anti-communism that McCarthy represented. But other New York intellectuals thought that the magazine seemed increasingly to be trying to persuade them to fall in with the status quo and not question it too closely. This was particularly seen as a problem for Jews because of their desire to be assimilated into the wider American society. The anti-semitism that had previously stopped many Jewish intellectuals from obtaining positions in universities was breaking down, and while this was obviously a good thing some writers worried that it might lead to conformity. Sociologist David Riesman asked, "Were not intellectuals of more use to this country when they had less use for it?" And Irving Howe was so disturbed by what was happening that he started *Dissent*, which by its very name indicated where it wanted to be in relation to the general situation in America. So far I've looked mostly at the political aspects of *Commentary*, and the magazine also printed literary criticism, fiction, and poetry, though when Norman Podhoretz took over as editor he upset poets by saying that he would edit their work as rigorously as he edited that of prose writers. Saul Bellow, Bernard Malamud, Philip Roth, Nelson Algren, and Delmore Schwartz all published fiction in *Commentary*, though Balint doesn't delve too deeply into their work. One novel that does receive some attention, though none of it appeared in the magazine, is Isaac Rosenfeld's *Passage From Home*. It was reviewed by Irving Howe, who praised it, and Daniel Bell described it as "a parable of alienation." The alienation factor was something .that intrigued American Jewish writers and intellectuals because of the discrimination that they often experienced and their consequent sense of apartness from the concerns of many other Americans. As noted above, this was changing but was still evident when Rosenfeld's book was published in 1946. It could be argued that Rosenfeld was something of a special case in that he made a point of rejecting attempts to absorb him into bourgeois society. He thought of the Jewish writer as "a specialist in alienation" and lived a life that could best be described as bohemian. Attitudes were altering, however, as opportunities for advancement opened up for Jews. In time the noted critic Leslie Fiedler could say, "if the system has been this good to us, it can't be as bad as we thought it was."

Elliott Cohen committed suicide in 1959 and control of *Commentary* passed to Norman Podhoretz who was astute enough to see that its previous obsession with communism was largely irrelevant as the paranoia of the Fifties declined. The times were changing and Podhoretz began to publish critical pieces about race, poverty, welfare, the developing Vietnam War, and brought in writers like Paul Goodman, Alfred Kazin, Dwight MacDonald, and Staughton Lynd to open up dialogues about these and other matters. Podhoretz could be seen as someone who wasn't afraid to admit that he was desperate to succeed in the New York intellectual hot-house. His book, *Making It*, unashamedly acknowledged that he wanted to be respected and to make a place for himself among people he admired (he was born in 1930 so was younger than them and hadn't been involved in the political turbulence of the 1930s). *Making It* wasn't liked by established figures such as Lionel and Diana Trilling, who considered it "crudely boastful," and one of Podhoretz's friends even thought he was going insane and ought to be committed. Podhoretz was intellectually tough enough to ride the storm and *Making It* is still worth reading for its account of a man scrambling up the ladder of success and for its picture of the New York intellectual scene of the 50s and 60s.

What had appeared to be a swing towards the left didn't last too long and the magazine soon began to react against what it saw as the excesses of the 60s. Podhoretz had, perhaps, shown his innate conservatism some years earlier when he wrote a piece for *Partisan Review* called "The Know-Nothing Bohemians" which was a savage attack on the Beats. And the rise of Black Power, feminism, gay rights, and the activities of the New Left, came under attack. In a way it's easy to see what bothered Podhoretz and his supporters. They weren't the only ones suspicious of many of the motives and actions of student activists and others. Their anti intellectualism was hard to take if you were used to the intellectual rigour of *Partisan Review* and *Commentary*, or indeed to any kind of literary or intellectual experience that demanded more than a passing glance at slogans and crude gestures. Balint rightly points out that, "unlike the 1930s, the 1960s did not produce much in the way of a body of radical literature."

This reaction may have had its virtues but it was only the start of an increasingly right-wing swing that included, among other things, almost-hysterical outbursts against gays, support for Ronald Reagan, a militant pro-Israel policy, enthusiasm for the invasion of Iraq, and much more of that nature. I'm not suggesting that such topics shouldn't be discussed in an intellectual magazine, but as even Balint (who worked for a time at *Commentary*) admits, the tone was often too shrill and there was a tendency to dismiss anyone with a different opinion as either misguided or motivated by a hatred of America. It's little wonder that, as the magazine became a mouthpiece for neoconservatives many of its one-time contributors drifted or were driven away. George Steiner was of the opinion that his work was ignored by *Commentary* because of his "doubts about Vietnam and my deepening fear about the development of Israel's policies and society." And Irving Howe said, "I contributed to *Commentary* when it was the natural voice of liberal Jewish debate."

Balint points out that, along with its right-wing politics, its coverage of the arts declined. Podhoretz had denounced "critics of the Left to whom art was a weapon, and who acclaimed or condemned novels for their positions on political and ideological matters," but he adds that "Podhoretz's own literary judgements - and by extension, the magazine's - had become ever more ideological." And he "began to see every product of the mind as something that reflected a political allegiance." Podhoretz, though, had achieved his ambition of "Making It" and in 2000, when George W.Bush was elected President, he wrote in enthusiastic terms about the dawn of a new day in American politics. His support for Bush didn't go unnoticed and in 2004 he was given the Presidential Medal of Honour, the nation's highest civilian award. For someone born in a poor part of Brooklyn to East European working-class Jewish parents it really must have seemed that he had made it.

I noted near the start of this review that the sub-title for this book is misleading, and Balint more or less admits it when he remarks that "from Franklin Roosevelt, who garnered 90 percent of the Jewish vote in 1940 to Barack Obama, who got 78 percent in 2008, Jews remained the most consistently liberal group in the country." And he goes on to say that the neoconservatives clustered around *Commentary* have never been able to come to terms with the fact that their fellow Jews can't or don't want to see that, according to the neoconservatives, they're not acting in their own self-interest. Perhaps they don't think that self-interest is the only reason for deciding which way to vote.

This is an informative book, tidily written and well-documented, and it adds to our knowledge of the New York intellectual scene.

RUNNING COMMENTARY: THE CONTENTIOUS MAGAZINE THAT TRANSFORMED THE JEWISH LEFT INTO THE NEOCONSERVATIVE RIGHT by Benjamin Balint.

Public Affairs. 290 pages. $26.95. ISBN 978 1 58648 749 2
Distributed in the U.K. by The Perseus Books Group.

PENGUIN PARADE

Anyone interested in little magazines, or in literature during the 1940s in Britain, will no doubt have come across copies of *Penguin New Writing* which ran for forty issues between 1940 and 1950. It published many well-known writers, along with new ones, some of whom went on to establish themselves in the literary world, and others who later disappeared from sight. I don't intend to start listing names from either category. My intention is to look at another publication from Penguin Books which, in my experience, is rarely mentioned when 1940s magazines are discussed. And that's a pity because, though not distinguishing itself with the poetry it featured, and not having illustrators of the calibre that John Lehman attracted to *Penguin New Writing*, it did spotlight some good short stories.

Penguin Parade was in existence before its now more-famous partner made an appearance. The first issue came out in November, 1937, and seems to have been popular enough to be reprinted in February of the following year. Edited by Denys Kilham Roberts, it aimed to be published at "(roughly) quarterly and later, possibly, at monthly intervals". It was, perhaps, an ambitious programme to follow, especially considering the still-shaky economic circumstances in Britain, and the uneasy political situation in Europe.

It's impossible, in a short survey like this, to point to all the contributors in each issue of *Penguin Parade*, so the ones I do mention are only a sample of those in its pages. Some of the writers are still remembered, while some may not cause any heads to nod in acknowledgement of their continued popularity. I'm not sure how many people will now recognise the name of James Stern, but in his day, which was probably the 1930s and 1940s, he was considered a first-rate writer of short stories. The initial issue of *Penguin Parade* featured his "The Man from Montparnasse", a well-written and amusing account of an encounter with a restless bohemian artist who spends more time drinking and talking about what he's going to do than actually doing it.

Another writer who may be little read today, though he achieved some notoriety in his lifetime, was James Hanley, whose novel, *Boy*, ran into censorship problems when it was published in a cheap edition in 1934. Its account of life at sea, which Hanley had experienced, got a little too near reality when it hinted at homosexuality. His story in *Penguin Parade* also had a sea-faring angle, with a sailor fighting to survive when he's flung into the water as his ship founders.

Sherwood Anderson, H.E. Bates, I.A.R. Wylie, and Herbert Read are all names that might be known to at least some contemporary readers, though I have to admit that I knew nothing about I.A.R. Wylie before coming across her name when writing this article. But she had an impressive list of publications, and some notes say that "Much of her work has been filmed by the leading American companies".

Stella Gibbons, who wrote *Cold Comfort Farm,* is still remembered, but what of Raymond Watkinson who, like Gibbons, was published in issue 3? He was born in Flixton, Manchester, and attended the Manchester School of Art, though he said that he was always more interested in poetry. I'm not convinced, on the evidence of the poem in *Penguin Parade*, that he had any great originality as a poet. Did he publish much poetry elsewhere? The biographical details mention that he was "left" in his politics and in 1937 was "engaged as an Art Teacher in an Elementary School near Manchester".

There are names that are listed in the contents (I'm skipping around various issues now), and attracted my attention when I first came across issues of the magazine. Joseph Vogel was an American writer, and I knew of him because of a novel, *Man's Courage*, that I'd read, and which is sometimes mentioned in books about radical writing in the United States in the 1930s. His story in *Penguin Parade* concerned an immigrant family from Poland attempting to make a success of things in America, but often meeting mishaps as the father stumbles in and out of failed business ventures.

Matters relating to the publishing schedule appeared to be running reasonably smoothly, and issues 4 and 5 appeared in 1938 and early 1939, and both went into later reprints. Leslie Halward was in issue 4. He had already been published in numerous prestigious magazines, and his collection of short stories, *To Tea on Sunday,* had been praised by critics. Does anyone read him now? The same can perhaps be said of Gerald Kersh, though some of his work has been reprinted in recent years. His "The Extraordinarily Horrible Dummy" in issue 6 was a briskly-told tale of a ventriloquist whose dummy takes over. As the man says as his mental state declines, "It isn't I who makes Micky talk. Micky makes me talk". Kersh wrote some excellent stories. I was lucky enough to come across several of his books in a charity shop recently. I got them for next-to-nothing (they were showing their age) and enjoyed most of what I read.

It's worth mentioning that also in issue 6 (1939) was a story by Martha Dodd, the daughter of the American Ambassador in Berlin in the 1930s. It was later shown that she had been spying for the Russians, obtaining information from a Nazi official she had been sleeping with while also having an affair with a Soviet agent. She had additionally passed on details from documents she had access to in the American Embassy. She was tracked by the FBI in the late-1940s and early-1950s and fled behind the Iron Curtain. Her illegal activities apart, she wrote a couple of novels, one of them, *Sowing the Wind,* about the coming to power of the Fascists in Germany in the 1930s, and a number of short stories. (See my "The Strange Case of Martha Dodd" in *Brits, Beats & Outsiders,* Penniless Press, 2012, for further information).

It's obvious that the start of the Second World War in September, 1939, had an effect on publishing, and only five more issues appeared on an annual basis, with none in 1944, between 1940 and 1945. It's interesting to speculate on the reason(s) for this. Paper rationing was introduced during the war, and *Penguin New Writing* was launched in 1940, so was there a decision to use resources for it and restrict publication of *Penguin Parade*? Denys Kilham Roberts continued as editor, so it doesn't seem to have been a case of him being summoned for service in the armed forces. Or maybe he was, but could still find time to edit the occasional issues of the magazine? A replacement editor could easily have been found, anyway. And sufficient material to fill both publications wasn't likely to be a problem. Little magazines of one kind or another flourished in the war years, despite the paper shortages and other problems. And it was a democratic period in terms of the number and range of people who wanted to express themselves in print.

It's indicative of the wartime conditions that names began to crop up that might not have done otherwise. The American novelist and short-story writer, Irwin Shaw, was in issues 8 (1941) and 9 (1942). Shaw was a war correspondent, so was possibly in London for a time. His "Weep in Years to Come" (issue 8) evoked the somewhat desperate gaiety of a young couple in New York on the eve of American involvement in the Second World War. Shaw was a first-rate writer of short-stories, and his "The Girls in Their Summer Dresses" is still anthologised. He also wrote a successful war novel, *The Young Lions*, though it probably hasn't survived as well as Second World War books by his contemporaries, Norman Mailer and James Jones.

Appearing alongside Shaw's contribution in issue 8 was a story by Ralph Bates who had served with the International Brigades during the Spanish Civil War. He wrote novels like *The Lean Men* and *The Olive Field* about life in Spain prior to the Civil War, and later about the war itself in his short-story collection, *The Miraculous Horde*. Bates was never a communist, though he co-operated with them until some of his views became unacceptable to the Party, and he decided it was safer not to return to Spain after he'd left to go on a speaking tour to drum up support for the Republicans.

In connection with Spain, issue 7 (1940) had a story by Arturo Barea set in Madrid during the war. Barea had worked for the Republican Government and escaped to England when Franco took over. His trilogy, *The Forge, The Track, The Clash*, is a classic account of his experiences growing up in poverty, soldiering with the Spanish Army in Morocco, and his activities during the Civil War.

The Yorkshire-born writer, Eric Knight, had stories in issues 9 (1942) and 10 (1943) which focused on where he came from, though he had moved to the United States with his family when he was a boy. He worked at various jobs, wrote several novels and short-stories, and spent time in Hollywood as editor of a film magazine and as a screenwriter. He's probably best remembered now as the author, under the name of Richard Hallas, of what is often referred to as a classic crime novel, *You Play the Black and the Red Comes Up*.

There wasn't any indication in issue 11 (1945) that it was the final issue in the first series of *Penguin Parade*. Denys Kilham Roberts was still around (he died in 1976) and active as an editor and writer generally. Without access to the Penguin archives, it's impossible to know why a decision was made to discontinue the magazine. Times were still tough for publishers in terms of obtaining paper and other materials, and there does seem to have been a decline in interest in little magazines once the war ended and both soldiers and civilians had to face up to the domestic demands and austerities of life in post-war Britain. By 1950 *Penguin New Writing, Horizon*, and many other publications had closed down, and the rest were on the brink of doing so in the next couple of years.

An attempt was made to revive *Penguin Parade* in 1947 when a second series was launched under the editorship of J.E. Morpurgo. Three issues appeared in 1947 and 1948, but the approach was different, as was made evident in the Foreword to the first issue: "Whereas the first series was devoted principally to the short story, to poetry, and to reportage, the second series will emphasise critical and informative writing". Morpurgo did also say that the "work of contemporary 'creative' artists obviously demands inclusion in any periodical that purports to reflect some aspects of life to-day", so some work by poets and fiction writers would appear, though "short stories of quality are very rare indeed", and "reportage, the utility furniture of war-time, has lost much of its freshness and usefulness". Morpurgo eventually became a professor at Leeds University, and his academic inclinations may have been in evidence in his comments.

I suppose it might be said that the idea was to give *Penguin Parade* a more intellectual base. And was that comment about the lack of "short stories of quality" a dig at the contents of the earlier series? It may have been true that there was a leaning towards stories that could be read quickly and easily while on guard duty, or fire watch, or in the breaks between shifts in a factory. But, looking at a few of the titles of essays that were in the three issues that Morpurgo edited, we see "Criticism and Reviewage", "Literature and the Libretto: An Uneasy Friendship", "The Psychological Aspect of Strikes", "War and the Writer", and "An English Successor to Van Dyck". It's not being insulting to the readers of those earlier issues of *Penguin Parade* to suggest that they wouldn't have wanted to sit down to read material like that when they were tired and hungry and wondering when and where the next bomb might fall. It's difficult to imagine what sort of readership Morpurgo had in mind for the revived *Penguin Parade*.

It's a personal intrusion, but when I read the essay on "Criticism and Reviewage" I came across the following observation: "Between criticism and reviewing it is possible to make a distinction. One difference is that reviews have to be readable". As a reviewer for many years, and having struggled to keep my eyes on the page while reading a lot of contemporary academic criticism, I tend to agree with that statement.

I'm not suggesting that any of the pieces in the "new" *Penguin Parade* were bad in themselves, and some of the essays aroused my interest, including one on the revolutionary, Auguste Blanqui, and another on jazz, though the latter gave no sign of its writer knowing anything about the music beyond its early origins. He probably didn't think that what came after the music he described had any real connection to jazz. Puritanism was often a characteristic of much writing about the music. The point I'm making is that the new series was directed at a different audience to the readers that, on the whole, most likely bought the first one. Whatever the aim, it clearly failed and *Penguin Parade* died permanently in 1948. I suspect that sales simply hadn't justified its continuation.

Out of necessity I had to be selective when mentioning specific writers and their stories in the first series. Space wouldn't have permitted me to refer to them all. As with any magazine of its period, a lot of the writers never established major or lasting reputations, though it is interesting to read the notes on contributors and see how many of them had published books, as well as work in a wide variety of publications. Or how others were relatively new to publishing (have you heard of E.C. Harris, Mary Milne, Thomas S. Faulks, Nina Gifford, Audrey Burton, Elisabeth Cluer, Edgar Howard, and Sidney Young?). I'm always fascinated by the names I come across and wonder what happened to the people concerned. Most writers eventually slip from view. They may have only written, or had published, a story or two, but they made a contribution to literature, no matter how minor.

HANK WILLIAMS

Between 1954 and 1957 I was serving as a soldier with the British Army in Germany. I used to tune my radio to AFN (the American Forces Network) in preference to the dull programmes broadcast by the BFN (British Forces Network). AFN had more jazz, and it also had quite a lot of country music of one sort or another. There were plenty of Southerners in the American forces stationed in Europe.

It was while listening to AFN that I grew to enjoy country music, something that most of my fellow jazz enthusiasts disapproved of. But the records I heard were to my liking. Hank Snow's lovely "The Garden of Roses (It's You, Only You that I Love)", and his "A Fool Such as I"; Hank Locklin's, "Send Me the Pillow (that You Dream on)"; Hank Thompson's "The Wild Side of Life"; Hank Penny's witty "Bloodshot Eyes". There seemed to be a lot of Hanks around, and most of all, I was always aroused by anything featuring Hank Williams. The others were usually entertaining, but Williams had a raw edge to his singing that seemed to go beyond the sentimental or amusing. There was an intensity missing in the work of the rest of them. The irony was that, by the time I was getting to appreciate Hank Williams, he was already dead, a casualty of the fast and hard living that success brought.

Williams was born in 1923 into a poor family in Alabama, living in a town that was largely a centre for "farmers, cotton pickers, migrant workers, loggers". His parents were well-mannered, church-going Baptists, with his mother the dominant person in the family, something that had a significant impact on his later life. Mark Ribowsky says that Williams was "brought up believing that he was white trash", though his mother always had aspirations towards respectability. But as Williams himself said when commenting on his singing: "To sing like a hillbilly, you had to have lived like a hillbilly. You had to have smelt a lot of mule manure".

Williams was probably exaggerating when he seemed to be suggesting that he had "smelt a lot of mule manure". It's more than probable that he had little experience of hard, physical work. Ribowsky says that Williams suffered from back problems from an early age. They weren't properly diagnosed then, and it was only much later that he was shown to have a form of spina bifida. It's likely that the pain he constantly experienced was, in part at least, the cause of his heavy drinking and recourse to addictive pain-killers as he got older. It was the more easily-available alcohol that came first and he was drinking from an early age and probably an alcoholic before he was twenty.

He was introduced to black music by a local store-owner, and he picked up guitar lessons from an itinerant black musician called "Tee Tot" (real name, Rufus Payne) who, ironically, would have liked to have played hillbilly music ("white man's blues") but had to work the streets to scrounge loose change. Williams was also hearing gospel music, country singers like Jimmy Rodgers, and the more-commercial sounds of cowboy singers like Roy Rogers and Gene Autry who appeared in Hollywood films. I saw many of their less-than-wonderful performances in the local cinemas of the industrial town I grew up in during the 1940s, and can't honestly say I was all that impressed by either Rogers or Autry. Perhaps I was waiting for something better to come along, as it did in Germany?

Williams never was a good student and soon dropped out of school. He was working with local musicians in his mid-teens, touring with a rodeo show, appearing on local radio, and playing in some rough places, usually referred to as honky-tonk joints. And drinking hard and beginning to gain something of a reputation as a ladies man : "One of the reasons he got into so many fights in the honky-tonks was that when a sweet thing came waltzing though the door, Hank disregarded the man whose arm she was on". His mother admitted to "being a little jealous at times," when she heard about his womanising, and that comment may have caused a few raised eyebrows. And she went on to say that she was always Hank's "first girl, and he never forgot it".

His mother, Lillie, certainly tried to control him, and he had to hand over any money he earned, and in return she would give him a small allowance. Things began to change when, in 1943, he met Audrey May Sheppard Guy, "a tall, striking, and married woman and mom, with curly blonde hair, high cheekbones, and an aquiline nose". Williams fell for her in a big way, and she began to exert an influence on his life and songs. She had ambitions to be a singer herself, but her talents were limited, and Audrey and Hank's insistence on her being allowed on stage to perform with him led to dissension among his backing musicians. But there's no doubt that much of his inspiration for composing music was due to his feelings about her : "At any given moment, he loved or hated Audrey Sheppard, but that mix of bravado and fear would be at the crux of almost every song he would write and sing from now on".

Needless to say, there was always friction between Williams' mother and his wife, as Audrey (another dominant personality) soon became, though there were always doubts about whether or not the marriage was legal. She had filed divorce papers, but the couple jumped the gun and got married before the divorce was properly finalised. It would come back to affect Williams' future actions, and even the legal tussles after his death. Various parties laid claims to different parts of the Williams' estate, including royalties from the sales of his records and sheet music. Williams married more than once, and fathered children with several women. Ribowsky provides full details, should anyone be interested. They're probably among the more sensational aspects of the singer's story.

In between his drinking and womanising, Williams attempted to further his musical interests, despite being his own worst enemy. He antagonised his fellow-musicians, turned up late for engagements, sometimes even missed them altogether, and when he was there, no-one could guarantee that he'd be sober enough to perform. Fred Rose became his manager and promoter, as well as occasionally assisting with the composition of songs. Ribowsky thinks that Rose and Frank Walker, President of MGM Reords, "found all sorts of ways to stiff him on `expenses' and deductions for studio time and records that were returned by store owners. Even though Hank would clear almost $20,000 more in royalties in 1950, he likely never made nearly what he was owed".

For Williams, the money he did get allowed him to live it up, but his drinking was out of control, and he had additionally taken to using drugs, including morphine, to deaden the pain he increasingly experienced from his back. A curious character named Doctor Horace Rapol "Toby" Marshall, had appeared on the scene, and could be relied on to supply Williams with a steady flow of drugs, of one kind or another. It later transpired that Marshall had no medical qualifications.

Williams had achieved his ambition of appearing on the Grand Ole Opry show, though he soon caused the people in charge to stop hiring him because of his unpredictable behaviour. Some musicians withdrew their service after experiencing his unreliability. Others would jump at the chance to work with him, at least until they realised what a chore it could be and how many jobs they lost when managers of clubs and theatres refused to employ Williams. He threw away an opportunity to go to Hollywood to appear in a film. There is a story that Williams, ill and certainly only too aware that his reputation was in ruins, walked on stage at one gig, looked at the audience and said, "Ya'll paid to see ole Hank, didn't ya? Well, you seen him", and walked off. Promoters lost thousands of dollars when he did things like that.

With Williams increasingly suffering, the end came on New Year's Day, 1953. He was being driven to an engagement in Canton, West Virginia, and was drinking, as usual, and picking up whatever drugs were available. There were problems because of the inclement weather conditions, and stops had to be made for food and other reasons. At one of them, Williams, lying in the back seat, was checked and found to be dead. It wasn't that simple, though, and some witnesses said they'd seen him outside the car, and even inside the roadside diner where it was parked. Williams might have been amused by the chaos that ensued as much when he was dead as when he was alive.

I've already referred to the bitter disputes that occurred when his estate came up for grabs, so won't waste any time discussing the details. What is more important is the music he left behind. There are a large number of recordings, some of which are admittedly more interesting than others. I recall (and after over sixty years my memory may be faulty) that among the records I heard in Germany were "Your Cheatin' Heart", "Half as Much", "Cold, Cold Heart", and "I Can't Help it (if I'm still in Love with You)". These were very much the songs that Williams either wrote or at least used to express his feelings about Audrey. Even after she divorced him, he still continued to hope that somehow they'd get back together again. And she, perhaps, never completely terminated their relationship, even though she knew that his drinking and womanising would always be there. His recording of "Ramblin' Man" could well have been his signature tune. He was simply too far gone to settle down, and they would always fight.

It could be that the songs I've referred to were heard more due to a couple of them having been picked up and moved out of the country scene and into the wider pop music world. Tony Bennett had a hit with "Cold, Cold Heart", and Rosemary Clooney with "Half as Much". There were other transfers from country into pop, with Jo Stafford recording "Jambalaya", and Frankie Laine "Hey, Good Lookin' (Something for the Boys"). The point I'm making is that, leaving aside the question of royalties payable when Williams was the composer ("Half as Much", wasn't one of his), he would have benefited from the extra exposure to his music that other artists' recordings could lead to.

Songs such as "Jambalaya", "Setting the Woods on Fire", "Kaw-liga", "Hey, Good Lookin", "Move it on Over", "Honky Tonkin", and others like them, indicated that Williams wasn't just a writer and singer of sad songs of unrequited love and unfaithful women. Touring honky-tonks around the southern states had taught him that people liked to have a good time, and hard-driving music was one way to ensure they did. It's easy to see the origins of what was known as "rockabilly", the combination of country and early rock-and-roll, in some of Williams' recordings.

There are other aspects of his music worth exploring, such as the sounds of the gospel music he'd heard as a child. "I Saw the Light" is probably the best-known example of Williams' religious recordings, if I can call them that, but he recorded many more, including some with Audrey. Despite all his transgressive behaviour, the drinking, fornicating, swearing, and violence, he couldn't shake off the religious influence, and in his own idiosyncratic way, he was a believer.

Hank takes an exhaustive look at the singer's life and music. Some might say that it's also exhausting in the way it piles up the details of marital battles (often of a physical as well as verbal nature), irresponsible behaviour in terms of missed engagements and lost opportunities, endless drinking, financial irregularities, numerous women, forgotten children, and the curious relationships that Williams had with his mother and Audrey. They were both dominant women and he seemed to need them. It's all very interesting, but I have to say that, in the end, I go back to the music. For all his failings as a man, Hank Williams created something that has lasted.

HANK : THE SHORT LIFE AND LONG COUNTRY ROAD OF HANK WILLIAMS

By Mark Ribowsky

Liveright Publishing. 472 pages. £22.99/$29.95. ISBN 978-1-63149-157-3

DEPRESSION FOLK

"Surprisingly, the Depression was also the scene of a great cultural spectacle against the unlikely backdrop of economic misery. The crisis kindled America's social imagination, firing enormous interest in how ordinary people lived, how they suffered, interacted, took pleasure in one another, and endured".

Ronald D. Cohen uses that quote from Morris Dickstein's *Dancing in the Dark: A Cultural History of the Great Depression* (Norton, 2009) on the first page of his book, and it seems to me apt to use it in my review. Dickstein's words really do point to what was almost an outpouring of literature, both poetry and prose, theatre, music, art, and much more. Even Hollywood was affected and some would suggest that the 1930s were years when it passed through one of its "golden ages".

Cohen's emphasis is on music, and particularly the area of it that is usually referred to as "folk music". And it's useful to cite his definition of what he includes when he talks about folk: "My story is rooted in a broad definition of folk music, including hillbilly (country) songs, rural blues, spirituals, cowboy songs, western swing, ethnic music and performers, singer-songwriters, labour songsters, and various others".

It's a wide range of music that Cohen covers, and some might raise an eyebrow at the inclusion of, for example, western swing, which had commercial potential. Bob Wills and his Texas Playboys were very popular in their day, and so was Spade Cooley. But there must have been many other bands playing a similar sort of music, often on a local basis, and presumably drawing on traditional sources for at least some of their basic material. With this in mind, it's only fair to accept Cohen's definition as a reasonable one.

Even if a singer or group achieved some wider recognition, their music usually had a basis in the local and what might loosely be termed the folk style. They often simply refined it to appeal to a wider audience. That was what happened with the Weavers, whose recordings of folk-like songs such as "Goodnight, Irene", "Old Paint", "Kisses Sweeter Than Wine", and "On Top of Old Smoky", were popular around 1950, at least until they were blacklisted. They had previously, though not under the name of the Weavers, used material which indicated their left-wing inclinations, and it caught up with them when Senator McCarthy and others began their investigations of supposed subversives.

Cohen refers to "labour songsters", and it needs to be noted that they are only a small part of what he deals with, though the sub-title of his book may tend to suggest otherwise. But the point he is making is that the research and recording that took place in the 1930s was sometimes done by enthusiasts who did have specific political links: "There were a few significant individuals, such as Charles and Pete Seeger and John and Alan Lomax, perhaps with connections to the Communist Party (CP) or its affiliates, but the large number of folklorists and musicians had no overt political agenda".

And even the people he names did not aim to document only radical or protest songs, which were probably in relatively short supply, anyway. Songs were sometimes produced in response to a particular event, such as a strike, but were often virtually forgotten when the strike ended. Cohen mentions Ella May Wiggins, who wrote songs when she was one of the Gastonia mill strikers in North Carolina in 1929, but they were fairly basic compositions and used well-known melodies. They were never recorded and mostly not relevant outside their immediate context. A recent book, *Martyr of Loray Mill* by Kristina Horton (McFarland, 2015), prints a few of Ella May's songs, one of the best-known of which was "Mill Mother's Lament", the music for which was taken from an earlier ballad, "Little Mary Phagan" :

> We leave our homes in the morning,
> We kiss our children goodbye
> While we slave for the bosses
> Our children scream and cry.

We don't know how this sounded when performed by Ella May because, as noted earlier, she didn't make any recordings, and she was, in fact, killed when vigilantes ambushed a truck taking her and other strikers to a union meeting.

How many working-class people, beyond the immediate audience that Ella May sang to, heard songs like this, or even read the texts when they were printed in left-wing magazines and newspapers, is debatable. It's more than likely that the reading audience could have been restricted to a small number of working-class radicals, often involved with the CP, and middle-class intellectual supporters of the party in cities like New York and Chicago. Cohen is right to point out that commercialised "protest" songs like "Brother, Can You Spare a Dime," or "Remember My Forgotten Man," powerfully performed at the conclusion of the Hollywood film, *Gold Diggers of 1933*, reached a bigger number of people and had a greater impact.

Roosevelt's ascendancy to the role of President brought action to counter the effects of the Depression. Various organisations were set up to provide employment for writers, painters, and many others in the general field of the arts. But there doesn't appear to have been any substantial support for the kind of music defined as folk by Cohen. That may have been because, on the surface, at least, much of it appeared to have commercial potential and its practitioners could therefore stand a chance of earning some money by playing it. It should have been obvious that many of those who sang folk songs for their own pleasure, or to entertain friends and neighbours, would never make a living doing so.

But their voices could be recorded, and the words of their songs transcribed. It would involve extensive travelling, and a dedication to the task in hand, to ensure that a documentary record was established before the often elderly performers died off and their songs were forgotten. The advent of radio in the 1920s, and the wide distribution of phonograph records, meant that even the most out-of-the-way communities could be in touch with the latest fashions in music. Alan Lomax said: "Commercial music via the radio, the movies and the slot phonograph is usurping the place of traditional and home-made music".

Alan Lomax, and his father John, were among the most dedicated of musicologists who took their frequently-cumbersome recording equipment into places like Kentucky and West Virginia, to track down versions of songs that had their origins in the British Isles and had survived due to the isolated nature of individuals and small communities in the Appalachians. They luckily had some backing from the Library of Congress, though they also faced opposition from conservative elements among both Republican and Southern Democrat politicians. The Lomaxes always had to tread carefully in terms of not appearing to favour songs with in-depth political content, or allowing their own political sympathies to become obvious. Alan Lomax, in particular, became a person of interest to the authorities, and Cohen says that the FBI eventually had a substantial file on him.

It is a fact that the Communist Party did take an interest in certain aspects of "grassroots music," especially if they seemed to have elements of "protest" about them. Black musicians and singers could be seen as representing their race at a time when the party was anxious to make an impression among black communities. It's unlikely that they ever did on any kind of mass scale, and performers like Josh White and Lead Belly probably appealed more to white left-wingers in New York and other major metropolitan areas. I would guess that blacks in general listened to blues singers who weren't making obvious political points, or to bands like those led by Count Basie, Duke Ellington, and others who attracted large audiences to the Savoy Ballroom in Harlem.

The same opportunism could be seen at work in the party's interest in white artists, though there seems to have been a degree of snobbishness evident, with the kind of spontaneous, and sometimes sentimental strike songs that someone like Ella May Wiggins wrote, looked down on. But then, most of the white working-class, when they listened to music, preferred country sounds, or, if they lived in large urban districts, the popular music they could hear on the radio or records. Swing was the music that accompanied the sit-in strikes of the 1930s.

In William Herrick's *Jumping the Line: The Adventures and Misadventures of an American Radical* (University of Wisconsin Press, 1998) there's a passage where he says that in all his time on the road in the thirties, he "not once encountered a wandering minstrel.....like Guthrie singing working class songs on the road. Once in a while you'd see a guy playing a uke or banjo on some street corner, his hat at his feet, hoping for a couple pennies. Buddy, can you spare a dime? Life is just a bowl of cherries. Three little words, I love you. Later, you might run into him at the Hooverville out of town".

In pointing out that a broad range of popular music (swing, country, etc.) probably appealed more to most people than songs with a political bias (and especially those which promoted a political group like the Communist Party), I'm not attempting to play down the hard work and dedication of Alan Lomax and many others who went out to collect songs, and sometimes even to encourage people to write them in response to their situations. Cohen mentions Don West,

Myles Horton, and Agnes "Sis" Cunningham as activists who could be found around the Highlander Folk School in Tennessee, and the School for Workers at the University of Wisconsin.

It couldn't have been easy to operate within a framework that included forces hostile to them, but they persevered and published collections of songs with titles like *Songs of the People; Commonwealth Labour Songs; Songs for Southern Workers, March and Sing!* and many others. As Cohen says: "The country was soon awash with labour songbooks, filled with songs gathered from a variety of sources, old and new". And the Communist Party, by now embarked on its Popular Front programme, began to look favourably on folk music.

There may be some irony in the fact that, as rural communities increasingly turned to the musical fare offered by radio and records, folk music seemed to gain some popularity in cities, especially New York. There were reasons for this. New York had a substantial left-wing population inclined to be sympathetic towards songs that seemed to express the interests and involvements of workers, blacks, and other groups. Not all such songs were political, of course, but the fact that they ostensibly originated among the people they were about gave them credibility. Record companies and publishers were located in New York. There were clubs that featured folk music. And the Communist Party, important while it supported folk music, had its headquarters in the city.

There were other reasons, often relating to individual circumstances. Some activists, in particular those from Southern States, found that their situations were precarious in terms of personal safety. Sis Cunningham left Oklahoma when the heat was turned on local communists. Police raided the Progressive Book Store in Oklahoma City. A full account can be found in *Books on Trial: Red Scare in the Heartland* by Shirley A. Weigand and Wayne A. Weigand (University of Oklahoma Press, 2007). Several people were arrested and charged with criminal conspiracy and convicted, though the judgements were later overturned. But the harassment had its effect in terms of persuading someone like Sis Cunningham that she would be safer in New York. Greenwich Village could offer sympathetic friends who didn't think that being a communist was a crime.

It was still true that, in Cohen's words: "While there was a progressive side to folk music promoting racial equality, labour unions, and economic democracy, it remained mostly connected with traditional, grassroots America along with somewhat of a patriotic tinge". Even when songs composed by local activists expressed a dissatisfaction with conditions they rarely, if ever, questioned the basic system. Dave McCarn's "Cotton Mill Colic", took a look at what it was like to be employed in the mills of North Carolina:

> I'm gonna starve, everybody will
> You can't make a living in a cotton mill.
> Patches on my britches, holes in my hat
> Ain't had a shave since my wife got fat.

The overall effect revolves around what was usually the main aim of most strikes – shorter hours and higher pay – and communists often quickly ran into trouble when they tried to introduce too much left-wing politics or anti-religious propaganda into a situation. Places like Gastonia and Marion in North Carolina had strong Methodist and Presbyterian traditions and didn't take kindly to anyone speaking against them. Northerners were frequently looked on with suspicion.

It's Cohen's contention that, whatever else was achieved, the activities of people like Alan Lomax laid the basis for what came later: "The stage was now set for the blossoming folk revival of the 1950s and after, spearheaded and symbolised by the movers and shakers of the Depression years: Woody Guthrie, Burl Ives, Pete Seeger, John and Alan Lomax, Josh White, Lead Belly, and so many others". These are names we remember, but what happened to those like Dave McCarn, who made a few records – "social protest songs, with a comical twist" – and then dropped out of sight? Cohen says that "he returned to North Carolina, where he worked in a variety of industrial jobs and ended up as a radio and TV repairman until his death in 1964 at the age of fifty-nine, having lived a hard life". You can hear his recording of "Cotton Mill Colic" on a collection of protest songs released in the UK on Not Now NOT2CD453.

There must have been others like him, including many who never got the opportunity to record, and who had little circulation outside their home towns. They perhaps knocked out some words for a picket line or union meeting, invariably setting them to well-known tunes, as the Wobblies did many years earlier, and that was it. When the strike was over they went back to work, unless they were blacklisted and had to go elsewhere for employment. And they were probably soon forgotten.

Depression Folk is a fascinating book and packs a great deal of information into its briskly-written pages. It doesn't have a bibliography, but there are extensive notes which provide details of many relevant books. I know that it's always possible to suggest other books that might be useful to anyone looking further into this subject, but two seem to me worth drawing attention to. Robert Cantwell's *When We Were Good: The Folk Revival* (Harvard University Press, 1996) and Robbie Lieberman's *"My Song is My Weapon": People's Songs, American Communism, and the Politics of Culture, 1930-50* (University of Illinois Press, 1989) are of interest.

DEPRESSION FOLK: GRASSROOTS MUSIC AND LEFT-WING POLITICS IN 30s AMERICA
By Ronald D. Cohen
University of North Carolina Press. 201 pages. $27.95 (paperback).
ISBN 978-14696-288-13

ESSAYISM

What is an essay? According to Brian Dillon, "the essay is first of all a type of measurement or judgement, not so much a test of itself, of its own powers, or its author's powers, as a weighing of something outside of itself." And, a little later, he says: "it aspires to express the quintessence or crux of its matter, thus to a sort of polish and integrity, and it wants at the same time to insist that its purview is partial, that being incomplete is a value in itself for it better reflects the brave and curious but faltering nature of the writing mind". Or how about, "The essay is often itself a fragment, or it may be made of fragments".

Reviewing a book full of useful quotations by the author, or from other writers, it's a temptation to carry on with excerpts, Brian Dillon's range of them being so wide and relevant. He refers more than once to Walter Benjamin's *Arcades Project*, the incomplete but fascinating work that Benjamin left behind when he committed suicide. I can see why Dillon thinks so highly of it. Benjamin's notion of presenting a picture of nineteenth century Paris through what is essentially a series of fragments is not dissimilar to Dillon's idea of discussing the nature of the essay by referring to the numerous practitioners of the form, ranging from Montaigne to Susan Sontag, and along the way taking in Sir Thomas Browne, Virginia Woolf, Cyril Connolly, and Elizabeth Hardwick, and quoting from their work.

He also writes about his own experiences as a writer, and when he quotes from someone else it is often to illustrate his own feelings about writing essays. He notes Adorno's comments with approval: "The essayist, he writes, does not feel the need to say all that can be said on a subject, and is content to use concepts that already exist in philosophy".

It's possible to write an essay about anything, even the idea of writing an essay, which is what Dillon has done. And an essay can include everything. It's not necessary to stick completely to the subject. Diversions can be entertaining, provided there's eventually a return to the main theme. Dillon's essay, or what can be seen as his series of interlinked essays, takes in a great deal of his personal history. He's suffered from depression, with its consequent effect on his day-to-day life and his relationships with other people.

There is an essay by Dillon about "anxiety" in which he talks about reviewing, a subject close to my own heart. I've done so much of it in the past fifty and more years, and it has often occurred to me that I've probably used up a lot of time that might have been better spent on other things. Reviewing, I suspect, is looked down on by writers who produce novels or complete books about a particular subject. They may well write reviews themselves, though usually only to supplement their income or promote their academic careers. And it's true that reviewing can distract from more creative work, assuming that the reviewer has ambitions in that line. Personally, I enjoy reviewing, especially when I have the opportunity to extend what I'm writing to a review/essay. Short reviews of a few hundred words can sometimes admittedly be little more than a necessary chore.

But, to be fair, Dillon mentions Cyril Connolly in *Enemies of Promise* referring to the dangers of reviewing. And there's a brilliant essay by Seymour Krim ("What's this Cat's Story?" in *Views of a Near-sighted Cannoneer,* Dutton, 1968), in which he writes about the "drug" of reviewing, with its chance to appear in print almost immediately, and its possibility of a quick reputation, not to mention quick earnings. And let's not forget the boost to the ego at seeing one's name in print. Much of what he says is true, but at the same time the reader can't help wondering if Krim wasn't destined anyway to be a reviewer and essayist rather than a novelist? "When are you going to write your novel?" someone once asked me, and it implied that novels are superior to other forms of writing. I've never had any desire to write one, nor thought that I could even if I wanted to. The form doesn't really excite me, and mostly I prefer to read a short story, an essay, a poem, a good, informative review. Writing reviews, and other bits and pieces, can lead to being dismissed as a "hack," but I think of myself as in a grand tradition if I am, and love to read about Grub Street and the purveyors of minor literary productions. I relate to John Dunton and the rest of the rabble.

Dillon also says that he enjoys, "the workaday feeling that everything I write has a modest journalistic ambition". And he talks about the need to always have something ready to be done: another review, a request for an article. I know the feeling and like to look at the little pile of books waiting to be read and reviewed. Dillon does ponder on his own inclinations to a style of composition, with its dominance of the necessary and the immediate, and he thinks that his addiction to "small forms" could be a way that allows him, "and perhaps many other writers to keep a killing anxiety at bay". Does the sense of completion when an essay is finished have the effect of calming worries about what comes next, at least temporarily?: "I like and loathe the fact that my writing life is so fractured, so contingent and occasional".

Looking at Cyril Connolly's failed ambitions, Dillon says that: "*The Unquiet Grave* begins with a sentence from which it cannot recover: 'The more books we read, the clearer it becomes that the true function of a writer is to produce a masterpiece and that no other task is of any consequence' ". It's not only Connolly's book that can't recover. A young would-be writer, or indeed any writer of moderate ambitions, might well be put off writing at all by adopting such a statement as a guide. My advice, for what it's worth, to anyone taking Connolly seriously, might be along the lines of: lighten up a little: "There seems", said I, "an unaccountable prepossession among all persons, to imagine that whatever seems gloomy must be profound, and whatever is cheerful must be shallow. They have put poor philosophy into deep mourning, and given her a coffin for a writing desk, and a skull for an inkstand". (Bulwer-Lytton: *Pelham or Adventures of a Gentleman,* 1828*)*.

It needs to be said that Dillon does suggest that not only great writing can sustain us in darker moments. Affected by his mother's death, he returned to reading what might best be described as expendable journalism: "At certain moments in my reading life there have been essays or articles that I had to keep rereading if I was to stay sane, or so it seemed. And sometimes in retrospect, or even at the time not quite worth the emotional, intellectual, existential weight I asked them to bear. Very few pages of the *NME* in 1985 really deserved to be pored over to the degree that I attended them in the days after my mother's death. On the other hand I quite see how the collected journalism of Lester Bangs could have kept me afloat in the night, treading in panic above my black sea of despair, with his sentimental swagger".

Reading *Essayism* I kept coming across comments that made me acknowledge my own shortcomings (are they? Or useful attributes in the circumstances?): "I was capable only of interesting myself in subjects I was already interested in", and "I was and remain quite incapable of mounting in writing a reasoned and coherent argument, never mind describing to myself, as the study of logic required, the parts and processes, more or less persuasive, of that argument". How comforting it can be to realise that someone else shares my occasional misgivings about what I do. Luckily, I don't think about them too much and instead get on with the next job.

Dillon's honesty about his battles with depression is affecting, and I don't want to play down his experiences in any way. And I think his comments are balanced in the sense of combining with other elements in his writing. I've already referred to his analysis of Cyril Connolly's work, and Connolly, for all his faults, was someone I quite admired, if only for the lucidity of his book reviewing. Hunting for a poem by the 1890s poet Theodore Wratislaw recently, I pulled an anthology from the shelf and tucked inside it found a review by Connolly, published in *The Sunday Times* dated 20th December, 1970, of the Penguin publication, *Poetry of the Nineties*. I'm not going to claim that Connolly's review made me buy the book. I was already curious about Ernest Dowson, Arthur Symons, Richard Le Gallienne, and others in 1970, and would have got the book, anyway. But what Connolly said interested me. Perhaps he was a failed writer – aren't we all, in one way or another? – but I liked what he wrote enough to have kept the review for almost fifty years. Someone should do the same for me. It would be pleasant to be remembered, if only for a fragment or two.

Elizabeth Hardwick is another fine essayist who Dillon writes about in an informed and sympathetic manner. He particularly refers to her essays about Dylan Thomas and Billie Holiday, which he thinks show that she "understood extremes". There are many other Hardwick pieces that remain in my mind from the books of hers that I have on my shelves: "Bartleby in Manhattan", "A Bunch of Reds" (about John Reed and Louise Bryant, and their roles in the Russian Revolution), "The Neglected Novels of Christina Stead". I'm being selective with my list. "The list is a venerable and inventive literary mode," Dillon quotes William Gass as saying. And is it that because selectivity is an essential component of a list? What we list indicates our own preferences, prejudices, and priorities.

"Essayism is tentative and hypothetical, and yet it is also a habit of thinking, writing and living that has definite boundaries". Boundaries can be useful, both in life and writing. On a practical level in literature, the notion of a boundary can help to eliminate unnecessary writing. I remember an anecdote about the American sociologist,

Ned Polsky, whose collection of essays, *Hustlers, Beats and Others* (Penguin, 1971) was a pleasure to read. He had an editorial post with a publisher of academic texts, and made himself unpopular because he would return book-length manuscripts with the comment that there was the basis for a good essay in the material, but that it was unnecessarily expansive otherwise. He knew the value of the essay form. I don't know if the anecdote was true or not, but I liked the idea of it.

Brian Dillon has written an intriguing book, or book-length essay, or collection of short, interlinked essays. Pinning labels on a piece of writing is always unsatisfactory. Have I written a review, an essay, a review/essay? I'm not going to spend too much time considering the question. I'd rather turn to collections of essays by writers like Elizabeth Hardwick, Joseph Epstein (see his *Wind Sprints*, Axios Press, 2016, for entertaining examples of short, meaning a page or two, essays), Leslie Fiedler, Theodore Solotaroff, John Clellon Holmes, and enjoy re-reading them.

And I must look again at the five issues of Saul Bellow's little magazine, *The Noble Savage,* which alongside contemporary essayists (1960-62) had a series called "Ancestors", featuring essays by D.H. Lawrence, Isaac Rosenfeld, Isaac Babel, Alexander Pushkin, and Samuel Butler. The latter's "Ramblings in Cheapside", opens with "Walking the other day in Cheapside I saw some turtles in Mr Sweeting's window, and was tempted to stay and look at them". It goes on to talk about, among other things, Handel, Mendelssohn, slugs, Aeschylus, Butler's dislike of books ("I believe I have the smallest library of any literary man in London, and I have no wish to increase it"), Bradshaw's Railway Guide, and a lady who always travelled accompanied by her parrots. I'm in danger of compiling another list. And I want to add to it. I'm just about to start reading Joachim Kalka's *Gaslight: Lantern Slides from the Nineteenth Century* (New York Review of Books, 2017). Interesting and entertaining essays, I hope.

ESSAYISM
By Brian Dillon
Fitzcarraldo Editions. 138 pages. £10.99. ISBN 978-1-910695-41-8

BROWSE

I've spent half of my life in bookshops of one kind or another, and even now, when bookshops seem to be in general decline, I like to find the ones that still manage to hang on in the face of competition from on-line sellers of both new and old books, and the seeming indifference of the general public. Whenever I arrive in a location I've not visited before the first question I ask is, "Is there a bookshop in town?" A second-hand one preferably, but a Waterstones, if necessary. There rarely is anywhere else for new books unless it's a Waterstones. Blackwells in a university town, perhaps. I'm not complaining. It's good to find any kind of bookshop still open.

I prefer the second-hand shops because they're where I might find something unusual. And they do still exist, I'm happy to say, though the quirkiness of their owners sometimes appears to work against their continuing for much longer. I was in Oldham recently and called at a little bookshop I'd visited some years ago. It was still there, but shuttered up, though books could be seen piled against an upstairs window. An enquiry at the premises next door elicited the information that the bookseller does still occasionally open his shop, though not on any sort of regular basis. He may be there if you call, he may not. Maybe it's his age that now determines the opening hours? I knew the bookseller about forty years ago when we were both involved with the IWW (Industrial Workers of the World) and if he's approaching my age he probably doesn't find it congenial to his health to spend too long in the unheated shop tucked away in a little side-street.

A bookseller in Manchester appears to spend much of his time in the café that you have to pass through to get to the bookshop. He's cheerful enough, but doesn't give the impression that he's all that concerned about selling any books, many of which are badly overpriced. He'd surely sell more if he reduced his prices. What's the point of having thousands of books simply gathering dust? A shop I went to in Cheltenham recently had a sign saying that all the books were half the marked prices. And I bought some. But the man in Manchester steadfastly holds to his principles. I can't help suspecting that the shop is a good reason for not going home, if he has one. It wouldn't surprise me to learn that he sleeps on the premises. Still, he runs a bookshop so, again, I shouldn't complain.

The oddball nature of many of the characters in the second-hand book trade is a feature of Iain Sinclair's lively piece in *Browse* about a now-defunct shop in Bohemia Road, St Leonard's-on-Sea. Bohemia Road was a good address. Sinclair, now well-known for his own books, was once a provider of second-hand books at a stall in Camden Passage. He also used to produce some fascinating catalogues often featuring Beat-related literature and pulp crime novels. I recall them with pleasure.

I can't claim that my own prowling has ever really been in search of overlooked scarce items. The book scouts that Sinclair writes about were more adept at that. I've never been too bothered about books as rare objects. I just wanted to read them, and a grubby hardback, a tattered paperback, a stained old literary magazine, can satisfy me just as much as books in pristine condition or the occasional perhaps-valuable item that I have come across by chance. I remember my delight when, in a now long-since closed shop on the edge of Stockport, I found a couple of American left-wing novels from the 1930s and got them cheap. It wasn't that they were valuable in money terms. But they were valuable to me for other reasons. And I couldn't help wondering who had once owned them? It was a time when the old Left was dying off, working-class autodidacts were disappearing, and their terraced houses were being demolished, or sometimes renovated. I could imagine the sons and daughters piling up Dad's books and selling them to the bookseller. Houses with shelves of old books don't fit in with gentrification.

The bookshops covered in *Browse* aren't all of the second-hand variety, by any means, and Ian Sansom's memoir of working at the original Foyles Bookshop in Charing Cross Road, with the nearby Pillars of Hercules pub, reminded me of the hours I spent in both places. There is still a Foyles, of course, though in a slightly different location, and I don't want to criticise it, but it seems too shiny and organised for my tastes. I feel happier in the remaining second-hand bookshops further down Charing Cross Road and in Cecil Court. Or in Judd Books and Skoob, both not far from Euston Station.

But I'm being too insular and only looking at bookshops in Britain. In *Browse,* Andrei Kurkov talks about a bookshop in "Chernivtsi in the middle of the Bukovina region in the south-west of Ukraine." The shop was called Bukinist, its name derived from the French *bouquiniste*, which inevitably brings to mind the bookstalls along the Seine in Paris. More memories, as it was from one of those stalls that I got a copy of the Olympia Press edition of William Burroughs' *The Naked Lunch.* That was in 1962, and the book was still banned in Britain, so I smuggled it home at the bottom of my rucksack.

Juan Gabriel Vasquez writes about bookshops in Bogota, and Yiyun Li a bookshop in Beijing. In Cairo, Alaa Al Aswany had a book signing session that overspilled into a discussion about the current political situation in Egypt and the need to protest against a corrupt government. There are articles about bookshops in Nairobi and Bologna. They're often described as meeting places for students, writers, and others who perhaps just like to browse and buy something they've discovered. And talk to each other.

I'm reminded of the splendid Compendium Bookshop in Camden Town and often meeting poets and novelists there. I took the American writer Seymour Krim to Compendium when he was trying to find a copy of *Evergreen Review* which had one of his pieces. And on another occasion I met the late John Platt and we adjoined to a nearby pub where he asked me to contribute to his magazine, *Comstock Lode*. And Nick Kimberley (later to have his own bookshop, Duck Soup), and after him Mike Hart, behind the counter at Compendium, were always good to talk to.

Bookshops are more than just places to buy books. Or they ought to be. Someone once said that at Compendium you could find Mike "at the heart of a group of autodidacts, musicians, writers, lowlifes and drunks." The shop, described as "the last outpost of bohemianism" in Camden Town, closed as the area became more commercialised. Also long gone is Turret Bookshop, which Bernard Stone over the years operated from various addresses in Kensington, Covent Garden, and elsewhere. Bernard always got out a bottle of wine or vodka, no matter the time of day when I called. And there were readings in his shop which were happy affairs with the drink flowing freely. Bernard was friendly towards little magazines and small press publications and held a good stock of them.

Bookshops in Delhi and Denmark, and along with them the stories of the writers who found the way to their doors, and benefited from the experience. Ali Smith frequented the only bookshop in Inverness, Michael Dirda made a journey to the Second Story Books warehouse in Rockville, Maryland, as a snowstorm threatened to develop. The thought of finding something unusual was enough to make him take a chance on being cut-off when it was time to return home.

This is a book for all those who love books and the shops that sell them. I've been to bookshops in Toronto, New York, Pittsburgh, Amsterdam, Cologne, Berlin, Zurich, Paris, Prague, Seville, Cardiff, Glasgow, Edinburgh, London, and too many others in towns and cities across England to list here. And I hope to continue going to them as long as I'm able to get there. Yes, I know I can easily find books on Abe Books, and I do use their service, but only to get a book I know about and need. And that's satisfying in its way, but not the same as suddenly stumbling on something I wasn't aware of, or even if I was I probably would never have bought and read had I not actually held it in my hands.

Not too long ago I came across a copy of Leonard Merrick's *While Paris Laughed* in a bookshop in Edinburgh and enjoyed it so much that I've since tracked down four other Merrick books. But I may never have read Merrick had I not picked up that copy of *While Paris Laughed* in a bookshop. It's a collection of stories about an impoverished poet called Tricotrin, and entertainingly plays to the popular notion of the bohemian life. A more realistic and downbeat version of that life can be found in Merrick's novel, *Cynthia*, with its struggling writer and his family, unreliable editors and wayward publishers, publications that never prosper, and a permanent lack of money. Some of it was probably based on Merrick's own experiences in the City of Light.

Merrick had been there long before George Whitman arrived in Paris. But Whitman was by nature a bohemian, and once settled in the city he began to work towards his dream of opening a bookshop that would cater for the numerous English-speaking writers and others who were also around. He eventually opened Le Mistral in 1951 and changed its name to Shakespeare and Company in 1964. It was still Le Mistral when I first went to find it in 1962. And there had been a Shakespeare and Company in Paris in the 1920s and 1930s, when Sylvia Beach ran it and Hemingway, Gertrude Stein, Ezra Pound, and many others of the famed expatriate community frequented the shop.

There have been other English-language bookshops in Paris over the years, of course. I recall The English Bookshop from my 1962 visit, and more recently the excellent Village Voice Bookshop in the rue

Princesse, though it's now sadly closed, a victim of the internet and the decline of the area it was in from one with a bohemian touch into a fashionable district of boutiques and trendy bars, The Village Voice was always good for new books from the United States, and for a chat with Michael Neal. The San Francisco Book Company still thrives with second-hand books on the rue Monsieur le Prince.

It's Shakespeare and Company, needless to say, that is the most well-known. It's lucky with its location, just across the river from Notre Dame, and I suppose the fact of it having survived there for over sixty years now justifies it being described as legendary. George Whitman's presence on the premises usually added to the atmosphere, and it wasn't unusual to find a couple of writers also hanging around. I mean a couple of published writers as well as the young, hopeful poets and would-be novelists who were encouraged to doss down in the rooms above the shop in return for a few hours helping out with the chores. Jeremy Mercer's *Books, Baguettes & Bedbugs,* published in 2005, is useful for giving an idea of what their experiences were like, though some other publications, usually undated, that emanated from the shop, often had short accounts of their time in the Tumbleweed Hotel by a variety of visitors.

I never did stay there myself, but the bookshop was always good for chance encounters. I remember seeing Ted Joans, the black Beat poet there one day, and renewing an acquaintanceship we'd started at the Berlin Literature Festival in 1977. And, on another occasion, coming across two slightly tipsy English poets and adjourning to a nearby bar. They were in Paris for an exhibition they never actually got to, the Kronenbourg proving too strong a counter-attraction, but one of them later commemorated our meeting with a poem in a book called *Following the Seine.*

A history of Shakespeare and Company was sure to be published at some stage, and it's heartening to find that it has come from the bookshop and not from an outside source. The encouraging thing is that it's not what might be called a conventional history. The facts are there, but they're interspersed with numerous photos and other illustrations, memoirs by people who called at or were involved with the bookshop at one time or another, and other odds and ends.

The shop had its ups and downs over the years, sometimes because of French bureaucracy, sometimes because of George Whitman's free-and-easy approach to being the proprietor of a bookshop. He was likely to disappear for lengthy periods and leave the business in the hands of people not suited to running it. The noted writer, Lawrence Durrell, fell out with Whitman because a book-signing at the shop was left to a couple of incompetent young people while Whitman was away, and consequently was a shambles. And there was a disastrous fire in 1990 that might have been caused by the "ancient electrical wiring" or "an errant cigarette from a careless customer". Or "was it the rejected poet who'd been lurking about?"

I've encountered some oddballs during my sixty or so years around the poetry scene and its hordes of poets, but the thought of one who might have been an arsonist is disturbing. Not every poet could be trusted, however, and thefts of books were a perennial problem. The poet Gregory Corso, living in the so-called Beat Hotel in Paris, was known to steal books from Shakespeare and Company, just as he did from Lawrence Ferlinghetti's City Lights bookshop in San Francisco. Whitman continued to tolerate him in the shop because he was a good poet.

Anecdotes about Whitman and Shakespeare and Company abound. During the 1968 demonstrations Whitman, a one-time communist in the 1930s, sympathised with the students and others who were battling with the police: "Throughout the violence, the bookshop was a refuge. George hosted all-night talk sessions, and he hid those who were trying to escape the CRS." When the fire broke out he took it in his stride and immediately set to work to put right the damage: "Don't mourn. Organise," he's reputed to have said, quoting the words of the IWW activist, Joe Hill. It might be appropriate, at this point, to mention Whitman's suspicions about the CIA monitoring both him and the shop because of his radical past and the shop's open policy about the sort of literature it stocked. He wasn't just being paranoiac, and it was a fact that the CIA was active in Paris. The writer Peter Matthiessen (author of the Cold War novel, *Partisans*) later admitted to working on behalf of the CIA during his time in the city in the 1950s.

And there is information about *The Paris Magazine*, edited by Whitman, the first issue of which came out in 1967, the second in 1984 and the third in 1989. Anyone familiar with little magazines, and their inconsistencies, will know that regularity and frequency of publication are not always priorities for them, but three issues in twenty-two years, and with a seventeen-years gap between the first and second, might be something of a record. The magazine has been revived in recent times and looks imposing and has some fashionable names in its contents list, but I still have a liking for those early, idiosyncratic issues that George Whitman published.

Shakespeare and Company is a wonderful book, well-produced, and as I mentioned earlier, full of photos and other documents that vividly bring to life the life and times of George Whitman and his bookshop. He died in 2011, though his daughter, Sylvia, had more or less taken over well before that and started "modernising" the shop. It has expanded and now has a café. As she probably correctly predicted, if it wasn't modernised it was in danger of becoming just a museum piece. I can feel nostalgic for the bookshop that I first experienced in 1962, but I can also understand that change is inevitable.

BROWSE: THE WORLD IN BOOKSHOPS
Edited by Henry Hitchings
Pushkin Press. 253 pages. £12.99. ISBN 978-1-782272-12-0

SHAKESPEARE AND COMPANY: A HISTORY OF THE RAG & BONE SHOP OF THE HEART
Edited by Krista Halverson
Shakespeare and Company. 384 pages. 35 Euros. ISBN 979-10-96101-00-9

CRIME TIME, 1972

Crime writing, according to Ross MacDonald, "is a device for seeing through to life itself", and his own books do this vividly as his private detective, Lew Archer, moves through the flashy, corrupt world of Southern California, opening the cupboards and watching the skeletons fall out. But how many English crime novels achieve more than a surface effect? Despite a mass of details designed to make them "realistic", they too often have an unreal aura in that the characters are cardboard cut-outs from the set of English types. The backgrounds they operate against are merely clichéd class areas. One can't read MacDonald without realising that he aims at something more than playing on the reader's social prejudices, or enticing him or her towards the showdown. With the average English novel, though, the puppets are paraded before us and then packed away in their places to live happily ever after. Or pay the penalty for what they've done. Perhaps we like to think that life really is that way?

All that is not to suggest that English crime novels are unreadable. Michael Gilbert's *The Body of a Girl* skips along in a lively manner, with tough Detective Chief Inspector Mercer out to solve a murder which relates to the activities of a gang of brutal London crooks, and eventually some of the leading lights of the small town where the action takes place.

What is especially interesting is Gilbert's picture of the police. He doesn't paint them black – there's a partly-bent copper, and another who likes an uncomplicated life, and fiddles the statistics to achieve it, but these are individuals rather than the norm – and the main impression is of a brave, capable and somewhat self-righteous bunch of men who see themselves as the thin line between the "public" and the forces of evil. There is, of course, an element of truth in this, but Gilbert only hints at the thought that, if not properly controlled, it's an attitude that might lead to a need to play God.

Emma Page's *Family & Friends* is a curious book, half-way between a women's magazine serial and one of the better social novels of the Fifties. Set in a provincial town, it has sequences of in-fighting between local businessmen, their wives and relations, but instead of ending with a broken marriage, or a flight to the anonymity of a big city, there are two murders. The author takes up two-thirds of the book in analysing her characters – or delineating their actions, rather – before the killings take place, and it struck me that the crime elements were almost an afterthought. Added to which, the people seem to function in a vacuum. The real strains and stresses of contemporary life pass them by. Provincial society is a lot more complex than Emma Page allows, and although murder might not be an everyday occurrence, a talented novelist could use it to rip apart that society.

The Singing Millionaire is clumsily constructed in places, and yet it does try to get beneath the skin of its main character and, by doing so, throws light on the dark world he inhabits. Philippe, drug addict and drifter, arrives in Istanbul where he meets up with John, a shambling wreck of a would-be poet, and Maggie, a weak-willed dreamer. He kills John with an overdose, seduces Maggie to his own habits, and then takes off for Marseilles, with a plan to blackmail his stepfather. Maggie, by now dependent on Philippe for her drugs, is the bait.

What happens next is central to the dénouement of the story, and it would be unfair to say more, but in its portrayal of a mind made perverse by self-indulgence the book does get near to the truth about certain of the types who perambulate their hazy way from Nepal to Istanbul and elsewhere. By showing how Philippe's twisted morality corrupts Maggie, juggles with his stepfather's feelings, and then justifies it all, Michael Pereira puts on paper one of the "gangsters of the new freedom", as Gershon Legman so aptly described them.

Events in Africa these days often have all the hallmarks of a crime story, with crooked deals, vicious policemen, shady politicians of various persuasions, and a seething, anonymous mass beneath the surface. Meredith Cutlack milks this turbulent milieu for all it's worth in *Blood Running South* as Bill Payne, free-lance journalist, flies to Rhodesia to get the lowdown on a sanction-breaking operation, and promptly finds himself up to the neck in trouble.

I wouldn't want to fault Cutlack's descriptions of the mood of Africa – he's been there, I haven't – but as a novel his book suffers from a too earnest attempt to establish and sustain the laconic, no-nonsense tone that reporters reputedly love. The ghosts of Hemingway-imitators hover over the pages as Payne drinks his way through problems, almost beds a sexy white girl, and meets up with some madmen in mercenary uniforms. But it's exciting in a slick sort of way and Cutlack's sympathies are with the right people.

For a more down-to-earth view of African life take a look at the title-story in Chinua Achebe's *Girls at War.* In it a young girl is crushed and corrupted by external forces as Nigerian society crumbles around her. Not all of Achebe's stories are as powerful as this one – a couple are student exercises, as he freely admits – but at their best they are marked by a refreshing directness of expression.

Finally, a look back to a period in Japanese history when a form of Christian Socialism attracted the hope and enthusiasm of members of the growing left-wing community. *Pillar of Fire* was first published in Japan in 1904, and its author was an opponent of the war with Russia. His views weren't popular – a wave of nationalist enthusiasm had swept the country, and neither authorities nor workers took kindly to the handful of socialists who dared to speak out against it – and Nage Kinoshita was constantly in trouble.

The book was banned in 1910, and it was not until the 1950s that an uncensored edition again became available. As a novel it is rather melodramatic, with the characters little more than hinges on which to swing social comments, but Kenneth Strong's long, scholarly introduction places it firmly in its historical context. Like certain minor British novels of the period it has value because of its links with political movements and ideas.

THE BODY OF A GIRL by Michael Gilbert. Hodder & Stoughton

FAMILY AND FRIENDS by Emma Page. Collins

THE SINGING MILLIONAIRE by Michael Pereira. Collins

BLOOD RUNNING SOUTH by Meredith Cutlack. Heinemann

GIRLS AT WAR by Chinua Achebe. Heinemann

PILLARS OF FIRE by Nage Kinoshita. Allen & Unwin

DOUGLAS HAYES

Let me first of all say that this is not a biographical essay, nor one in the spirit of literary criticism. I know nothing at all about Douglas Hayes, and there is little or no information about him on the internet. What I'm writing is simply a response to finding a grubby and tattered old copy of a 1962 paperback edition of his novel, *The Comedy Man*, in a charity shop. I bought it and thought it one of the funniest and most pleasurable novels I've read for a long time.

"Pleasurable"? Ah, now that's a word likely to upset those who feel the need to look for significance or seriousness in anything they read. Some years ago, 1990 to be precise, there was an anthology, published by the magazine, *Antaeus,* under the title "Literature as Pleasure," in which a number of well-known writers talked about the pleasure they got from reading. There is, of course, a great deal of pleasure to be gained from reading widely, and Madison Smartt Bell is quoted as saying: "Reading, say, the latest Elmore Leonard gives me pleasure. Reading Dostoevsky gives me pleasure too. Is there a qualitative difference between these two experiences?"

The collection was also prefaced with a number of quotations, one of which was William Carlos Williams's, "If it ain't a pleasure it ain't a poem," something that often came to mind during my fifty years reviewing poetry. I also liked Doris Lessing's view that, "There is only one way to read, which is to browse in libraries and bookshops, picking up books that attract you, reading only those, dropping them when they bore you". I once met a man who claimed to have started at "A" in the fiction shelves of Aberdeen Public Library and worked his way through the alphabet, stopping reading if a book lost his attention. He reckoned to have read quite a few interesting books, and abandoned a lot of dull ones.

Doris Lessing' advice is worth taking note of, and a policy I worked out for myself years ago, and why I ignore hyperbole about this prize or that award, and the latest fashionable young novelist, and prefer to wander around bookshops, old and new, where they still exist, and disturb the dust in charity shops.

But to return to Douglas Hayes. It seems obvious that he had worked extensively in the theatre in a number of positions, including stage management and acting. *The Comedy Man* (it was, incidentally, made into a film with Kenneth More in 1963) is about the lives and misadventures of actors who seem to spend most of their time "resting" between engagements which are often only too brief and usually poorly paid. Hayes wasn't writing about successful actors, though he sometimes brings in characters who had known their five minutes of fame and then faded from sight due to a variety of problems, ranging from drink to a failure to make the right decisions regarding career moves. They're now reduced to queuing with the rest in an effort to persuade a shady agent to find them a couple of days work as a film extra, or a walk-on part in a second-rate play in a third-rate theatre.

It's obvious that Hayes had lived the life of an obscure and struggling actor. After reading *The Comedy Man*, I tracked down some of his other books, such as The *Shy Young Man, Quite a Good Address,* and *A Player's Hide*, working on my normal basis of finding them where I can and never paying too much for them. I'm not a collector wanting pristine copies complete with dustjackets. Paperback or hardback, beer-stained or with a shopping list or telephone numbers scribbled on a blank page, I'm happy provided all the pages are there for me to read.

The Comedy Man is probably the best of Hayes's books, or at least the best of those I've read. Perhaps I should say that it's the one that gave me most pleasure. But that isn't to say that the others don't have a lot to offer. They're lively and the details they provide about working on a film set, with its endless disruptions, doing commentaries for inane TV commercials, providing the voice of a parrot for a play where the parrot on stage can't be relied on to talk when necessary, and trying to persuade fumbling amateur actors in a local theatre group to play to the audience and not each other, ring true. They also refer to the sort of jobs, like working in a chocolate-biscuit factory, that "resting" actors have to take to make ends meet. A bit-part actor I knew told me that the only speaking part he ever had ("There's a gentleman to see you, sir") was left on the cutting room floor when the film was released. He also pointed me to a large-scale historical film in which he was one of a group of cowled monks wending their way into an abbey. "I'm the third from the front on the left," he said, "the one whose candle is shaking. There was a bar on the set and the leading players, several well-known actors, weren't stand-offish and insisted we drank with them". I think Douglas Hayes would have recognised his experiences.

If the books are at least semi-autobiographical, *The Shy Young Man* comes early in the account as the hero leaves home, and after some early experiences, is hired by "Harry Sparks and the Sparklers: Your Family Concert Party", working in the North, and doing a bit of everything, on-stage and off. A move to London, and then another trip North for "A Season of weekly Repertory" finds the young theatrical in digs with a widow who has an attractive eighteen-year old daughter. The inevitable happens, and the daughter gets pregnant. What complicates matters is that he's been sleeping with the mother, too, and she's also pregnant. References to Chamberlain and Munich place the story in context and the "shy young man" is relieved of responsibility for his actions by the start of the war in 1939. He's due to be conscripted and the women have, in the meantime, each met men who, though aware of their condition, are interested in marrying them.

It's not my intention to summarise the plots of the Hayes novels I've read. They're probably what might best be described as "picaresque" in the sense that they have a sequence of events that don't necessarily add up to some important conclusion. Things happen, characters come and go, the humour in situations is exploited, even when it might verge on the tragic. Taking pity on a decrepit old actor down on his luck, the young actor in *Quite a Good Address*, allows him to stay in his lodgings. He eventually has to force him to leave, his habits and behaviour being dirty and disruptive, but as the old man points out to him, there might come a time when he'll get too old for most parts in plays, he won't have clean clothes to go for an interview, or his memory will begin to fail him and he won't be able to remember his lines. Beneath the entertaining veneer of bohemianism there's an underlying feeling that theatrical life is precarious, and poverty a presence even when times appear to be good.

Shabby bedsits, pubs with coal fires, dole offices, pawnshops, old army greatcoats worn to keep warm. It's a world that has long gone, or mostly so. The dole office and pawnshops still exist, though with different names to describe them. But I suspect that the kind of life, and the sort of circumstances, Hayes was writing about didn't seem too relevant as the 1960s developed and the increasing affluence of the 1970s began to change tastes. I don't think "Harry Sparks and the Sparklers" would have been in great demand anymore. And a lot of theatres in the provinces were beginning to go out of business. So, perhaps all the social changes that became evident from the 1960s on were partly responsible for Hayes slipping from fashion as a writer and so being “forgotten”.

As I said earlier, I know very little about Douglas Hayes, and I’m not even sure when his last book was published (the early 1970s?) or when he died. I’d be interested if someone came up with a little information about him, but it’s not essential to have it. A writer is known by his work, and I’ve read enough of Douglas Hayes’s to know that he wrote some good books, and that reading them has given me a great deal of pleasure.

CLANCY SIGAL

Clancy Sigal wrote a book called *Going Away: A Report, a Memoir* that was marketed as a novel, but which was essentially an autobiographical account of how and why he left the United States in the late-1950s. It wasn't his first published book. *Weekend in Dinlock*, which appeared in 1960, preceded it, and pointed to the fact that Sigal was by that time living in Britain.

Weekend in Dinlock was interesting in that it was about the friendship between an American radical and a young British miner who was also a talented artist. It was, in fact, based on Sigal's association with Len Doherty, a miner from the North East who was also a novelist. It's a sad question to raise, but does anyone read Doherty these days? He published three novels, became a journalist, and died in 1983. *Weekend in Dinlock* was widely read, but didn't always impress those on the political left in Britain. It didn't paint a picture of working-class life in a pit village as being anything other than it was, with heavy drinking and narrow-mindedness being integral parts of it.

Sigal had been introduced to Doherty by Doris Lessing, and they had in common their membership of the Communist Party in their respective countries. And it was the communist connection that had pushed Sigal into deciding that departing from America was, in the circumstances of the Cold War and anti-communist feeling, a wise move. He naturally gravitated towards left-wing circles in London, and for several years had an affair with Doris Lessing. He appears, in fictional form as Saul Green, in her novel, *The Golden Notebook*. She, in turn, is portrayed as Rose O'Malley in Sigal's novel, *The Secret Defector*.

Sigal's left-wing inclinations were shaped by his parents. His father, described as "a gun-toting labour organiser", came and went in an irregular way, and he was brought up by his mother, who also happened to be heavily involved in left-wing politics and union organising. His book, *A Woman of Uncertain Character: The Amorous and Radical Adventures of My Mother Jennie (Who always Wanted to be a Respectable Jewish Mom) by Her Bastard Son* is a racy account of what it was like growing up in Chicago in the 1930s and 1940s with parents, and their friends and acquaintances, often engaged in factional fights with other left-wingers: "There is hardly a Jewish clan of their generation that was not bitterly split between the 'ists' – socialists versus Communists or both against the Trotskyists who didn't like the de Leonists who loathed the Cannonites who despised the Shachtmanites who – and on and on". It's an amusing aside to Sigal's early years that he said that the first time he'd been in prison was when he was five years old. His mother had been arrested for her union organising activities, and she took her son to prison with her.

After army service, Sigal returned to Chicago and attempted to find a place for himself as a union organiser for the United Automobile Workers (UAW), but the union was starting to purge communists and their supporters from its ranks. Sigal moved to the West Coast, but continued with his radical activities. He once claimed that he had been fired from Columbia Studios when he was found using their copying facilities to run off political leaflets.

Much later, when he was living in London, Sigal had other involvements, perhaps not political in the usual sense, but certainly considered radical at the time. Always good at turning his experiences into lightly-disguised fiction, Sigal's *Zone of the Interior* had its basis in his relationship with the controversial anti-psychiatrist, R.D. Laing. What was noticeable about Sigal was the fact that he always managed to deal with a subject with an element of humour built into the narrative. It was as if he was looking at himself and wondering how he had become involved in whichever situation he was in. The humour was, perhaps, a kind of survival technique.

But it's probably for *Going Away: A Report, a Memoir* that Sigal will be most remembered. In it the narrator leaves the West Coast where he had been active, in various ways, in the film industry, and drives across the United States. On the way he visits old friends and finds them inevitably altered. The McCarthy years have had their effect and one-time union and political activists are keeping their heads down. They're often family men now, and need to hold onto their jobs. The American Left has effectively fallen apart. Alongside the encounters with old and new friends there are loving descriptions of the landscapes, both urban and rural, that are observed. Some commentators have almost linked Sigal's book to Jack Kerouac's *On the* Road, but with Sigal showing a greater social and political awareness.

I don't think Sigal meant to stay away from America as long as he did – his original intention was to spend six months in Paris, writing *Going Away* : he did and inevitably got to know Simone de Beauvoir and other intellectuals and political activists – but it was thirty years before he made a permanent move back to his homeland. In those thirty years he'd written his various books, worked for the BBC, and *The Guardian*, *The Observer, Encounter*, and other publications, and generally built up a reputation as a lively and sometimes combative journalist. A book about his adventures in England is scheduled to be published in 2018.

When he did return to America, he lived in California, got married, taught at the University of Southern California, and was once again involved with films, sometimes as a screenwriter. He was the principal screenwriter for the film, *Frida*, about the life of the Mexican artist, Frida Kahlo. The final book published during his lifetime was *Black Sunset: Hollywood Sex, Lies, Glamour, Betrayal and Raging Egos*, a fast-moving account of his sometimes bizarre experiences working as a talent agent in Hollywood in the 1950s.

I always read anything that Clancy Sigal wrote whenever I came across it in book form or in the pages of newspapers and magazines. He was never dull. And he could always tell a good story. He was spoken of as being in a class with other Chicago-related writers like James T. Farrell and Nelson Algren. There are much worse ways to be remembered.

ROY FISHER 1930-2017

Roy Fisher never became a "popular poet", in the sense of his work being widely known and printed in the sort of anthologies that appeal to a broad public. I recall him once saying that he didn't have a "party piece" poem, the kind that he could perform regularly and be recognised by. On the whole, his work didn't lend itself to being quoted from to emphasise a point of view. I think his audience was largely confined to fellow-poets, a few informed readers of poetry and, after a time, various academics. One or two, like Eric Mottram, had supported him all along, but it took others some years to catch up, if they ever did. When it came to the response to Fisher's work by the literary establishment generally, Donald Davie probably got it right when he said that he was the victim of "the blindness and condescension of the metropolis to writing which is provincial in its origins or subject matter".

Fisher was born in 1930 in Birmingham, and the city, and the Midlands generally, figured prominently in his poetry throughout his lifetime. His early long poem, *City,* published in 1961 by Migrant Press, was an example of how he could use the facts of his background in verse that was shaped by his reading of American and European modernist poets. It was certainly different from the kind of poetry that was then being produced by most English writers, and it's perhaps significant that many of the first people to recognise its qualities were Americans like Robert Creeley and Denise Levertov, who wrote about Fisher in the influential American magazine, *Kulchur*, in 1962.

It was Gael Turnbull who, in the early-1950s, introduced Fisher to the work of William Carlos Williams, Creeley, Charles Olson, and Louis Zukofsky. He also encouraged him to send poems to Cid Corman's magazine, *Origin.* Fisher certainly learned a great deal from reading American poets, but he was also interested in Continental art and writing, and he always retained his own voice and concerns. Tom Pickard made a filmed documentary about Fisher, and it was tellingly called, *Birmingham's What I Think With.*

Most of Fisher's early work appeared in little magazines and small press pamphlets, though the adventurous Fulcrum Press did publish several books by him in the 1960s. It was only in the late-1970s that a somewhat bigger publisher, Carcanet Press, brought out one of his books, and this was followed by his being taken up by Oxford University Press in 1980. It gave him some status (Oxford eventually did several books by him) but, as usual, the London-centred literary critics and commentators largely ignored him. Bloodaxe Books published his later collections.

He had worked in schools and colleges, and for a number of years was a lecturer in the American Studies Department of Keele University. Fisher was also a talented jazz pianist. He had started playing with local jazz groups in the Birmingham area while still a teenager, and was influenced by what was known as Chicago-style jazz. Pee Wee Russell and Bud Freeman were the kind of musicians he admired. Later, he was skilled enough to be employed as an accompanist for Bud Freeman when the American tenor-saxophonist toured Britain. And I recall Fisher playing with Slim Gaillard at the *Beat Dreams/Plymouth Sounds* convention in Plymouth in 1987.

I knew and liked Roy Fisher. He was a good man and a fine poet. I'm happy that, in a small way, I was able to promote his work at a time when very few other people were paying attention to it. I can't make any great claims for what I did, which amounted to a few short reviews in *Tribune* (see below) and *Ambit.* I also used some of his poems in *Move* and *Palantir*, a couple of magazines I edited in the Sixties and Seventies. But it pleases me to think that I knew him and valued his writing.

The flash merchants of literature sometimes seem to get all the attention, but it should never be forgotten that the really memorable work is often being done by writers who don't get spotlighted on television or written up in the glossies. Roy Fisher is one such man, a skilled and talented poet and prose writer who has worked quietly for years, publishing in obscure magazines, at times more appreciated abroad than here, and only in recent years having his writings issued in relatively easy-to-obtain editions.

His *Collected Poems* appeared in 1969 and drew on the most significant of his work from the preceding twelve or so years. And *The Ship's Orchestra,* a complex and compact prose work, was published in 1966. Both were slim volumes. Fisher never over-writes, and his prose and poetry is carefully constructed and only presented on the page when it has been shaped into the precise form that he wants.

Now we have a new collection of poems, and it proves that Fisher is going from strength to strength. He states that his poems are "propositions or explorations rather than reactions to personal experience", and that is true enough. But at the same time the feeling of his background – the provinces – comes through. It is not that Fisher describes anything in detail, and often what he does describe is something (a painting, for example) outside his main physical environment, but rather that the tone of his poems suggests the measure of his life. *Matrix* is an extremely exciting achievement.

The Cut Pages is a new prose work, and again one can see how Fisher aims to explore instead of sketch. He is not content to tell a "story", or reflect on a set scene or situation. And when he does describe it is to isolate the image.

We have heard a lot in recent years about collage and cut-up techniques, and so on. It's true that *The Cut Pages* can perhaps be viewed in that light, and dipped into accordingly. But to do so is to lose its essence. The whole book is balanced and unless one accepts it as it is, and considers it at its own pace, then the overall value is debased. Fisher is not easily understood, and the reader must be prepared to work with him.

Roy Fisher is a rare individual in contemporary English writing. He doesn't belong to any "school", issue any manifestos, lead any group. But what he is doing, with his care for language and form, is of real importance.

MATRIX by Roy Fisher. Fulcrum Press.

THE CUT PAGES by Roy Fisher. Fulcrum Press.

THOUGHTS ON MUSIC AND LITERATURE

In an essay called "Let the Good Times Roll", published in *Jazz & Blues* (February, 1972), and later reprinted in my *Bohemians, Beats and Blues People* (Penniless Press, 2013), I quoted from Abbie Hoffman's *Woodstock Nation* to show how, in the early-1950s, dissident whites turned to black rhythm-and-blues in preference to the mediocre mass-popular music of the day. Another book in which the author refers to the cultural influence of black music was Charles Plymell's *The Last of the Moccasins*, loosely described as a novel, but in fact a racy, autobiographical account of growing up in and around Wichita, and his eventual involvement in the San Francisco art scene.

The book has a great deal of life, and Plymell's experiences were wider than those of many purely-literary types, but it is his brief acknowledgement of the social/cultural impact of rhythm-and-blues that primarily interests me. Here he is talking about Wichita in the 1950s: "The town was wide open. I spent a lot of time in small Spadeclubs listening and jiving to such later big names as Chuck Berry, Bo Diddley, Fats Domino. Fats Domino had done some real down home hillbilly-motown stuff before he was famous. Jimmy Mammy came by and said listen here to this, man. We sat for hours listening to Fats Domino singing 'Don't leave me this way', 'Please don't leave me' and 'Rosemary'. He came to the Mambo Club and we were there to greet him. He drove up in his old dented Cadillac from Louisiana. What was nice about it then you could see all the 'stars' in some little dive on a Saturday night if you watched the billboards down in spade town. They came to gig in their own clubs before white people picked up on them. Also some of the jazz musicians had come down from Kansas City after the Norman Granz concerts busted up".

This clearly indicates how white artists and bohemians were already picking up on rhythm-and-blues long before the wider pop-music audience discovered it. And people like Plymell were prepared to accept the music in its original form, not in the watered-down versions that white-dominated radio stations and record companies favoured. I don't think it was cultural slumming, either, because Plymell, like many of his kind, was alienated enough from American society to relate to ghetto music in a spontaneous manner, There are other references to blues and jazz scattered around *The Last of the Moccasins*, and I would guess that anyone interested in post-1945 socio-cultural matter will find it of interest.

Plymell arrived in San Francisco in the 1960s, but Michael McClure had been active there since the hectic days of the Beat movement. You can find his poems in most of the magazines and anthologies that helped launch the new literature into the public eye. I have to say that my own liking for McClure's poetry is mainly limited to his early work, but a man who claims to "have blossomed in an aura of jazz, William Blake and the visionary surrealists" has something interesting about him.

McClure's *The Mad Cub* appeared in print in 1970, and it is this book that has some appeal for jazz enthusiasts. It consists of two long stories, on the surface somewhat out of character with the rest of his writings, but still of interest in themselves. The title-story, the action of which appears to take place around 1950, has a few references to bop and the people who made a cult, and a life-style, out of the music. The following passage is significant when we recall the decline of bop as the 1940s came to an end: "Robertson goes on to tell us about the height of Bop. Last year was the great last year of music. The classic days of Bop have fallen into decadence and last year's heroes sleep in spotted overcoats in hallways this year. (I hardly believe, but later I see it with my own eyes; hallucinated beboppers sleeping in the hallways of old friends who will not open the door for them because they have become mad and unfashionable and would steal their host's shoes if there was a chance of pawning them to keep a barbiturate habit going….)".

If the Plymell and McClure books deal with aspects of the "underground" mood of America, and in doing so throw light on later cultural developments, then Brian Jackson's *Working Class Community* is worth reading for the way in which it deals with what was, I suppose, "underground" in England in the 1950s. Jackson charts the ups-and-downs of a jazz club founded in Huddersfield in 1952, and in existence for the following thirteen years. Of course, it's a vastly different reading experience to Plymell and McClure, even allowing for the fact that they're working in fictional form, and the comparative weakness – in experience and activity - of the English version of an "underground" is obvious.

There was, I think, an "underground" similar to the American one, but it only existed in London, and in the minds of a few individuals scattered around the country. I should make it clear that Jackson nowhere claims to be dealing with an "underground" as such. His thesis is based on the idea of a jazz club as an extension of working-class experience, and it is my analysis that suggests wider social/cultural applications.

If we accept the limitations of Jackson's survey, however, the book is well worth reading, and anyone with knowledge of the provincial jazz scene will find his chapter on the club to the point and well-informed. It makes one realise how jazz in the 1950s provided provincial bohemia with a focal point. But let me quote from Jackson's opinions as to why the club was founded, and what it meant in terms of a refuge from the larger society: "I think what happened originally was that a group of working-class boys at grammar school found themselves at odds with the social and academic demands of their school. 'I hated the etiquette, the sugar tongs part of it'. Yet at the same time they were excited and enthusiastic and the colour and music of jazz satisfied them in a way that the GCE demands of the schoolroom never could. They fell in love with the literature of jazz too – the prostitution, violence, drugs of New Orleans went along with its music, vitality, imagination. If the life of New Orleans was an exaggerated image of working-class life, the stimulated, generalised emotions of jazz were a hazy image of what the world of art could offer. The school provided the first and didn't particularly lead to the second".

Now one may not necessarily agree with everything Jackson says – that reference to "the stimulated, generalised emotions of jazz" will, no doubt, bother some people, though it seems to me valid when applied to the sort of music churned out in provincial clubs. But read in the context of his book in its broad sense, his comments on the jazz club are of interest.

Before leaving this subject, I'd like to quote from an interview with Roy Fisher, poet, prose writer, jazz pianist, in which he reminisced about jazz in the provinces: "I always thought that a lot of the audience were young Conservatives, it was rather worrying. By modern standards they were very straight. We used to go round in open-necked cricket shirts in opposition to the dance club circuit where you wore a drape evening suit. Then there was this curious boom, you know, with people like Kenny Ball and Chris Barber and every provincial city had a Trad Band which was composed of teachers and bank clerks and insurance men kicking their heels up at night. And they were mostly very fat-arsed bands". The interviewer said that he always thought of that scene as an "early underground", and Fisher replied, 'It was underground. You were slightly persecuted, hounded from pub to pub' ". That last statement ties in with much of what Brian Jackson says in *Working Class Community*.

In my article, "What's Your Song, King Kong?", on jazz slang in *Jazz and Blues* (August/September, 1971), later reprinted in *Bohemians, Beats and Blues People*, I mentioned the phrase, "out of sight", and pointed to its use in Stephen Crane's *Maggie: A Girl of the Streets*, first published in 1892. I suggested that it may have been of white origin, but some later reading led me to doubt this. "Out of sight", as an assertion that something is good or favourable, is used by certain of the characters in Paul Laurence Dunbar's *The Sport of the Gods*, a novel of black life which first appeared in 1902. Dunbar was a black writer, born in 1872, and his main aim in his book was to show how a black family forced to leave the South and move to New York, slowly disintegrates under the social and economic pressures of the big city. At times, the book does have something of the flavour of a moral tract, but it's necessary to be fair and understand the conditions of the period to fully appreciate the book's tone.

After all, one can read nineteenth-century English novels of slum-llfe – Mrs Gaskell's *Mary Barton* and Arthur Morrison's *A Child of the Jago*, to name just two well-known examples – and smile at their occasional earnestness, but had one been around in 1840s Manchester or 1890s London, and known at first-hand the levels of poverty and despair, there might have been a different reaction. Likewise, New York at the beginning of the twentieth-century was a cruel place for any poor person. And more so for a poor black person. Still, Dunbar does seem to have been somewhat similar to Arthur Morrison in that, while accepting that social and economic conditions could corrupt, he had little hesitation in condemning the corrupted once they were in that state.

Insofar as relevance to jazz or popular music is concerned, Dunbar's novel gives a good picture of life in a Northern city at a time when the mass black movement of the 1890-1914 period was under way. A census of blacks in Manhattan in 1910 reported a total of 60,534. Of those, only 14,309 had actually been born in New York State. The rest had drifted in from elsewhere – mainly the South. Thus Dunbar's account covers the conditions which created the social background for a lot of jazz.

Dunbar himself was not unfamiliar with the music scene of his time. He was an acquaintance of black entertainers and musicians, and wrote the lyrics for Will Marion Cook's "Jes Lak White Fo'ks" and "Clorindy". Some of the scenes in his novel are set in a club where show-biz types, gamblers, musicians, journalists, etc. hang out. In the contrast between their speech, and that of the "respectable" blacks Dunbar contrasts them to, one can sense the beginnings of a kind of night-life personality – the hustler and the hipster.

In particular, there is Sadness, a layabout whose precision of speech, and his flippancy, are a mask for his bitterness. Sadness is a prototype hipster, cool and nearly always withdrawn. He is aware of the need that drives losers to seek each other's company: "Poor Wallace, who is just coming in, and who looks like a jaunty ragpicker, came here about six months ago with about two thousand dollars, the proceeds from the sale of a house his father had left him. He'll sleep in one of the club chairs tonight, and not from choice. He spent his two thousand learning. But, after all, it was a good investment. He begins to know already how to live on others as they have lived on him. The plucked bird's beak is sharpened for other's feathers. From now on Wallace will live, eat, drink and sleep at the expense of others, and will forget to mourn his lost money. He will go on in this way, until broken and useless, the poorhouse or the potter's field gets him. Oh, it's a fine rich life, my lad. I know you'll like it. I said you would the first time I saw you. It has plenty of stir in it, and a man never gets lonesome. Only the rich are lonesome. It's only the independent who depend upon others".

It's not a long jump from this to McClure's be-boppers sleeping in hallways. Although Sadness vividly describes the lifestyle and eventual fate of people like himself, Dunbar can't refrain from adding a moral comment: "He belonged to a peculiar class, one that grows larger and larger each year in New York and which has imitators in every large city in this country. It is a set which lives, like the leech, upon the blood of others, that draws its life from the veins of foolish men and women, that prides itself upon its well-dressed idleness and has no shame in its voluntary pauperism. Each member of the class knows every other, his methods and his limitations, and their loyalty to one another makes of them a great hulking, fashionably uniformed fraternity of indolence".

It's intriguing to wonder what Dunbar would have thought had he lived to see the types he so scathingly dismisses eventually made into culture heroes (hipsters, and some of the characters admired by devotees of Beat literature) in the post-1945 period. It might well have convinced him of the correctness of his assertion that the city in general has a corrupting influence.

The Sport of the Gods has admittedly little, if any, direct relationship to jazz, but it seems to me a fascinating background document. I should mention that there is one reference to rag-time, an early precursor of jazz. An acquaintance tells Sadness that "dancing is the poetry of motion", and he replies, "Yes, and dancing to rag-time is the dialect poetry".

The statistics I quoted when discussing *The Sport of the Gods* were culled from Gilbert Osofsky's *Harlem: The Making of a Ghetto*, which is sub-titled *Negro New York, 1890-1930*. This is primarily a sociological study, concerned to analyse the development of Harlem as a major black centre, but Osofsky does devote one well-documented chapter to the white "discovery" of Harlem in the 1920s as a place of exotic music – Duke Ellington's "jungle" sounds – and excitement. But the whole book deserves to be read. You can't divorce music (and especially jazz and popular music) from its social background.

The books I've referred to are Charles Plumell's *The Last of the Moccasins* (City Lights Books, San Francisco, 1971); Michael McClure's *The Mad Cub* (Bantam Books, New York, 1970); Brian Jackson's *Working Class Community* (Penguin Books, Harmandsworth, 1972); Paul Laurence Dunbar's *The Sport of the Gods* (Collier Books, New York, 1970); Gilbert Osofsky's *Harlem: The Making of a Ghetto* (Harper & Row, New York, 1968). The Roy Fisher interview I mentioned appeared in *Sad Traffic 5* (Seaview Publications, Barnsley, 1971).

Contents of Jim Burns' previous essay collections

Beats, Bohemians and Intellectuals *Trent Books 2000*

Radicals, Beats and Beboppers *PPP (2011)*

Brits, Beats & Outsiders *PPP (2012)*

Bohemians, Beats and Blues People *PPP* (2013)

Artists, Beats and Cool Cats *PPP* (2014)

Rebels, Beats and Poets *PPP* (2015)

Anarchists, Beats & Dadaists *PPP* (2016)

Paris, Painters, Poets *PPP (*2017)

DID2101148

#0326 - 220118 - C0 - 229/152/15 - PB - DID2101148